IET SECURITY SERIES 20

Artificial Intelligence for Biometrics and Cybersecurity

IET Book Series in Advances in Biometrics – Call for authors

Book Series Editor: Val Moliere, Senior Consultant Commissioning Editor, The IET

This Book Series provides the foundation on which to build a valuable library of reference volumes on the topic of Biometrics. Proposals for coherently-integrated co-authored or edited contributions are welcome for consideration. Please email your proposal to vmoliere@theiet.org or to the IET at: author_support@theiet.org.

Published titles in this series include:

Voice Biometrics: Technology, trust and security, edited by Carmen García-Mateo, Gérard Chollet 2021: This edited book presents the state of the art in voice biometrics research and technologies, including implementation and deployment challenges in terms of interoperability, scalability and performance, and security.

Hand-Based Biometrics: Methods and technology, edited by Martin Drahanský; 2018: Hand-based biometrics identifies users by unique features in their hands, such as fingerprints, palmprints, hand geometry, and finger and palm vein patterns. This book explores the range of technologies and methods under development and in use for hand-based biometrics, with evaluations of the advantages and performance of each.

Iris and Periocular Biometric Recognition, edited by Christian Rathgeb, Christoph Busch; 2017: This book provides an overview of scientific fundamentals and principles of iris and periocular biometric recognition. It covers an introduction to iris and periocular recognition; a selective overview of issues and challenges; soft biometric classification; security aspects; privacy protection and forensics; and future trends.

Mobile Biometrics, edited by Guodong Guo, Harry Wechsler; 2017: This book covers the use of biometrics on mobile/smart phones. An integrated and informative analysis, this is a timely survey of the state-of-the-art research and developments in this rapidly growing area.

User-Centric Privacy and Security in Biometrics, edited by Claus Vielhauer; 2017: User-Centric Privacy and Security in Biometrics explores how developments in biometrics will address security and privacy aspects. The book surveys and evaluates how biometric techniques can enhance and increase the reliability of security strategies in a variety of applications.

Age Factors in Biometric Processing, edited by Michael Fairhurst; 2013: This book explores the implications of ageing on biometric technologies, and how such factors can be managed with practical situations.

Artificial Intelligence for Biometrics and Cybersecurity

Technology and applications

Edited by
Ahmed A. Abd El-Latif, Mohammed Adel Hammad,
Yassine Maleh, Brij B. Gupta and Wojciech Mazurczyk

The Institution of Engineering and Technology

Published by The Institution of Engineering and Technology, London, United Kingdom

The Institution of Engineering and Technology is registered as a Charity in England & Wales (no. 211014) and Scotland (no. SC038698).

The Institution of Engineering and Technology
Futures Place
Kings Way, Stevenage
Hertfordshire SG1 2UA, United Kingdom

www.theiet.org

British Library Cataloguing in Publication Data
A catalogue record for this product is available from the British Library

ISBN 978-1-83953-547-5 (hardback)
ISBN 978-1-83953-548-2 (PDF)

Typeset in India by MPS Limited

Contents

About the editors

Ahmed A. Abd El-Latif (SMIEEE, MACM) received the BSc degree with honours rank in mathematics and computer science in 2005 and MSc degree in computer science in 2010, all from Menoufia University, Egypt. He received his PhD degree in computer science and technology at Harbin Institute of Technology (H.I.T.), Harbin, P.R. China in 2013. He is an associate professor of computer science at Menoufia University, Egypt, and at EIAS Data Science Lab, College of Computer and Information Sciences, Prince Sultan University, Saudi Arabia. In more than 17 years of his professional experience, he published over 280 papers in journals/conferences, including 10 books with over 9,000 citations. He was also selected in the 2022, 2021 and 2020 Stanford University's ranking of the world's top 2% scientists. He has been involved in government and international funded R&D projects related to the widespread use of artificial intelligence for 5G/6G networks. He has received many awards: State Encouragement Award in Engineering Sciences 2016, Arab Republic of Egypt; the best PhD student award from Harbin Institute of Technology, China 2013; Young scientific award, Menoufia University, Egypt 2014. He is a fellow at Academy of Scientific Research and Technology, Egypt. His areas of interests are cybersecurity, 5G/6G wireless networks, post-quantum cryptography, artificial intelligence of things, AI-based image processing, information hiding, dynamical systems (discrete-time models: chaotic systems and quantum walks). He is the leader of mega grant programme 'Research of network technologies with ultra-low latency and ultra-high density based on the widespread use of artificial intelligence for 6G networks'. Dr Abd El-Latif is the chair/co-chair of many Scopus/EI conferences. He is the EIC of *International Journal of Information Security and Privacy*, and the series editor of *Advances in Cybersecurity Management* (https://www.routledge.com). He is also an academic editor/associate editor for the set of indexed journals (Scopus journals' quartile ranking).

Mohammed Adel Hammad received his PhD degree in 2019, School of Computer Science and Technology, Harbin Institute of Technology, Harbin, China. He is an assistant professor in the Faculty of Computers and Information, Menoufia University, Egypt. He is currently a researcher in EIAS Data Science Lab, College of Computer and Information Sciences, Prince Sultan University. His research interests include biomedical imaging, bioinformatics, cybersecurity, digital forensics, IoT, computer vision, machine learning, deep learning, pattern recognition and biometrics. He has published more than 50 papers in international SCI-IF journals.

Furthermore, he has served as an editorial board member in *PLoS One* journal, an editorial board member in *BMC Bioinformatics* journal, an associate editor in *IJISP*, a topics board editor in *Forensic Sciences* (MPDI) journal, a guest editor in many international journals such as *IJDCF*, *Sensors* (MDPI) and *Information* (MDPI). He has been a reviewer of more than 500 papers for many prestigious journals and listed in the top 2% of scientists worldwide (according to the recently released list by Stanford University, USA in 2022).

Yassine Maleh is an associate professor of cybersecurity and IT governance at Sultan Moulay Slimane University, Morocco. His research studies cover information security and privacy, Internet of Things security, wireless and constrained network security and IT governance. He has published over 70 papers, 10 edited books and 3 authored books. He is editor-in-chief of the *International Journal of Information Security and Privacy* and serves as an associate editor for *IEEE Access and the International Journal of Digital Crime and Forensics (IJDCF)*. He is also the series editor of *Advances in Cybersecurity Management*. He is a senior member of the IEEE and a member of the International Association of Engineers (IAENG). Yassine is also the founding chair of the IEEE Consultant Network Morocco and the founding president of the African Research Center of Information Technology & Cybersecurity.

Brij B. Gupta is working as a director of the International Center for AI and Cyber Security Research and Innovations, and a full professor with the Department of Computer Science and Information Engineering (CSIE), Asia University, Taiwan. In his more than 18 years of professional experience, he has published over 500 papers in journals/conferences, including 35 books and 11 patents with over 21,000 citations. He has received numerous national and international awards, including Canadian Commonwealth Scholarship (2009), Faculty Research Fellowship Award (2017), MeitY, GoI, IEEE GCCE outstanding and WIE paper awards and Best Faculty Award (2018 and 2019), NIT KKR, respectively. Prof. Gupta was selected for 2022 Clarivate Web of Science Highly Cited Researchers in Computer Science. He was also selected in the 2022, 2021 and 2020 Stanford University's ranking of the world's top 2% scientists. He is also a visiting/adjunct professor with several universities worldwide. He is also an IEEE senior member (2017) and also selected as a 2021 distinguished lecturer in IEEE CTSoc. Dr Gupta is also serving as member-in-large, Board of Governors, IEEE Consumer Technology Society (2022–24). Prof. Gupta is also leading IJSWIS, IJSSCI, STE and IJCAC as Editor-in-Chief. Moreover, he is also serving as a lead-editor of a book series with CRC and IET press. He also served as TPC members in more than 150 international conferences as well as an associate/guest editor of various journals and transactions. His research interests include information security, cyber physical systems, cloud computing, blockchain technologies, intrusion detection, AI, social media and networking.

Wojciech Mazurczyk is a professor at the Institute of Computer Science and Head of the Computer Systems Security Group (CSSG) in the Faculty of Electronics and Information Technology, Warsaw University of Technology (WUT), Poland. He is an accredited cybercrime expert, trainer and a member of the Academic Advisory Network for Europol EC3 (European Cybercrime Center) as well as a founder and a coordinator of the Criminal Use of Information Hiding (CUIng) Initiative launched in cooperation with Europol EC3. He is a member of the Working Group 3— Secure ICT Research and Innovation of the Network and Information Security (NIS) Public-Private Platform for the European Commission. He is an IEEE senior member and Technical Committee Affiliate Member of IEEE Information Forensics and Security, a EURASIP member and a founding member of EURASIP 'Biometrics, Data Forensics and Security' (B.For.Sec.) Special Area Team. He is a co-author and co-editor of several research books and holds two patent applications. He received a PhD degree with honours in telecommunications from Warsaw University of Technology (WUT), Poland.

Preface

As the world becomes increasingly digitized, the need for robust security measures to protect against cyberthreats has never been more urgent. The use of biometrics and artificial intelligence (AI) is playing an increasingly critical role in achieving these security goals. This book, *Artificial Intelligence for Biometrics and Cybersecurity Technology and Applications*, provides an in-depth exploration of the intersection of these two fields and how they can be leveraged to provide enhanced security measures.

The book begins with an introduction to the key concepts of AI, biometrics and cybersecurity, providing readers with a solid foundation for the subsequent chapters. Chapter 2 focuses on the use of AI in biometrics and cybersecurity, exploring how these technologies are used to protect against various threats, such as identity theft, data breaches, and cyber-attacks.

Chapters 3–9 provide a comprehensive overview of various techniques and methods used in biometrics and cybersecurity. These chapters cover a range of topics, including performance evaluation of biometric security, leveraging generative adversarial networks and federated learning for enhanced cybersecurity, face recognition methods with federated learning, biometric authentication using ECG signals, email phishing detection methods, securing hardware coprocessors against piracy and intelligent authentication systems using graphical one-time passwords.

The book concludes with Chapter 10, which summarizes the key takeaways from the preceding chapters and provides insights into the future of AI, biometrics and cybersecurity. The authors hope that readers will find this book informative and thought-provoking, and that it will inspire further research in this exciting and rapidly evolving field.

The authors would like to express their gratitude to all the contributors and reviewers who made this book possible. They hope that this book will serve as a valuable resource for researchers, academics, students and professionals working in the fields of AI, biometrics and cybersecurity.

Editors,
Ahmed A. Abd El-Latif, Mohammed Adel Hammad, Yassine Maleh, Brij B. Gupta and Wojciech Mazurczyk

Chapter 1

Introduction

Mohamed Hammad[1,2] and Ahmed A. Abd El-Latif[1,3]

In today's digital age, the convergence of Artificial Intelligence (AI) and biometric security systems has become increasingly vital for ensuring the authenticity and security of digital identities [1]. Biometric security systems, a key component of this technological revolution, rely on the utilization of unique biological traits to authenticate individuals, such as electrocardiogram (ECG), electroencephalogram, fingerprints, iris scans, and facial recognition [2–15]. By leveraging these distinctive biological traits, biometric security systems provide a robust and reliable means of verifying individuals' identities. These systems offer several advantages over traditional authentication methods, such as passwords or personal identification numbers (PINs), which can easily be compromised or forgotten. Biometric authentication is convenient, as it requires individuals to present their unique traits for identification, eliminating the need for additional tokens or passwords.

The applications of biometric security systems span across various domains, including access control, surveillance, and banking and finance [16–18]. Access control systems are crucial for maintaining security in high-risk environments, such as government agencies, corporate offices, and restricted areas. Biometric authentication has become an integral part of access control solutions, offering a higher level of security compared to traditional methods like keys, ID cards, or passwords. By using biometric traits such as fingerprints, iris patterns, or facial features, access control systems can accurately verify the identity of individuals and grant access only to authorized personnel. This enhances overall security, prevents unauthorized entry, and minimizes the risks associated with stolen or forged credentials.

Surveillance systems leverage biometric technologies to identify individuals in real time, facilitating law enforcement agencies in investigations and enhancing public safety. By integrating facial recognition capabilities into surveillance cameras, these systems can automatically detect and match faces against databases of known individuals. This enables law enforcement to track suspects, locate missing

[1] EIAS Data Science Lab, College of Computer and Information Sciences, Prince Sultan University, Saudi Arabia

[2] Department of Information Technology, Faculty of Computers and Information, Menoufia University, Egypt

[3] Department of Mathematics and Computer Science, Faculty of Science, Menoufia University, Egypt

persons, and enhance situational awareness in public spaces. Biometric surveillance systems contribute to crime prevention, rapid response to incidents, and the identification of individuals involved in criminal activities.

In the banking and finance sector, biometric authentication has become increasingly important to ensure secure access to accounts and transactions. Traditional methods such as PINs or passwords can be compromised, leading to identity theft and financial fraud. Biometric authentication provides a robust solution by linking an individual's unique biological traits, such as fingerprints or iris patterns, to their banking activities. This enhances security, reduces the risks associated with stolen credentials, and protects sensitive financial information. Biometric authentication also offers convenience to customers, eliminating the need to remember complex passwords or carry physical tokens for transactions.

Moreover, biometric security systems have also found applications in border control, healthcare, and time and attendance management. Border control agencies utilize biometric technologies to verify the identities of travelers, enhancing border security and facilitating smoother immigration processes. In the healthcare sector, biometric authentication ensures secure access to electronic health records, preventing unauthorized access to sensitive patient information. Biometric time and attendance systems accurately record and verify employee attendance, eliminating time theft and ensuring accurate payroll management.

The applications of biometric security systems continue to expand, driven by advancements in technology and the need for enhanced security and convenience. However, it is crucial to address concerns regarding privacy, data security, and ethical use of biometric information. Striking the right balance between security and individual privacy is paramount in deploying biometric systems responsibly and ethically across different domains.

Despite their numerous benefits, biometric security systems also face several challenges that necessitate further advancements. One of the primary concerns lies in the accuracy and reliability of biometric systems [19]. Environmental conditions, such as lighting, pose challenges to image capture and quality, affecting the performance of facial recognition or iris scanning systems. Similarly, variations in fingerprint patterns due to factors like moisture, dirt, or changes in the skin can impact the accuracy of fingerprint recognition systems. To overcome these challenges, ongoing research focuses on developing algorithms and techniques that are robust to variations in environmental conditions and improve the overall accuracy of biometric systems.

Additionally, the vulnerability of biometric data to attacks and privacy breaches calls for robust security measures to safeguard individuals' sensitive information [20]. Biometric systems are vulnerable to attacks where an individual attempts to impersonate or deceive the system using fake or altered biometric data. For example, facial recognition systems can be fooled by presenting a photograph or a mask instead of a real face. This necessitates the development of anti-spoofing techniques that can detect and prevent such attacks. Advancements in liveness detection methods, such as analyzing micro-movements or utilizing in-depth information, are being explored to enhance the security of biometric systems.

Furthermore, the security and privacy of biometric data are critical considerations. Biometric information, such as fingerprints, iris scans, or facial features, are unique to individuals and highly sensitive. Protecting this data from unauthorized access, data breaches, or misuse is of utmost importance. Robust encryption, secure storage mechanisms, and strict access control policies are essential to safeguard biometric data. Additionally, privacy regulations and ethical guidelines play a significant role in ensuring that individuals' biometric information is collected, stored, and used responsibly, with explicit consent and transparency.

Standardization and interoperability are also challenges in the biometric security domain. As biometric technologies continue to evolve, it is crucial to establish common standards and protocols to ensure compatibility and seamless integration across different systems and devices. This enables interoperability between various biometric systems, facilitates information sharing, and supports collaborative efforts in enhancing security measures.

To address these challenges and enhance the performance of biometric security systems, researchers have turned to AI approaches, which have shown promising results. AI techniques, particularly machine learning (ML) algorithms, enable biometric systems to adapt and improve their performance over time. By analyzing vast amounts of biometric data, AI algorithms can identify intricate patterns and make accurate predictions, leading to more reliable authentication processes. ML algorithms empower biometric systems to adapt and improve their performance over time. By analyzing large volumes of biometric data, these algorithms can learn and identify intricate patterns and relationships that exist within the data. This ability allows the algorithms to make accurate predictions and decisions during the authentication process. As more data is processed, the algorithms can refine their models, leading to enhanced accuracy and reduced error rates.

One notable advantage of AI in biometric systems is its ability to handle variations in environmental conditions and data quality. Traditional biometric systems may struggle when faced with challenges such as poor lighting conditions or low-quality images. However, ML algorithms can be trained to recognize and account for such variations. By learning from diverse and representative datasets, these algorithms can adapt to different environmental conditions and improve their performance, increasing the robustness of biometric systems.

AI techniques also facilitate the development of advanced feature extraction methods. In biometric systems, accurate feature extraction plays a crucial role in identifying unique patterns and characteristics from biometric data. With AI, researchers can leverage deep learning algorithms to automatically extract relevant and discriminative features from biometric data. Deep neural networks, for example, can learn hierarchical representations of facial features or fingerprint patterns, capturing more nuanced details that aid in accurate identification.

Furthermore, AI-based approaches enable continuous learning and adaptation. As new data becomes available, ML algorithms can update their models, incorporating the latest information to enhance their performance. This adaptability ensures that biometric systems remain effective even as new challenges or variations emerge.

The integration of AI and biometric security systems also allows for the development of multimodal biometrics, where multiple biometric traits are combined for enhanced accuracy and security. AI algorithms can effectively fuse information from different biometric modalities, such as combining facial recognition with iris scans or voice recognition. This multimodal approach improves the overall reliability of biometric authentication, as it reduces the likelihood of false positives or false negatives.

Moreover, the integration of AI algorithms into biometric security systems enables the detection and mitigation of potential attacks. By continuously learning and training on large datasets, these systems can effectively identify anomalous patterns and distinguish between legitimate users and impostors. This capability enhances the system's ability to counteract attacks and ensures a higher level of security.

AI algorithms can analyze various aspects of biometric data, such as behavioral patterns or physiological responses, to detect signs of fraudulent activities. For example, in behavioral biometrics, AI algorithms can analyze typing rhythms, gesture patterns, or voice characteristics to establish a unique user profile. Any deviation from this established profile can trigger an alert, indicating a potential security breach.

ML techniques, including anomaly detection algorithms and neural networks, enable biometric systems to identify unusual or suspicious behavior. By training on a wide range of normal and abnormal patterns, AI algorithms can learn to recognize and flag potential threats in real time. These algorithms can adapt and update their models based on new attack methods, ensuring that the system remains resilient to evolving threats.

Furthermore, the integration of AI with biometric security systems enables proactive defense mechanisms. AI algorithms can simulate and predict potential attack scenarios, allowing system administrators to anticipate vulnerabilities and strengthen security measures. This proactive approach helps identify and address potential weaknesses before they can be exploited, minimizing the risk of successful attacks.

Another benefit of AI in biometric security is its ability to detect and counteract spoofing attempts. Biometric systems are vulnerable to various spoofing techniques, such as presenting fake fingerprints or using facial images to deceive facial recognition systems. AI algorithms can be trained to recognize these spoofing patterns by analyzing discrepancies between genuine and fake biometric traits. This enables the system to reject fraudulent attempts and maintain the integrity of the authentication process.

In-depth exploration of the intersection among AI, biometrics, and cybersecurity is presented in the book titled *Artificial Intelligence for Biometrics and Cybersecurity*. The book consists of *12* chapters that cover a wide range of topics related to the use of AI in biometric security systems and cybersecurity. It will cover the fundamental concepts of biometric recognition, including face recognition, ECG identification, and more. The book will delve into the advancements in AI techniques, such as ML, deep learning, neural networks, and their application in biometric systems. Furthermore, it will explore the integration of biometric technologies with cybersecurity protocols, including secure authentication, access control, and intrusion detection systems.

The book delves into biometric authentication systems, network security and cybersecurity for Internet of Things (IoT). It offers real-world case studies that demonstrate the practical implementation and effectiveness of AI in biometrics and cybersecurity. The book also explores the evaluation of biometric security systems, including performance metrics, methods, and tools for testing and analysis. It emphasizes the importance of standardized evaluation protocols and benchmark datasets for future research in this field.

In-depth discussions are dedicated to advanced technologies such as generative adversarial networks (GANs) and federated learning (FL) and their applications in cybersecurity. The potential of GANs in generating synthetic data for training ML models and simulating cyber-attacks, as well as the collaborative and privacy-preserving nature of FL, are explored. The book also covers the development and achievements of face recognition technology using FL, considering both its success and the privacy protection concerns associated with it.

Furthermore, the book investigates the utilization of ECG as a biometric tool for human identification and authentication. It examines the unique qualities of ECG and provides a framework for adopting ML approaches in developing ECG-based biometric authentication methods. Additionally, the book evaluates deep learning models for detecting email phishing attacks and highlights the potential of these models in enhancing cybersecurity defenses.

In-depth insights are provided into securing IoT hardware through biometric-based methodologies, such as fingerprint, facial, and palmprint biometrics. These techniques offer protection against counterfeiting, cloning, piracy, and fraudulent intellectual property ownership claims. The book emphasizes the incorporation of biometric security during the design process to ensure minimal overhead and easy isolation of counterfeited designs.

Finally, the book proposes a graphical password authentication method as an alternative to traditional alphanumeric passwords. This method offers improved security, memorability, and usability through a graphical one-time password scheme. It provides protection against common graphical password attacks and is designed to be easily remembered and used. In order to provide readers with a convenient and accessible resource, the book includes a dedicated table (Table 1.1)

Table 1.1 Abbreviation summary—a comprehensive compilation of abbreviation discussed throughout the book for quick reference and easy navigation

Abbreviation	Full form
AI	Artificial Intelligence
ECG	Electrocardiogram
EEG	Electroencephalogram
ID	Identification
PIN	Personal identification number
IoT	Internet of Things

(Continues)

Table 1.1   (*Continued*)

Abbreviation	Full form
GANs	Generative adversarial networks
FL	Federated learning
AFIS	Automated fingerprint identification systems
GDPR	General data protection regulation
FPR	False positive rate
FNR	False negative rate
EER	Equal error rate
FAR	False acceptance rate
FRR	False rejection rate
ROC	Receiver operating characteristic
FTE	Failure to enroll rate
FTA	Failure to acquire rate
PCR	Polymerase chain reaction
STR	Short tandem repeat
FP	False positive
FN	False negative
TP	True positive
TN	True negative
TPR	True positive rate or sensitivity, recall and hit rate
TNR	Specificity or true negative rate
PPV	Precision or positive predictive value
MCC	Matthew's correlation coefficient
AUR	Area under the curve
NIST	National Institute of Standards and Technology
ISO	International Organization for Standardization
FMR	False match rate
MFA	Multifactor authentication
GPL	General Public License
NBIS	NIST Biometric Image Software
BEF	Biometric evaluation framework
OBI	Open biometrics initiative
BSPA	Biometric security and privacy analysis
PFM	Partial joint momentum
FV	Joint validation
LBP	Local binary patterns
ML	Machine learning
DTW	Dynamic time wrapping
FLDA	Fisher's linear discriminant analysis
K-NN	K-Nearest neighbor
PCA	Principal component analysis
LDA	Linear discriminant analysis
GMM	Gaussian mixture modeling
PAR	Pulse active ratio
DCT	Discrete cosine transform
SVM	Support vector machine
RMSE	Root mean square error
RF	Random forest
RNN	Recurrent neural networks

(Continues)

Table 1.1   (Continued)

Abbreviation	Full form
LSTM	Long short-term memory
Bi-LSTM	Bidirectional long short-term memory
ReLU	Rectified linear unit
BRNN	Bidirectional recurrent neural network
FERC	Federal Energy Regulatory Commission
Pc	Probability of coincidence
DSP	Digital signal coprocessors
FIR	Finite impulse response
IIR	Infinite impulse response
IP	Intellectual property
IT	Information technology
GSCM	Global supply chain and management
SoC	System-on-chip
HLS	High-level synthesis
CIG	Colored interval graph
RAT	Register allocation table
RTL	Register transfer level
OTP	One time password
TOTP	Time-based one-time password
HOTP	HMAC-based one-time password
PKI	Public key infrastructure
CA	Certificate authority

that summarizes all the abbreviation discussed throughout the chapters. This table serves as a handy reference guide, enabling readers to quickly locate and review the various shortcuts presented in the book.

In this book, we have organized the content into *12* chapters, each focusing on a specific aspect of AI, biometrics, and cybersecurity. The following chapters provide a comprehensive exploration of the subject matter:

- **The second chapter** highlights that biometric systems have significantly improved with the help of advancements in technology and AI, making them more accurate, reliable, and secure than before. However, several challenges such as data quality, privacy, and security still need to be addressed. AI approaches such as data preprocessing, pattern recognition, deep learning, and behavioral biometrics are being used to overcome these challenges and make biometric systems more accurate and reliable. The chapter emphasizes the importance of ensuring that biometric systems are developed and deployed in a responsible and transparent manner, protecting individual privacy and data security while complying with ethical and legal guidelines. The ultimate goal is to maximize the benefits of biometric systems while minimizing their potential risks as they continue to evolve and become more prevalent.

- **The third chapter** emphasizes the importance of evaluating the performance and security of biometric systems to ensure their effectiveness and reliability.

The chapter provides an overview of biometric security, the metrics used for performance evaluation, and the methods and tools available for evaluating biometric systems. Biometric security performance evaluation requires a combination of testing, analysis, and simulation to assess accuracy, speed, and robustness, and standardized evaluation protocols and benchmark datasets are needed for future research. The recommendations for biometric security performance evaluation include the adoption of standardized protocols, relevant performance metrics, and regular monitoring and evaluation of biometric systems to ensure optimal performance and security. Open-source tools and platforms can facilitate widespread adoption of best practices and ensure that biometric systems are secure, reliable, and effective. Overall, biometric security performance evaluation is critical for ensuring the effectiveness and reliability of biometric systems in various applications.

- **The fourth chapter** states that the use of ML and deep learning algorithms, particularly GANs and FL, in cybersecurity can effectively detect and respond to cyber threats while preserving data privacy. GANs can be used to generate synthetic data for training ML models and simulate cyber-attacks for testing cybersecurity defenses, while FL enables multiple parties to collaborate and train a model without sharing their data with a central server, enhancing model accuracy and mitigating the risks of data breaches. The chapter suggests several directions for future research, including the use of GANs for generating diverse network traffic, FL for training ML models in decentralized environments, and developing adaptive and resilient cybersecurity defenses. The conclusion also highlights potential areas of research for GANs and FL in image security, such as image encryption, steganography, and search engine security, as well as privacy-preserving image analysis techniques. Overall, the use of GANs and FL in cybersecurity and image security has shown promising results, and future research can explore further advancements to develop more robust and secure techniques.

- **The fifth chapter** discusses the development and achievements of face recognition technology using FL. It highlights the success of deep neural networks in face recognition but also raises concerns about privacy protection. The chapter provides an overview of FL and traditional face recognition technology and analyzes the progress made in face recognition technology under the FL framework. The chapter concludes by discussing potential future developments and identifying possible problems.

- **The sixth chapter** discusses the use of ECG as a biometric tool for human identification and authentication in highly secured systems. ECG is a nearly unique human feature with several key qualities to assess its usage as a biometric system, including universality, uniqueness, permanence, collectability, and circumvention. The chapter also provides an overview of biometrics and the two primary subcategories of physiological and behavioral characteristics. The chapter presents a framework for the proper adoption and adjustment of ML approaches for developing ECG-based biometric authentication methods.

- **The seventh chapter** evaluates deep learning models for detecting email phishing attacks using CNN, recurrent neural networks (RNN), long short-term memory (LSTM), and bidirectional long short-term memory models on a dataset of phishing and legitimate emails. The LSTM model achieved the highest accuracy of 99.41%, outperforming all other models, while the RNN model had the worst accuracy. The chapter highlights the potential of deep learning models for detecting email phishing attacks and underscores the need for further research to develop more effective and reliable approaches. The findings have practical implications for the development of email phishing detection systems and provide a foundation for future research in this area.

- **The eighth chapter** discusses the importance of ensuring the security of hardware used in IoT systems to prevent security threats such as data leakage and device malfunctioning. The chapter focuses on biometric-based methodologies, such as fingerprint, facial, and palmprint biometrics, to secure IoT hardware coprocessors against piracy and isolate counterfeited designs. Biometric security is incorporated during the high-level synthesis phase of the design process to ensure minimal design overhead and easy isolation of counterfeited designs. The palmprint biometric approach provides higher tamper tolerance, while the fingerprint biometric approach has a smaller probability of coincidence.

- **The ninth chapter** examines the weaknesses of alphanumerical passwords and explores graphical authentication as a potential alternative. The proposed solution is a graphical one-time password scheme where users select four picture passwords and enter their (x,y) coordinates on a 4×4 matrix. The system includes decoy images and is designed to protect against common graphical password attacks while being easy to remember and use. The chapter concludes that graphical authentication is a viable replacement for alphanumerical passwords and offers improved security, memorability, and usability.

- **The tenth chapter** highlights the pivotal role of AI in social cybersecurity and its ability to address emerging threats in the realm of social media. It underscores the importance of collaboration between stakeholders, including social media platforms, AI developers, and regulatory bodies, to ensure responsible and effective use of AI in social cybersecurity. By leveraging AI-driven approaches and embracing best practices, we can establish a more secure and resilient social media landscape for users worldwide.

- **The last chapter** before the conclusion emphasizes the need to strike a balance between harnessing the potential benefits of AI in social cybersecurity and addressing the ethical and privacy concerns associated with its implementation. It calls for collaboration between stakeholders, the adoption of multi-stakeholder governance frameworks, and the continuous monitoring and adaptation of ethical and privacy practices as technology evolves.

Each chapter delves into the respective topics, offering detailed insights, practical examples, and discussions on the latest advancements in the field.

Together, these chapters provide a comprehensive guide for readers interested in exploring the intersection of AI, biometrics, and cybersecurity.

Generally, this book provides in-depth insights and analysis of the opportunities and challenges presented by the intersection of AI, biometrics, and cybersecurity. It offers a comprehensive overview of AI in biometric security systems, covering various topics ranging from authentication and performance evaluation to advanced technologies and real-world case studies. The book aims to equip researchers, professionals, and students with a thorough understanding of the potential, implications, and future directions of AI in biometrics and cybersecurity.

References

[1] Horowitz, M. C., Allen, G. C., Saravalle, E., Cho, A., Frederick, K., and Scharre, P. (2018). *Artificial Intelligence and International Security*. Center for a New American Security.

[2] Hammad, M., Iliyasu, A. M., Elgendy, I. A., and Abd El-Latif, A. A. (2022). End-to-end data authentication deep learning model for securing IoT configurations. *Human-Centric Computing and Information Sciences*, 12(4).

[3] Prakash, A. J., Patro, K. K., Hammad, M., Tadeusiewicz, R., and Pławiak, P. (2022). BAED: a secured biometric authentication system using ECG signal based on deep learning techniques. *Biocybernetics and Biomedical Engineering*, 42(4), 1081–1093.

[4] Hammad, M., Ibrahim, M., and Hadhoud, M. M. (2016). A novel biometric based on ECG signals and images for human authentication. *International Arab Journal of Information Technology*, 13(6A), 959–964.

[5] Sakr, A. S., Pławiak, P., Tadeusiewicz, R., and Hammad, M. (2022). Cancelable ECG biometric based on combination of deep transfer learning with DNA and amino acid approaches for human authentication. *Information Sciences*, 585, 127–143.

[6] Hammad, M., and Wang, K. (2017, April). Fingerprint classification based on a Q-Gaussian multiclass support vector machine. In *Proceedings of the 2017 International Conference on Biometrics Engineering and Application* (pp. 39–44).

[7] Yadav, J. K. P. S., Jaffery, Z. A., and Singh, L. (2020). A short review on machine learning techniques used for fingerprint recognition. *Journal of Critical Reviews*, 7(13), 2768–2773.

[8] Aljuboori, A. M., and Abed, M. H. (2022). Finger knuckle pattern person identification system based on LDP-NPE and machine learning methods. *Bulletin of Electrical Engineering and Informatics*, 11(6), 3521–3529.

[9] Uz, T., Bebis, G., Erol, A., and Prabhakar, S. (2009). Minutiae-based template synthesis and matching for fingerprint authentication. *Computer Vision and Image Understanding*, 113(9), 979–992.

[10] Kumar, A., and Passi, A. (2010). Comparison and combination of iris matchers for reliable personal authentication. *Pattern Recognition*, 43(3), 1016–1026.

[11] Thavalengal, S., Bigioi, P., and Corcoran, P. (2015). Iris authentication in handheld devices-considerations for constraint-free acquisition. *IEEE Transactions on Consumer Electronics*, 61(2), 245–253.

[12] Morampudi, M. K., Prasad, M. V., and Raju, U. S. N. (2020). Privacy-preserving iris authentication using fully homomorphic encryption. *Multimedia Tools and Applications*, 79, 19215–19237.

[13] Azouji, N., Sami, A., and Taheri, M. (2022). EfficientMask-Net for face authentication in the era of COVID-19 pandemic. *Signal, Image and Video Processing*, 16(7), 1991–1999.

[14] Huang, D. Y., Lin, C. L., and Chen, Y. Y. (2022). Securable networked scheme with face authentication. *IET Biometrics*, 11(2), 97–108.

[15] Nguyen, H. H., Marcel, S., Yamagishi, J., and Echizen, I. (2022). Master face attacks on face recognition systems. *IEEE Transactions on Biometrics, Behavior, and Identity Science*, 4(3), 398–411.

[16] Gupta, S., Kacimi, M., and Crispo, B. (2022). Step and turn—a novel bimodal behavioral biometric-based user verification scheme for physical access control. *Computers & Security*, 118, 102722.

[17] Humphrey, D. (2022). Sensing the human: biometric surveillance and the Japanese technology industry. *Media, Culture & Society*, 44(1), 72–87.

[18] Ahamed, J., Maisha, M., Labiba, Z., Islam, M. A., and Nandi, D. (2022, March). A review report on the fingerprint-based biometric system in ATM banking. In *Proceedings of the Second International Conference on Computing Advancements* (pp. 522–529).

[19] Salman, A. S., Salman, A. S., and Salman, O. S. (2022). Using behavioral biometrics of fingerprint authentication to investigate physical and emotional user states. In *Proceedings of the Future Technologies Conference (FTC) 2021*, Volume 2 (pp. 240–256). Springer International Publishing.

[20] Bandari, V. (2023). Enterprise data security measures: a comparative review of effectiveness and risks across different industries and organization types. *International Journal of Business Intelligence and Big Data Analytics*, 6(1), 1–11.

Chapter 2

AI in biometrics and cybersecurity

Mohamed Hammad[1,2] and Ahmed A. Abd El-Latif[1,3]

This chapter provides an overview of the role of biometrics and artificial intelligence (AI) in enhancing cybersecurity. The chapter starts by defining biometrics and explaining the different types of biometric systems. It then delves into the challenges associated with traditional authentication methods and how biometric systems address these challenges. The chapter also discusses the use of AI in biometric systems, including machine learning techniques for identifying and authenticating users. Finally, the chapter highlights the importance of the integration of biometric and AI technologies in cybersecurity and the potential for future developments in this field.

2.1 Introduction

In the ever-evolving digital landscape, the adoption of biometric security systems has witnessed a significant rise, owing to their remarkable accuracy and efficiency in verifying individuals' identities. Biometric systems leverage distinct biological traits, such as fingerprints, facial recognition, and iris scans, to authenticate users and grant them access to various digital systems [1–12]. By relying on these inherent and unique characteristics, biometric security systems offer a robust and reliable means of identity verification, revolutionizing the way we secure our digital assets.

Despite their undeniable advantages, biometric security systems face a set of challenges that necessitate continuous research and innovation. One of the primary concerns is the attainment of high accuracy rates in biometric authentication [13]. Factors such as variations in environmental conditions, data quality, and the potential for spoofing attempts can hinder the reliability of these systems. Ensuring that biometric systems achieve consistently accurate results, even in diverse operating environments, remains a crucial objective for researchers and practitioners in the field.

[1]EIAS Data Science Lab, College of Computer and Information Sciences, Prince Sultan University, Saudi Arabia
[2]Department of Information Technology, Faculty of Computers and Information, Menoufia University, Egypt
[3]Department of Mathematics and Computer Science, Faculty of Science, Menoufia University, Egypt

Another challenge lies in the reliability of biometric systems, particularly in scenarios where individuals' biological traits may change over time. For instance, facial features can be altered due to aging or facial hair, while fingerprints may undergo temporary changes due to environmental factors. Adapting biometric systems to accommodate such variations and ensuring their continuous reliability is an ongoing endeavor within the research community.

Moreover, the susceptibility of biometric systems to attacks poses a significant concern for their widespread implementation. As biometric data becomes more prevalent in various applications, it becomes an attractive target for malicious actors seeking to exploit vulnerabilities. Adversarial attacks, presentation attacks, and replay attacks are among the potential threats that biometric systems must withstand [14]. Robust security measures and countermeasures are essential to safeguarding individuals' biometric data and maintaining the integrity of the authentication process.

To address these challenges and bolster the security of biometric systems, researchers have turned to the integration of Artificial Intelligence (AI) approaches, which have demonstrated promising outcomes. AI techniques, particularly those based on machine learning algorithms, offer a valuable means of enhancing the accuracy, reliability, and security of biometric systems [15]. By leveraging AI, biometric systems can continually learn from vast amounts of data, adapt to changing conditions, and improve their performance over time.

Machine learning algorithms enable biometric systems to identify intricate patterns, mitigate the impact of environmental variations, and discern genuine users from impostors. Through continuous learning and training, AI-powered biometric systems can refine their decision-making processes, resulting in more accurate and reliable authentication outcomes. Furthermore, AI algorithms can identify anomalies and potential attacks, enhancing the robustness of biometric systems and bolstering their resistance against adversarial attempts.

This chapter provides an overview of the history, challenges, terminologies, and fundamental concepts of biometrics and their security impacts. It highlights the importance of biometric security systems and how they have evolved over time. It discusses the challenges faced by biometric systems, including the limitations of traditional authentication methods, the need for increased accuracy and reliability, and the susceptibility to attacks. Additionally, the chapter provides an overview of the terminologies and fundamental concepts used in biometric security systems, such as biometric modalities, error rates, and enrollment and verification processes.

This chapter also highlights the role of AI in biometric security systems and cybersecurity. AI-based approaches, such as machine learning, have shown promising results in enhancing the accuracy and reliability of biometric systems. These approaches use algorithms that can learn and adapt to changes in the biometric data, improving the performance of the system over time. Additionally, the chapter discusses the security impacts of biometric data collection and use, including privacy concerns and potential ethical dilemmas.

2.2   History of biometric systems

The history of biometric systems stretches back thousands of years, with the use of unique physical or behavioral characteristics to identify individuals finding their roots in ancient civilizations [16]. Early societies relied on visual cues, such as facial features and body marks, to distinguish and recognize individuals from one another. However, it was during the nineteenth century that the concept of biometrics gained formal recognition and the first biometric system was developed [17].

Throughout history, various civilizations recognized the significance of individual identification. In ancient Egypt, Rome, and China, for example, facial features were used to identify individuals for administrative, commercial, and security purposes. These early applications of biometrics laid the groundwork for the modern understanding of the field.

The formalization of biometrics as a scientific discipline can be attributed to the work of Sir Francis Galton, who published the influential book *Fingerprints* in the late nineteenth century. Galton extensively explored the uniqueness and permanence of fingerprints, which became a cornerstone for their use in identification [17]. His research sparked further investigation into biometrics and ultimately led to the development of the first biometric system.

Edward Henry, an English police officer, made significant contributions to the field of biometrics with his pioneering work on fingerprint identification. In 1892, Henry introduced the Henry Classification System, a practical method for fingerprint classification and identification. This system standardized fingerprint patterns and principles, enabling the efficient identification of individuals based on their fingerprints. Henry's breakthrough set the stage for subsequent advancements in biometric technology.

Since the introduction of fingerprint identification systems, biometric technology has undergone continuous refinement and expansion. Advances in science, technology, and computing have facilitated the integration of additional biometric modalities, including iris scans, voice recognition, DNA analysis, and gait recognition. These modalities provide unique advantages and further enhance the accuracy and reliability of biometric systems.

One of the earliest documented instances of biometrics being used dates back to ancient Babylon, where fingerprints were used on clay tablets for business transactions [18]. The Chinese were also known to use handprints on official documents during the Qin Dynasty (221–206 BC) [19]. In the fourteenth century, the Persian mathematician Al-Khwarizmi described using fingerprints as a means of identifying people in his book, *The Book of Cryptographic Messages* [20].

The concept of using fingerprints for identification traces its roots back to the late nineteenth century when Sir Francis Galton, a renowned scientist and cousin of Charles Darwin, brought the uniqueness of fingerprints into the limelight. Galton's groundbreaking work on fingerprints, highlighted in his influential book titled *Fingerprints*, shed light on their distinctiveness and proposed their utilization for identification purposes. This pivotal publication served as the catalyst for the development of the first fingerprint identification system, pioneered by Edward Henry, an English police officer, in 1892 [21].

Galton's exploration of fingerprints revealed an astonishing truth: no two individuals possess identical ridge patterns on their fingertips. This intrinsic uniqueness forms the foundation of fingerprint identification, transforming it into a powerful tool for distinguishing individuals and establishing their identities. Henry recognized the potential of fingerprints as a reliable means of identification and embarked on developing a systematic approach to harnessing this phenomenon.

Drawing upon Galton's research, Henry introduced the Henry Classification System, an innovative framework that organized fingerprints into distinct categories based on their ridge patterns and other identifiable features. This system revolutionized the field of forensic science, providing investigators with a structured method for comparing and matching fingerprints collected from crime scenes with those of known individuals. The Henry Classification System marked a significant milestone in the history of fingerprint identification, establishing the groundwork for subsequent advancements in the field.

Over time, fingerprint identification systems evolved and adopted new technologies, transitioning from manual comparison to automated processes. Today, biometric security systems extensively utilize fingerprint recognition as a key component for identity authentication and access control. Advancements in imaging technology, such as high-resolution scanners and sophisticated algorithms, have elevated the accuracy and reliability of fingerprint recognition systems to unprecedented levels.

The integration of fingerprint recognition technology has found widespread applications in various domains, including law enforcement, border control, banking, and smartphone security. Its effectiveness in verifying individuals' identities with a high degree of certainty has propelled its adoption in critical areas where security and confidentiality are paramount.

By leveraging AI, fingerprint recognition systems can learn from vast datasets, adapt to different fingerprint variations, and continuously improve their performance. Machine learning models can analyze intricate patterns, identify minutiae, and effectively distinguish genuine fingerprints from fabricated or altered ones. Furthermore, the integration of AI enables fingerprint recognition systems to detect anomalies, such as spoofing attempts or forged fingerprints, bolstering their resistance against fraudulent activities.

The field of biometric technology has witnessed remarkable advancements and transformations over the course of several decades. This journey can be traced back to significant milestones in the mid-twentieth century, where pioneering breakthroughs introduced various biometric modalities for identification purposes. This in-depth introduction delves into the evolution of biometric technology, highlighting key developments such as the commercial application of photographs for identification in 1936, the introduction of voiceprints in the 1950s, and the emergence of facial recognition technology in the 1960s [22].

In 1936, a pivotal moment in the history of biometrics occurred with the introduction of the first commercial application of a biometric system. This innovative system relied on the utilization of photographs to identify and track criminals. By capturing and comparing facial features, law enforcement agencies gained a valuable tool for identifying individuals involved in criminal activities. The adoption of this early form of biometric technology marked a significant step forward in enhancing identification processes, allowing for more accurate and efficient criminal investigations.

The following decade witnessed another groundbreaking development in biometric technology with the introduction of voiceprints. In the 1950s, researchers recognized the unique characteristics embedded within an individual's voice and its potential for identification purposes. Voiceprints, similar to fingerprints, possess distinct patterns that are specific to each individual. By analyzing and comparing these patterns, voice recognition systems gained traction as a reliable biometric modality. This breakthrough opened new avenues for voice-based identification and authentication, finding applications in telephone security, voice-controlled systems, and forensic investigations.

The decade 1960s marked a significant milestone in biometric technology with the development of facial recognition systems. Researchers and engineers began exploring the intricate features and nuances of human faces, seeking ways to leverage these characteristics for identity verification. Early facial recognition systems utilized primitive algorithms to extract and compare facial features, paving the way for advancements in the field. Although these early systems were limited in accuracy and performance, they laid the foundation for future breakthroughs in facial recognition technology.

Over time, biometric technology continued to evolve and mature, incorporating advancements in computer vision, pattern recognition, and machine learning. The convergence of these disciplines empowered biometric systems to become more accurate, reliable, and capable of handling large-scale applications. Today, facial recognition technology has reached unprecedented levels of sophistication, enabled real-time identification, and tracked individuals in various settings, including law enforcement, border control, and secure access control systems.

Furthermore, the fusion of multiple biometric modalities, such as fingerprints, voiceprints, iris scans, and facial recognition, has led to the development of multimodal biometric systems. These systems leverage the strengths of each modality to enhance identification accuracy and overcome the limitations of individual biometric traits. By combining multiple sources of biometric data, multimodal systems provide robust and reliable identification solutions, ensuring a higher level of security and reducing the risk of false positives or negatives.

The development of computers and advanced algorithms in the latter half of the twentieth century paved the way for more sophisticated biometric systems. In the 1970s, automated fingerprint identification systems (AFIS) were developed, which used digital imaging technology and pattern recognition algorithms to match fingerprints. The first AFIS was installed in the United Kingdom in 1974 [23].

In the 1980s and 1990s, biometric technology continued to improve, with the introduction of iris recognition, retinal scanning, and facial thermography. In 1998, the International Biometric Group was formed, which helped to standardize biometric technology and establish guidelines for its use [23].

Today, biometric systems are used in a wide range of applications, from security and law enforcement to healthcare and financial services [24–26]. They are used to authenticate individuals for access to secure facilities, to track employee attendance and timekeeping, and to prevent identity theft and fraud. Biometric technology is also increasingly used in mobile devices, such as smartphones and tablets, to enable secure authentication and identity verification [27,28].

In recent years, the widespread adoption of biometric systems has raised concerns regarding privacy and data security [29]. Biometric data, consisting of unique physical or behavioral characteristics, holds sensitive and personal information about individuals. Therefore, safeguarding this data from unauthorized access or misuse is crucial.

To address these concerns, significant advancements have been made in encryption and secure storage techniques. Encryption algorithms are employed to encode biometric data, ensuring that it remains protected during transmission and storage. Additionally, secure storage systems, such as encrypted databases and secure servers, are implemented to safeguard biometric templates and prevent unauthorized access.

One approach to enhancing privacy in biometric systems is through the use of template protection techniques. Rather than storing the raw biometric data, biometric templates are derived from the original data and securely stored. Template protection methods, such as cryptographic transformations or fuzzy commitment schemes, ensure that the stored templates cannot be reverse engineered to retrieve the original biometric data. This adds an extra layer of security and privacy to biometric systems.

Furthermore, regulations and standards have been established to govern the collection, storage, and usage of biometric data. Privacy laws, such as the General Data Protection Regulation in Europe, impose strict guidelines on the handling of personal data, including biometric information. These regulations aim to protect individuals' privacy rights and ensure that organizations handling biometric data adhere to stringent security and privacy measures.

While concerns about privacy and data security persist, ongoing research and development efforts are focused on addressing these challenges. Collaborative efforts between academia, industry, and regulatory bodies aim to develop robust and secure biometric systems that prioritize privacy and data protection. This includes the development of privacy-enhancing technologies, such as secure multiparty computation, differential privacy, and homomorphic encryption, which enable secure processing and analysis of biometric data while preserving individual privacy.

As biometric technology continues to evolve, it is expected to play an increasingly important role in identity authentication and verification. Biometric systems offer numerous advantages over traditional methods, such as passwords or PINs, as they provide a more reliable and convenient means of identification. Biometric characteristics are unique to individuals and cannot be easily replicated or stolen, making them inherently secure.

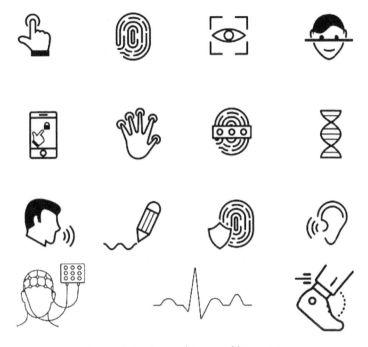

Figure 2.1   Several types of biometrics

With ongoing advancements in biometric technology, we can anticipate improvements in accuracy, efficiency, and user experience. Emerging trends, such as the integration of AI and machine learning algorithms, enable intelligent and adaptive biometric systems capable of identifying complex patterns and detecting anomalies. These advancements not only enhance the security and reliability of biometric systems but also contribute to the widespread adoption of biometrics across various sectors, including finance, healthcare, and transportation [30].

Biometrics can be classified into two broad categories: physiological and behavioral [31]. Figure 2.1 shows the different types of biometrics.

- **Physiological biometrics**: This type of biometrics is based on a person's physical characteristics, such as fingerprints, facial features, iris or retinal patterns, palm prints, or DNA. These characteristics are unique to each individual and remain constant over time.
- **Behavioral biometrics**: This type of biometrics is based on a person's behavior, such as typing rhythm, gait, signature, or voice. These characteristics are not necessarily unique to each individual, but they can still be used for identification purposes.

There are several motivations for using biometric systems [32]:

Security: Biometric systems can be used to enhance security by providing a reliable way to identify individuals. Biometric characteristics are difficult to replicate, making it more difficult for unauthorized individuals to gain access to secure facilities or information.

Convenience: Biometric systems can provide a convenient way for individuals to authenticate themselves, eliminating the need to remember passwords or carry identification cards. This can be particularly useful in settings where speed and efficiency are important, such as in airports or at large events.

Accuracy: Biometric systems can provide a high level of accuracy in identification, especially when compared to traditional identification methods such as passwords or identification cards. This can help to prevent identity theft and reduce fraud.

Cost savings: Biometric systems can help to reduce costs associated with traditional identification methods such as producing and distributing identification cards or maintaining password management systems.

Compliance: Biometric systems can help organizations to comply with regulations and standards related to security and identity verification, such as Healthcare Information Portability and Accountability Act (HIPAA) in the healthcare industry or Payment Card Industry Data Security Standard (PCI DSS) in the payment card industry.

Despite the potential benefits of biometric systems, there are also concerns related to privacy, data security, and the potential for misuse. As such, it is important for organizations to implement appropriate safeguards and procedures to ensure that biometric data is collected, stored, and used in a responsible and ethical manner. Biometric systems are used in a variety of applications, including the following:

- **Law enforcement**: Biometric systems have long been used by law enforcement agencies for identification and tracking of suspects. AFIS are commonly used to compare fingerprints found at a crime scene with those in a database of known criminals. Facial recognition technology is also used to identify suspects in surveillance footage [33].
- **Access control**: Biometric systems are commonly used to control access to secure facilities such as data centers, airports, and military bases. Biometric authentication can be used in conjunction with other security measures such as keycards and passwords to ensure that only authorized personnel are granted access. For example, some companies use facial recognition technology to verify employee identities before granting them access to certain areas of the building [34].
- **Time and attendance tracking**: Biometric systems are also used to track employee attendance and timekeeping. This helps to prevent time fraud and ensures that employees are paid accurately for the hours they work. For example, some companies use fingerprint scanners to record employee clock-in and clock-out times [35].
- **Healthcare**: Biometric systems are increasingly being used in healthcare settings to improve patient safety and prevent medical errors. For example, some hospitals use palm vein scanners to verify patient identities before administering medication or performing medical procedures [36].
- **Banking and financial services**: Biometric systems are used to enhance security and prevent fraud in banking and financial services. For example,

some banks use facial recognition technology to verify the identities of customers opening new accounts or accessing online banking services [37].

- **Border control**: Biometric systems are used in border control to verify the identities of travelers entering and leaving a country. For example, some airports use facial recognition technology to match passengers to their passports and verify their identities before allowing them to board a flight [38].
- **Mobile devices**: Biometric systems are increasingly being incorporated into mobile devices such as smartphones and tablets to improve security and provide a convenient way for users to authenticate themselves. For example, some smartphones use fingerprint scanners or facial recognition technology to unlock the device or authorize payments [39].

In conclusion, the history of biometric systems spans several centuries, from ancient Babylon to the modern day. Biometric systems have been used for a variety of purposes, including identification, authentication, and access control. The development of modern biometric systems has been driven by advances in technology, including computer vision, machine learning, and AI. While biometric systems have the potential to provide significant benefits in terms of security, convenience, and accuracy, there are also concerns related to privacy, data security, and the potential for misuse. As such, it is important for organizations to carefully consider the ethical and legal implications of implementing biometric systems, and to take appropriate steps to safeguard biometric data and protect individuals' rights.

2.3   Challenges of biometric systems

While biometric systems have the potential to provide significant benefits, there are also several challenges associated with their use [6,34,40]. These challenges include the following:

- **Accuracy**: Biometric systems are only as accurate as the biometric traits they are measuring. While some biometric traits, such as fingerprints, are highly accurate, others, such as facial recognition, can be less reliable. Inaccurate biometric systems can result in false positives (when the system incorrectly identifies a person) or false negatives (when the system fails to identify a person).
- **Privacy**: Biometric systems can raise concerns related to privacy, particularly in cases where biometric data is collected without individuals' knowledge or consent. There is also a risk that biometric data could be stolen or used for unauthorized purposes, such as identity theft or surveillance.
- **Security**: Biometric systems can be vulnerable to security threats such as hacking or data breaches. If biometric data is stolen or compromised, it could be used to impersonate individuals or gain access to secure systems.
- **Bias**: Biometric systems can be biased if the underlying data used to train the system is not representative of the population as a whole. This can result in incorrect identification or exclusion of certain groups of individuals.

- **Cost**: Biometric systems can be expensive to implement and maintain, particularly for organizations with large numbers of users or complex systems.
- **User acceptance**: Some individuals may be reluctant to use biometric systems due to concerns related to privacy, security, or cultural beliefs.

To address these challenges, organizations implementing biometric systems should take steps to ensure that they are accurate, secure, and compliant with applicable laws and regulations [41]. This includes implementing appropriate data security measures, providing transparency and choice around the collection and use of biometric data, and conducting ongoing testing and evaluation to ensure that the system is working as intended. Organizations should also be mindful of the potential for bias in biometric systems and take steps to ensure that they are inclusive and representative of the populations they serve. Finally, organizations should work to educate users about the benefits of biometric systems and address any concerns or questions they may have about their use.

AI approaches can also be used to help overcome the challenges associated with biometric systems in several ways [42–47]:

- *Accuracy*: AI can be used to improve the accuracy of biometric systems by using machine learning algorithms to better identify and classify biometric traits. By analyzing large amounts of data and learning from past mistakes, AI can help to reduce false positives and false negatives in biometric systems.
- *Privacy*: AI can be used to improve the privacy of biometric systems by using techniques such as differential privacy to protect sensitive data. This involves adding random noise to data to prevent individuals from being identified, while still allowing for useful information to be extracted.
- *Security*: AI can be used to improve the security of biometric systems by identifying and mitigating potential threats, such as hacking or data breaches. AI-based anomaly detection systems can help to identify unusual patterns of activity that may indicate a security threat, while machine learning algorithms can be used to predict and prevent potential attacks.
- *Bias*: AI can be used to reduce bias in biometric systems by improving the diversity and representativeness of training data. This involves using techniques such as data augmentation, where synthetic data is generated to increase the diversity of the training set, and bias mitigation techniques, where algorithms are used to detect and correct bias in data.
- *Cost*: AI can be used to reduce the cost of biometric systems by automating certain tasks and improving the efficiency of data processing. For example, AI-based facial recognition systems can be used to automatically detect and recognize individuals in large crowds, reducing the need for manual identification processes.
- *User acceptance*: AI can be used to improve user acceptance of biometric systems by providing a more seamless and natural user experience. For example, AI-based voice recognition systems can be used to authenticate users without the need for physical contact, while AI-based emotion recognition systems can be used to tailor the user experience to the individual's emotional state.

Overall, AI approaches can help to address many of the challenges associated with biometric systems, improving their accuracy, privacy, security, and user acceptance [42–47]. However, it is important to ensure that AI-based biometric systems are transparent, explainable, and ethical, with appropriate safeguards in place to protect individual rights and privacy.

2.4 Terminologies and fundamental concepts of biometric systems

Biometric systems are based on a variety of fundamental concepts and terminologies. Some of the key concepts and terms used in biometric systems include the following:

- **Biometric trait**: A biometric trait is a distinctive physical or behavioral characteristic that serves as a means of identifying individuals in various systems and applications [48]. These traits encompass a wide range of features, including fingerprints, which are unique patterns of ridges and valleys on the fingertips; facial features, such as the shape of the eyes, nose, and mouth; iris patterns, the intricate structures found in the colored part of the eye; voiceprints, which capture the distinctive vocal characteristics of an individual; and gait patterns, which refer to the unique walking style of a person. These biometric traits provide valuable information that can be captured, analyzed, and compared against reference data to establish and verify an individual's identity. By leveraging these diverse biometric characteristics, organizations and institutions can enhance their security measures and streamline various processes that require reliable and accurate identification.
- **Template**: A template serves as a digital representation of a biometric trait and plays a vital role in the identification and authentication process. It encompasses the essential information extracted from biometric data, capturing the distinct characteristics and features specific to an individual. Through advanced algorithms and analysis, templates are generated by identifying and isolating the unique patterns and traits within the biometric data, such as fingerprints, facial features, iris patterns, voiceprints, or gait patterns. These templates provide a compact and standardized representation of the biometric trait, allowing for efficient storage and comparison against reference templates during the identification process. By utilizing templates, biometric systems can achieve accurate and reliable identification, enabling secure access control, streamlined authentication procedures, and various other applications where precise identification is essential [49].
- **Enrollment**: Enrollment is a crucial step in the implementation of a biometric system, facilitating the registration and incorporation of an individual's biometric data. This process involves capturing the desired biometric trait, such as fingerprints, facial features, iris patterns, voiceprints, or gait patterns, through specialized sensors or devices. The collected biometric data is then subjected to rigorous analysis and processing, extracting unique characteristics, and

creating a template that represents the individual's biometric identity. This template is securely stored within the biometric system's database for future reference and comparison during identification or verification procedures. Enrollment ensures that each individual's biometric data is properly recorded, standardized, and associated with their respective identity within the system. By accurately capturing and storing biometric templates during the enrollment process, biometric systems can effectively authenticate individuals and provide secure access control, enhanced identity management, and a wide range of applications that rely on precise identification [50].

- **Verification**: Verification is a fundamental step in biometric systems that aims to confirm the identity of an individual using their unique biometric data. In the verification process, the biometric data of an individual, such as fingerprints, facial features, iris patterns, voiceprints, or gait patterns, is captured using specialized sensors or devices. This captured biometric data is then compared to a preexisting template stored in the system's database. The template serves as a reference point, containing the extracted and encoded features of the individual's biometric trait. By employing advanced algorithms and pattern-matching techniques, the system analyzes the captured biometric data and compares it to the stored template. The objective is to determine whether a match exists between the presented biometric data and the template. If a match is found within a certain threshold of acceptance, the system confirms the individual's identity. Verification plays a crucial role in various scenarios, including access control systems, financial transactions, and secure authentication processes. By utilizing biometric data and the process of verification, organizations can enhance security, reduce fraud, and ensure reliable and accurate identification of individuals [49].

- **Identification**: Identification is a fundamental function of biometric systems that aims to determine the identity of an individual when their identity is unknown. In the process of identification, the biometric data of an individual, such as fingerprints, facial features, iris patterns, voiceprints, or gait patterns, is captured using specialized sensors or devices. This captured biometric data is then compared to a database of stored templates within the system. The templates in the database represent the biometric data of known individuals. The system analyzes the captured biometric data and compares it to the templates in the database using advanced algorithms and pattern-matching techniques. The objective is to find a match or a close similarity between the presented biometric data and one of the stored templates. If a match is found within a certain threshold of acceptance, the system identifies the individual and retrieves their corresponding identity from the database. Identification is commonly used in scenarios where the identity of individuals needs to be established, such as law enforcement, border control, and large-scale access control systems. By leveraging biometric data and the process of identification, organizations can enhance security, streamline processes, and accurately identify individuals even when their identity is unknown [51].

- **False positive**: A false positive refers to a situation in which a biometric system erroneously identifies an individual as a match, even though there is no actual match between the presented biometric data and the stored templates. False positives are considered errors in biometric identification. They occur when the system incorrectly associates the captured biometric data with a stored template, leading to a mistaken identification. False positives can happen due to various factors, including technical limitations, environmental conditions, and the quality of the biometric data itself. These errors can result in unauthorized access or the misidentification of individuals, potentially compromising the security and integrity of the system. Biometric systems strive to minimize the occurrence of false positives by employing sophisticated algorithms, improving the accuracy of data capture devices, and setting appropriate thresholds for matching criteria. Continuous research and development efforts are dedicated to enhancing the reliability and performance of biometric systems, reducing the occurrence of false positives, and ensuring the overall effectiveness and trustworthiness of biometric identification [52].

- **False negative**: A false negative occurs when a biometric system fails to identify an individual as a match, even though there is a genuine match between the presented biometric data and the stored templates. In other words, it is an error where the system incorrectly rejects a valid match. False negatives can happen due to various reasons, such as technical limitations, poor quality of biometric data, variations in the captured data compared to the stored templates, or inadequate matching algorithms. When a false negative occurs, it means that the system fails to recognize the true identity of an individual who should have been identified. This can lead to denied access to authorized individuals, security breaches, and inconvenience in various applications such as access control or identity verification processes. To minimize the occurrence of false negatives, biometric systems undergo rigorous testing, calibration, and optimization to ensure optimal performance. Advanced algorithms, high-quality data capture devices, and appropriate threshold settings are employed to improve accuracy and reduce the chances of false negatives. Continuous research and development efforts are focused on enhancing the sensitivity and reliability of biometric systems, aiming to achieve a balance between security and user convenience while minimizing false negatives and maximizing correct identifications [52].

- **Matching score**: A matching score serves as a crucial quantitative measure in biometric systems, representing the extent of similarity between a given biometric sample and a stored template. It provides a numerical value that gauges the likeness or correlation between the presented biometric data and the reference template. This matching score plays a vital role in determining the presence of a match and effectively managing the rates of false positives and false negatives within the system. By comparing the matching score to predefined thresholds, the system can make accurate decisions about match verification or identification. It allows for controlling the balance between accepting legitimate matches and minimizing erroneous identifications, ensuring the system's reliability and security are maintained at optimal levels [53].

- **Biometric performance metrics**: Biometric performance metrics play a crucial role in assessing the accuracy and effectiveness of biometric systems. These metrics provide quantitative measures that enable the evaluation of system performance. The false positive rate (FPR) indicates the probability of incorrectly identifying an individual who should not be granted access, while the false negative rate (FNR) represents the likelihood of failing to identify an individual who should be granted access. These two metrics collectively measure the system's reliability and its ability to balance security and convenience. Another significant metric is the equal error rate (EER), which signifies the point at which the FPR and FNR are equal. The EER serves as an important benchmark for comparing different biometric systems, as it reflects the system's overall performance in terms of both false positives and false negatives. These biometric performance metrics provide valuable insights into the strengths and limitations of a system, aiding in its optimization and continual improvement [54].

- **Sensor**: A sensor is an essential component of biometric systems, responsible for capturing the required biometric data from individuals. Different types of sensors are employed based on the specific biometric trait being measured. For instance, a fingerprint sensor utilizes specialized technology to capture and analyze the unique ridge patterns present on an individual's fingertip. This sensor employs various techniques such as optical imaging or capacitive sensing to accurately capture the distinct fingerprint characteristics. Similarly, a camera is commonly used to capture facial features by capturing images or videos of an individual's face. The camera sensor detects and records various facial attributes, including the shape, contours, and proportions of facial structures, enabling subsequent analysis and identification. These sensors are designed with precision and sensitivity to capture biometric data accurately and reliably, ensuring the integrity of the biometric system and enabling effective authentication processes [55].

- **Feature extraction**: Feature extraction plays a crucial role in biometric systems as it involves identifying and extracting distinct characteristics from biometric data that aid in differentiating individuals. In the case of fingerprints, feature extraction focuses on capturing key attributes such as the location and orientation of ridges and valleys. This process involves analyzing the fingerprint image and detecting specific ridge patterns, minutiae points (e.g., ridge endings, bifurcations), and other relevant details. By extracting and quantifying these unique features, a compact representation, often referred to as a template, is created. This template serves as a condensed digital representation of the individual's biometric trait, enabling efficient storage, comparison, and matching processes within the biometric system. Feature extraction algorithms leverage advanced techniques, such as image processing, pattern recognition, and machine learning, to ensure accurate and reliable extraction of discriminative features across different biometric modalities, enhancing the overall performance and effectiveness of the biometric system [56].

- **Biometric fusion**: Biometric fusion is an essential concept in biometric systems that involve integrating multiple biometric modalities to enhance the system's accuracy, reliability, and overall performance. By combining different biometric traits, such as facial recognition and voice recognition, the system can leverage the unique strengths of each modality to increase the likelihood of correct identification and improve the overall robustness of the system. Biometric fusion techniques aim to exploit the complementary nature of different modalities, as each modality captures distinct aspects of an individual's identity. For instance, while facial recognition focuses on facial features, such as the shape of the face and unique landmarks, voice recognition analyzes vocal characteristics like pitch, tone, and speech patterns. By fusing these modalities, the system can achieve a higher level of confidence in identification by cross verifying the results obtained from each modality, reducing the chances of false positives and false negatives. Biometric fusion algorithms employ sophisticated methodologies, including feature-level fusion, score-level fusion, and decision-level fusion, to effectively combine and interpret the information obtained from multiple biometric sources. This integration of modalities in biometric fusion contributes to the advancement of biometric systems, enabling improved accuracy and reliability in diverse real-world applications, such as access control, identity verification, and forensic investigations [57].
- **Liveness detection**: Liveness detection plays a crucial role in biometric systems by verifying the authenticity and vitality of the biometric sample being presented. It is designed to prevent spoofing attacks, where an imposter tries to deceive the system using fake representations like photographs, masks, or artificial replicas. Liveness detection techniques employ various methods to differentiate between live individuals and fraudulent attempts. These methods often leverage physiological or behavioral characteristics that are difficult to replicate artificially. For example, in the case of facial recognition, liveness detection algorithms may analyze subtle facial movements, such as blinking, changes in skin texture, or response to challenges like asking the individual to smile or turn their head. These dynamic cues help confirm the presence of a live person. Similarly, in fingerprint recognition, liveness detection algorithms may analyze characteristics like blood flow, finger pressure, or even response to thermal stimuli to ensure the presence of a live finger. By incorporating liveness detection into biometric systems, the vulnerability to spoofing attacks is significantly reduced, enhancing the security and reliability of the system. Liveness detection is a rapidly evolving field, constantly advancing with the emergence of new technologies and techniques to stay ahead of sophisticated spoofing attempts. Continuous research and development in liveness detection are crucial to maintaining the integrity and trustworthiness of biometric systems in various domains, including law enforcement, border control, and financial institutions [58].
- **Biometric database**: A biometric database is a secure repository that stores biometric templates for identification and verification purposes. These

templates contain unique features extracted from individuals' biometric data, such as fingerprints or facial scans. To protect the privacy and integrity of this sensitive information, stringent security measures are implemented. Access to the database is tightly controlled through authentication mechanisms and encryption techniques. Physical security measures and regular monitoring ensure that the database is protected from unauthorized access and tampering. Compliance with data protection regulations and ongoing research contribute to continuously improving the security of biometric databases. By maintaining the trust and integrity of these databases, organizations can rely on them for accurate identification and verification in various applications [59].

- **Multimodal biometrics**: Multimodal biometrics is a technique that combines multiple biometric modalities to enhance the accuracy and reliability of biometric systems. By leveraging the strengths of different biometric traits, such as fingerprint, iris, face, voice, or behavioral characteristics, multimodal biometrics aims to overcome the limitations of relying on a single modality. Integrating multiple modalities provides a more comprehensive and robust identification or verification process, reducing the risk of false positives (incorrectly accepting an unauthorized person) and false negatives (failing to recognize an authorized person). The system captures and analyzes data from multiple sources, applying sophisticated algorithms to fuse and match the biometric information. This fusion of modalities enhances the overall performance of the biometric system, making it more resilient to spoofing attacks and capable of handling variations in individuals' biometric characteristics. By embracing multimodal biometrics, organizations can achieve higher accuracy and security in their identification and authentication processes, ensuring reliable and trustworthy outcomes [60].

- **Biometric encryption**: Biometric encryption is an advanced security technique that leverages biometric data to encrypt sensitive information, ensuring its confidentiality and integrity. By combining the unique attributes of an individual's biometric trait, such as fingerprints, iris patterns, or voiceprints, with encryption algorithms, biometric encryption provides a highly secure and personalized approach to data protection. During the encryption process, the biometric data is transformed into a mathematical representation or template, which serves as the encryption key. This key is then used to encrypt the desired information, such as files or messages. To decrypt the data, the same biometric trait is required for authentication, ensuring that only authorized individuals with matching biometric characteristics can access the decrypted information. Biometric encryption offers an additional layer of security by incorporating the inherent uniqueness of biometric traits, making it significantly more challenging for unauthorized individuals to gain access to the encrypted data [61].

Understanding these concepts is important for developing and deploying effective and reliable biometric systems. By combining different modalities, using advanced sensor technology, and implementing strong security measures, it is possible to build biometric systems that are accurate, secure, and efficient.

2.5   AI in biometric security systems and cybersecurity

The use of AI in biometric security systems has become increasingly popular due to its ability to enhance the accuracy and efficiency of such systems. AI can be used to address several challenges faced by biometric systems, including those related to data quality, performance, and security. The following are some ways in which AI is being used in biometric security systems and cybersecurity [62–65]:

- **Data quality improvement**: AI algorithms can be used to improve the quality of biometric data by removing noise, filling gaps, and enhancing the resolution of images or videos. This can help improve the accuracy of biometric systems by providing higher quality data for analysis [66].
- **Data preprocessing**: Before being analyzed by biometric algorithms, biometric data often needs to be preprocessed to improve its quality. AI can be used to automate and optimize this process, including tasks such as image enhancement, segmentation, and normalization [67].
- **Pattern recognition**: AI-based algorithms are well suited for pattern recognition tasks, making them ideal for identifying and matching biometric data. For example, AI algorithms can be trained to recognize facial features or fingerprint patterns, making it easier to identify and verify individuals [66].
- **Deep learning**: Deep learning is a type of AI that uses neural networks to learn and analyze complex patterns in data. Deep learning can be used to improve the accuracy and reliability of biometric systems by training algorithms to recognize complex patterns in biometric data [68].
- **Liveness detection**: AI algorithms can be used to detect and prevent fraud by verifying the liveness of an individual providing biometric data. For example, AI can be used to detect whether a face or fingerprint is being presented by a live individual or a fake representation, such as a photograph or a mask [69].
- **Biometric template protection**: Biometric templates are unique representations of an individual's biometric data, such as a fingerprint template or facial recognition template. It is important to protect these templates from unauthorized access or misuse. AI can be used to develop secure methods for storing and protecting biometric templates, such as encryption or biometric watermarking [70].
- **Security and encryption**: AI can be used to enhance the security of biometric systems by encrypting biometric data and protecting it from unauthorized access. AI algorithms can be used to develop secure encryption methods that use biometric data as the key [71].
- **Continuous authentication**: Biometric systems can also be used for continuous authentication, which involves verifying an individual's identity on an ongoing basis during a session or transaction. AI can be used to develop algorithms that continuously monitor biometric data and detect anomalies that may indicate unauthorized access or fraudulent activity [72].
- **Threat detection**: AI can be used to detect and respond to cybersecurity threats in real time. For example, AI-based algorithms can be used to

monitor network traffic and detect anomalous behavior that may indicate a cyberattack [73].

- **Behavioral biometrics**: In addition to physiological biometrics, such as fingerprints or facial recognition, behavioral biometrics can also be used to identify individuals based on unique patterns of behavior, such as typing rhythm or mouse movements. AI can be used to analyze and identify these patterns, allowing for more robust authentication and fraud detection [74].
- **Adversarial attacks**: Biometric systems can be vulnerable to adversarial attacks, in which an attacker attempts to manipulate or deceive the system. AI can be used to develop algorithms that can detect and defend against such attacks, by identifying patterns of behavior or data that are inconsistent with legitimate use [75].
- **Multimodal fusion**: As previously mentioned, combining multiple biometric modalities can improve the accuracy and reliability of biometric systems. AI can be used to develop algorithms that effectively fuse different biometric modalities, such as facial recognition and voice recognition, to achieve higher accuracy rates [76].

AI is playing an increasingly important role in the development and deployment of biometric security systems and cybersecurity. By leveraging AI's capabilities in areas such as pattern recognition, data processing, and continuous monitoring, biometric systems can be made more accurate, reliable, and secure.

2.6   Conclusion

In conclusion, biometric systems have come a long way since their inception in ancient times, and advancements in technology and AI have enabled biometric systems to be more accurate, reliable, and secure than ever before. Despite the many benefits of biometric systems, there are still several challenges that need to be addressed, including issues related to data quality, privacy, and security.

To overcome these challenges, AI approaches are being used in various ways, such as data preprocessing, pattern recognition, deep learning, liveness detection, security and encryption, threat detection, biometric template protection, multimodal fusion, continuous authentication, and behavioral biometrics. By leveraging AI's capabilities, biometric systems can be made more accurate, reliable, and secure, and can be used for a wide range of applications, such as border control, law enforcement, access control, and mobile devices.

However, it is important to ensure that biometric systems are designed and implemented in a way that protects individual privacy and data security, and that they comply with ethical and legal guidelines. As biometric systems continue to evolve and become more prevalent, it is crucial that they are developed and deployed in a responsible and transparent manner, with the goal of maximizing their benefits while minimizing their potential risks.

References

[1] Hammad, M., Ibrahim, M., and Hadhoud, M. M. (2016). A novel biometric based on ECG signals and images for human authentication. *International Arab Journal of Information Technology*, 13(6A), 959–964.

[2] Sakr, A. S., Pławiak, P., Tadeusiewicz, R., and Hammad, M. (2022). Cancelable ECG biometric based on combination of deep transfer learning with DNA and amino acid approaches for human authentication. *Information Sciences*, 585, 127–143.

[3] Penny, W. D., Roberts, S. J., Curran, E. A., and Stokes, M. J. (2000). EEG-based communication: A pattern recognition approach. *IEEE Transactions on Rehabilitation Engineering*, 8(2), 214–215.

[4] Seha, S. N. A. and Hatzinakos, D. (2020). EEG-based human recognition using steady-state AEPs and subject-unique spatial filters. *IEEE Transactions on Information Forensics and Security*, 15, 3901–3910.

[5] Hammad, M. and Wang, K. (2017, April). Fingerprint classification based on a Q-Gaussian multiclass support vector machine. In *Proceedings of the 2017 International Conference on Biometrics Engineering and Application* (pp. 39–44).

[6] Maltoni, D., Maio, D., Jain, A. K., and Prabhakar, S. (2009). *Handbook of Fingerprint Recognition* (Vol. 2). London: Springer.

[7] Chen, J., Shen, F., Chen, D. Z., and Flynn, P. J. (2016). Iris recognition based on human-interpretable features. *IEEE Transactions on Information Forensics and Security*, 11(7), 1476–1485.

[8] da Costa, R. M. and Gonzaga, A. (2012). Dynamic features for iris recognition. *IEEE Transactions on Systems, Man, and Cybernetics, Part B (Cybernetics)*, 42(4), 1072–1082.

[9] Islam, S. M., Davies, R., Bennamoun, M., Owens, R. A., and Mian, A. S. (2013). Multibiometric human recognition using 3D ear and face features. *Pattern Recognition*, 46(3), 613–627.

[10] Saber, S., Amin, K., Pławiak, P., Tadeusiewicz, R., and Hammad, M. (2022). Graph convolutional network with triplet attention learning for person re-identification. *Information Sciences*, 617, 331–345.

[11] Saber, S., Meshoul, S., Amin, K., Pławiak, P., and Hammad, M. (2023). A multi-attention approach for person re-identification using deep learning. *Sensors*, 23(7), 3678.

[12] Prakash, A. J., Patro, K. K., Hammad, M., Tadeusiewicz, R., and Pławiak, P. (2022). BAED: A secured biometric authentication system using ECG signal based on deep learning techniques. *Biocybernetics and Biomedical Engineering*, 42(4), 1081–1093.

[13] Hammad, M., Liu, Y., and Wang, K. (2018). Multimodal biometric authentication systems using convolution neural network based on different level fusion of ECG and fingerprint. *IEEE Access*, 7, 26527–26542.

[14] Hammad, M. and Wang, K. (2019). Parallel score fusion of ECG and fingerprint for human authentication based on convolution neural network. *Computers & Security*, 81, 107–122.

[15] Patel, V. M., Chellappa, R., Chandra, D., and Barbello, B. (2016). Continuous user authentication on mobile devices: Recent progress and remaining challenges. *IEEE Signal Processing Magazine*, 33(4), 49–61.

[16] Wayman, J. L., Jain, A. K., Maltoni, D., and Maio, D. (eds.) (2005). *Biometric Systems: Technology, Design and Performance Evaluation*. Berlin: Springer Science & Business Media.

[17] Samal, A. and Iyengar, P. A. (1992). Automatic recognition and analysis of human faces and facial expressions: A survey. *Pattern Recognition*, 25(1), 65–77.

[18] Minaee, S., Abdolrashidi, A., Su, H., Bennamoun, M., and Zhang, D. (2023). Biometrics recognition using deep learning: A survey. *Artificial Intelligence Review*, 1–49.

[19] Li, P., Yang, S., Qi, R., Zhu, H., Zhang, Q., and Wang, Q. (2021). Handprints on bricks from the Jin-Yuan Period (1115–1368 CE) of Inner Mongolia, China—A case of art experiments by laborers. *Journal of Archaeological Science: Reports*, 37, 102983.

[20] Al-Kadit, I. A. (1992). Origins of cryptology: The Arab contributions. *Cryptologia*, 16(2), 97–126.

[21] Berry, J. and Stoney, D. A. (2001). The history and development of fingerprinting. *Advances in Fingerprint Technology*, 2, 13–52.

[22] Clarke, N. L. and Furnell, S. M. (2007). Advanced user authentication for mobile devices. *Computers & Security*, 26(2), 109–119.

[23] Jain, A. K., Nandakumar, K., and Ross, A. (2016). 50 years of biometric research: Accomplishments, challenges, and opportunities. *Pattern Recognition Letters*, 79, 80–105.

[24] Hammad, M., Pławiak, P., Wang, K., and Acharya, U. R. (2021). ResNet-Attention model for human authentication using ECG signals. *Expert Systems*, 38(6), e12547.

[25] Hammad, M., Iliyasu, A. M., Elgendy, I. A., and Abd El-Latif, A. A. (2022). End-to-end data authentication deep learning model for securing IoT configurations. *Human-Centric Computing and Information Sciences*, 12(4).

[26] Wang, J. S. (2021). Exploring biometric identification in FinTech applications based on the modified TAM. *Financial Innovation*, 7(1), 42.

[27] Zhang, W. Z., Elgendy, I. A., Hammad, M., *et al.* (2020). Secure and optimized load balancing for multitier IoT and edge-cloud computing systems. *IEEE Internet of Things Journal*, 8(10), 8119–8132.

[28] Sedik, A., Hammad, M., Abd El-Latif, A. A., *et al.* (2021). Deep learning modalities for biometric alteration detection in 5G networks-based secure smart cities. *IEEE Access*, 9, 94780–94788.

[29] Romanou, A. (2018). The necessity of the implementation of privacy by design in sectors where data protection concerns arise. *Computer Law & Security Review*, 34(1), 99–110.

[30] Furnell, S. and Clarke, N. (2012). Power to the people? The evolving recognition of human aspects of security. *Computers & Security*, 31(8), 983–988.

[31] Hammad, M., Zhang, S., and Wang, K. (2019). A novel two-dimensional ECG feature extraction and classification algorithm based on convolution neural network for human authentication. *Future Generation Computer Systems*, 101, 180–196.

[32] Dargan, S. and Kumar, M. (2020). A comprehensive survey on the biometric recognition systems based on physiological and behavioral modalities. *Expert Systems with Applications*, 143, 113114.

[33] Smith, M. and Miller, S. (2022). The ethical application of biometric facial recognition technology. *AI & Society*, 1–9.

[34] Gates, K. A. (2011). *Our Biometric Future: Facial Recognition Technology and the Culture of Surveillance* (Vol. 2). New York, NY: NYU Press.

[35] Sani, Y. M., Umeh, M. P., and Adamu, M. (2019). Biometric finger prints security system for clock-in and clock-out for primary school. *i-manager's Journal on Pattern Recognition*, 6(3), 7.

[36] Fletcher, R. R., Raghavan, V., Zha, R., Haverkamp, M., and Hibberd, P. L. (2014, October). Development of mobile-based hand vein biometrics for global health patient identification. In *IEEE Global Humanitarian Technology Conference (GHTC 2014)* (pp. 541–547). Piscataway, NJ: IEEE.

[37] Chen, X., You, X., and Chang, V. (2021). FinTech and commercial banks' performance in China: A leap forward or survival of the fittest? *Technological Forecasting and Social Change*, 166, 120645.

[38] Khan, N. and Efthymiou, M. (2021). The use of biometric technology at airports: The case of customs and border protection (CBP). *International Journal of Information Management Data Insights*, 1(2), 100049.

[39] Lee, P. (2017). Prints charming: How fingerprints are trailblazing mainstream biometrics. *Biometric Technology Today*, 2017(4), 8–11.

[40] Vacca, J. (2007). *Biometric Technologies and Verification Systems*. Amsterdam: Elsevier.

[41] Humphreys, E. (2008). Information security management standards: Compliance, governance and risk management. *Information Security Technical Report*, 13(4), 247–255.

[42] Liang, Y., Samtani, S., Guo, B., and Yu, Z. (2020). Behavioral biometrics for continuous authentication in the internet-of-things era: An artificial intelligence perspective. *IEEE Internet of Things Journal*, 7(9), 9128–9143.

[43] Berghoff, C., Neu, M., and von Twickel, A. (2021). The interplay of AI and biometrics: Challenges and opportunities. *Computer*, 54(9), 80–85.

[44] Jaswal, G., Kanhangad, V., and Ramachandra, R. (eds.). (2021). *AI and Deep Learning in Biometric Security: Trends, Potential, and Challenges*. Boca Raton, FL: CRC Press.

[45] Rüb, M., Herbst, J., Lipps, C., and Schotten, H. D. (2022, October). No one acts like you: AI based behavioral biometric identification. In *2022 Third*

International Conference on Next Generation Computing Applications (NextComp) (pp. 1–7). Piscataway, NJ: IEEE.

[46] Abdullahi, S. B., Khunpanuk, C., Bature, Z. A., Chiroma, H., Pakkaranang, N., Abubakar, A. B., and Ibrahim, A. H. (2022). Biometric information recognition using artificial intelligence algorithms: A performance comparison. *IEEE Access*, 10, 49167–49183.

[47] Gavrilova, M. L. and Monwar, M. (2013). *Multimodal Biometrics and Intelligent Image Processing for Security Systems*. IGI Global.

[48] Xiao, Q. (2007). Technology review-biometrics-technology, application, challenge, and computational intelligence solutions. *IEEE Computational Intelligence Magazine*, 2(2), 5–25.

[49] Jain, A. K., Ross, A., and Prabhakar, S. (2004). An introduction to biometric recognition. *IEEE Transactions on Circuits and Systems for Video Technology*, 14(1), 4–20.

[50] Matyas Jr, S. M. and Stapleton, J. (2000). A biometric standard for information management and security. *Computers & Security*, 19(5), 428–441.

[51] Shen, W., Surette, M., and Khanna, R. (1997). Evaluation of automated biometrics-based identification and verification systems. *Proceedings of the IEEE*, 85(9), 1464–1478.

[52] Dunstone, T. and Yager, N. (eds.). (2009). *Biometric System and Data Analysis: Design, Evaluation, and Data Mining*. Boston, MA: Springer US.

[53] Yager, N. and Dunstone, T. (2008). The biometric menagerie. *IEEE Transactions on Pattern Analysis and Machine Intelligence*, 32(2), 220–230.

[54] Rajasekar, V., Premalatha, J., and Sathya, K. (2021). Cancelable iris template for secure authentication based on random projection and double random phase encoding. *Peer-to-Peer Networking and Applications*, 14, 747–762.

[55] Chaki, J., Dey, N., Shi, F., and Sherratt, R. S. (2019). Pattern mining approaches used in sensor-based biometric recognition: A review. *IEEE Sensors Journal*, 19(10), 3569–3580.

[56] Delac, K. and Mislav G. (2004). A survey of biometric recognition methods. In *Proceedings of 46th International Symposium on Electronics in Marine (Elmar-2004)*. Piscataway, NJ: IEEE.

[57] Gudavalli, M., Raju, S. V., Babu, A. V., and Kumar, D. S. (2012, March). Multimodal biometrics—Sources, architecture and fusion techniques: An overview. In *2012 International Symposium on Biometrics and Security Technologies* (pp. 27–34). Piscataway, NJ: IEEE.

[58] Hammad, M., Luo, G., and Wang, K. (2019). Cancelable biometric authentication system based on ECG. *Multimedia Tools and Applications*, 78, 1857–1887.

[59] Maio, D., Maltoni, D., Cappelli, R., Wayman, J. L., and Jain, A. K. (2002). FVC2000: Fingerprint verification competition. *IEEE Transactions on Pattern Analysis and Machine Intelligence*, 24(3), 402–412.

[60] Sanjekar, P. S. and Patil, J. B. (2013). An overview of multimodal biometrics. *Signal & Image Processing*, 4(1), 57.

[61] Soutar, C., Roberge, D., Stoianov, A., Gilroy, R., and Kumar, B. V. (1999). Biometric encryption. In *ICSA Guide to Cryptography* (Vol. 22, p. 649). New York, NY: McGraw-Hill.

[62] Pooyandeh, M., Han, K. J., and Sohn, I. (2022). Cybersecurity in the AI-based metaverse: A survey. *Applied Sciences*, 12(24), 12993.

[63] Zhang, Z., Ning, H., Shi, F., *et al.* (2022). Artificial intelligence in cyber security: research advances, challenges, and opportunities. *Artificial Intelligence Review*, 1–25.

[64] Yamin, M. M., Ullah, M., Ullah, H., and Katt, B. (2021). Weaponized AI for cyber attacks. *Journal of Information Security and Applications*, 57, 102722.

[65] Taddeo, M. (2019). Three ethical challenges of applications of artificial intelligence in cybersecurity. *Minds and Machines*, 29, 187–191.

[66] Anantrasirichai, N. and Bull, D. (2022). Artificial intelligence in the creative industries: A review. *Artificial Intelligence Review*, 55, 1–68.

[67] Ngugi, L. C., Abelwahab, M., and Abo-Zahhad, M. (2021). Recent advances in image processing techniques for automated leaf pest and disease recognition— A review. *Information Processing in Agriculture*, 8(1), 27–51.

[68] Grekousis, G. (2019). Artificial neural networks and deep learning in urban geography: A systematic review and meta-analysis. *Computers, Environment and Urban Systems*, 74, 244–256.

[69] Nigam, A., Pasricha, R., Singh, T., and Churi, P. (2021). A systematic review on AI-based proctoring systems: Past, present and future. *Education and Information Technologies*, 26(5), 6421–6445.

[70] Rathgeb, C. and Busch, C. (2012). Multi-biometric template protection: Issues and challenges. *New Trends and Developments in Biometrics*, 173–190.

[71] Tarif, E. B., Wibowo, S., Wasimi, S., and Tareef, A. (2018). A hybrid encryption/hiding method for secure transmission of biometric data in mul-timodal authentication system. *Multimedia Tools and Applications*, 77, 2485–2503.

[72] Peng, J., Choo, K. K. R., and Ashman, H. (2016). User profiling in intrusion detection: A review. *Journal of Network and Computer Applications*, 72, 14–27.

[73] Vähäkainu, P. and Lehto, M. (2019, February). Artificial intelligence in the cyber security environment. In *ICCWS 2019 14th International Conference on Cyber Warfare and Security: ICCWS 2019* (p. 431). Oxford: Academic Conferences and Publishing Limited.

[74] Ryman-Tubb, N. F., Krause, P., and Garn, W. (2018). How artificial intel-ligence and machine learning research impacts payment card fraud detec-tion: A survey and industry benchmark. *Engineering Applications of Artificial Intelligence*, 76, 130–157.

[75] Khalaf, B. A., Mostafa, S. A., Mustapha, A., Mohammed, M. A., and Abduallah, W. M. (2019). Comprehensive review of artificial intelligence

and statistical approaches in distributed denial of service attack and defense methods. *IEEE Access*, 7, 51691–51713.

[76]   Shekhar, S., Patel, V. M., Nasrabadi, N. M., and Chellappa, R. (2013). Joint sparse representation for robust multimodal biometrics recognition. *IEEE Transactions on Pattern Analysis and Machine Intelligence*, 36(1), 113–126.

Chapter 3

Biometric security performance: analysis methods and tools for evaluation and assessment

Mohamed Hammad[1,2] and Ahmed A. Abd El-Latif[1,3]

3.1 Introduction

Biometric security is a method of identifying individuals based on their unique biological characteristics, such as fingerprints [1–3], electrocardiogram [4–8], facial features [9–12], iris patterns [13–15], or voiceprints [16–18]. Biometric security has become increasingly popular in recent years as it offers a more secure and reliable means of authentication compared to traditional methods such as passwords or PINs, which can easily be compromised [19]. Biometric security is of great importance in many industries, including finance [20], healthcare [21–23], personal reidentification [24,25], and government [26–28], as it can help prevent fraud, identity theft, and other forms of cybercrime. For example, biometric authentication is widely used in banking and financial institutions [20] to prevent unauthorized access to sensitive data or transactions. Biometric authentication is also used in healthcare systems [21–23] to ensure that only authorized personnel have access to patient records. Figure 3.1 shows examples of biometrics.

This chapter aims to provide a comprehensive survey of the various methods used to analyze the performance of biometric security systems. The chapter will begin by providing an overview of the background of biometric security, including a definition of biometric security and the different types of biometric technologies used. The chapter will then delve into the various metrics used to evaluate the performance of biometric security systems, including false acceptance rate (FAR), false rejection rate (FRR), receiver-operating characteristic (ROC) curve, equal error rate (EER), failure to enroll (FTE) rate, and failure to acquire (FTA) rate. The chapter will then examine the different methods used to evaluate the performance of biometric security systems, including testing and evaluation standards, performance testing procedures, and performance testing protocols. The chapter will also discuss various

[1]EIAS Data Science Lab, College of Computer and Information Sciences, Prince Sultan University, Saudi Arabia
[2]Department of Information Technology, Faculty of Computers and Information, Menoufia University, Egypt
[3]Department of Mathematics and Computer Science, Faculty of Science, Menoufia University, Egypt

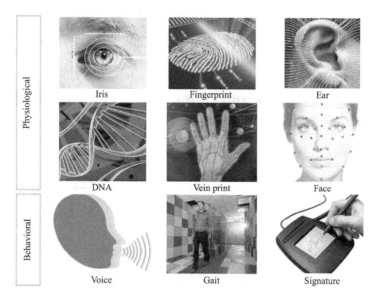

Figure 3.1   Examples of biometric security

tools available for biometric security performance testing, analysis, and evaluation, including open-source and proprietary tools. In addition, the chapter will explore the security vulnerabilities of biometric security systems and the various threat models and attacks that these systems may face. The chapter will also discuss the different countermeasures and mitigation techniques that can be used to prevent and mitigate these attacks.

Finally, the chapter will present several case studies of biometric security performance evaluation, highlighting best practices and lessons learned from these evaluations. The chapter will conclude with a summary of key findings, implications for future research, and recommendations for biometric security performance evaluation.

3.2   Background

Biometric security involves using unique biological characteristics to verify the identity of an individual [29]. This section will provide a definition of biometric security and explore the different types of biometric technologies used in security, as well as the advantages and disadvantages of using biometric security. Biometric security involves the use of biological characteristics, such as fingerprints, facial recognition, iris patterns, voiceprints, or DNA, to verify the identity of an individual [30]. This technology is based on the principle that every person has a unique set of biological characteristics that can be used to establish their identity. Biometric security systems capture these unique biological characteristics and store them in a database, which can be used to authenticate individuals when they attempt to gain access to a secure area or perform a secure transaction [31]. There are several types of biometric technologies used in security, including the following:

1. Fingerprint recognition [1–3]: This technology involves capturing an individual's fingerprint using a sensor device and processing it to extract unique features such as ridge patterns and minutiae points. These features are then compared against a preexisting database of stored fingerprints to determine the individual's identity. Fingerprint recognition has gained significant popularity due to the high level of distinctiveness and stability of fingerprints, making it a reliable and widely adopted biometric modality for various applications, including access control, forensic investigations, and mobile device authentication. The process typically involves several stages, such as image acquisition, preprocessing, feature extraction, and matching, where advanced algorithms and pattern recognition techniques are employed to ensure accurate and efficient fingerprint recognition.

2. Facial recognition [9–12]: This technology utilizes cameras or imaging devices to capture an individual's facial features, including the arrangement of eyes, nose, mouth, and other facial landmarks. The captured facial image is then processed and analyzed using sophisticated algorithms to extract distinctive features and create a unique facial template. This template is compared against a database of pre-enrolled facial templates to determine the identity of the individual. Facial recognition has gained widespread attention and application due to its nonintrusive nature and the ubiquity of camera-equipped devices. It has found applications in various domains, such as law enforcement, surveillance systems, access control, and personalized user experiences in mobile devices. The facial recognition process involves multiple stages, including face detection, alignment, feature extraction, and matching, where advanced computer vision and machine learning techniques are employed to accurately identify individuals based on their facial characteristics.

3. Iris recognition [13–15]: Iris recognition technology relies on capturing a high-resolution image of an individual's iris, which is the colored portion of the eye surrounding the pupil. The intricate patterns within the iris, including the crypts, furrows, and rings, are unique to each individual and remain stable over time. The iris image is captured using specialized cameras that illuminate the eye with near-infrared light to enhance the visibility of the iris patterns. The captured iris image is then subjected to preprocessing steps, such as segmentation and normalization, to isolate the iris region and enhance its features. Next, feature extraction algorithms are applied to extract distinct iris features, such as the arrangement of texture patterns or local intensity variations. These features are transformed into a compact template that represents the individual's iris characteristics. During the verification or identification process, the stored iris templates are compared against the newly captured iris image using advanced matching algorithms, such as the Hamming distance or

correlation-based methods. Iris recognition is known for its high accuracy, robustness, and resistance to tampering or forgery, making it suitable for various applications, such as border control, national identification systems, and secure access control in high-security environments.

4. Voice recognition [16–18]: Voice recognition technology utilizes the unique characteristics of an individual's voice to establish their identity. The process begins with the capture of a voice sample, typically through a microphone or a telecommunication device. The captured voice signal is then subjected to preprocessing, which involves removing background noise, normalizing the signal, and segmenting it into smaller units, such as phonemes or speech frames. Feature extraction techniques are applied to extract relevant vocal features, such as pitch, intensity, spectral patterns, and formant frequencies. These features are used to create a voiceprint or a vocal template that represents the individual's unique voice characteristics. During the verification or identification process, the captured voice sample is compared to the stored voiceprints in a database using various algorithms, such as dynamic time warping or the Gaussian mixture models. The matching process involves measuring the similarity between the extracted features of the captured voice and those in the stored templates. Voice recognition finds applications in voice authentication, speaker identification, and voice-based access control systems. It offers the advantage of being nonintrusive and convenient, as it does not require physical contact or specialized equipment.

5. DNA recognition [32]: DNA recognition technology utilizes the unique genetic code found within an individual's DNA to establish their identity. The process begins by obtaining a sample of the individual's DNA, typically through methods such as swabbing the inside of the cheek or collecting blood samples. The DNA sample is then processed in a laboratory to extract and isolate the specific genetic markers that are used for identification. These markers, known as DNA profiles, are composed of sequences of nucleotides that vary between individuals. The extracted DNA profiles are compared to a stored database of DNA profiles to determine a match. This comparison is typically performed using advanced DNA analysis techniques, such as polymerase chain reaction and short tandem repeat analysis. DNA recognition is widely used in forensic investigations, paternity testing, and genetic profiling. It is known for its high accuracy and reliability, as DNA sequences are highly unique to each individual, making it a powerful tool for identification purposes.

We can highlight the advantages and disadvantages of biometric security as the following:

•   Advantages of biometric security are as follows:
    –   Improved security: Biometric security offers enhanced levels of security compared to traditional methods of authentication, such as passwords or PINs. This is primarily due to the uniqueness and difficulty in replicating an individual's biological characteristics used in biometric systems. Unlike passwords or PINs, which can be forgotten, shared, or easily

guessed, biometric traits are inherently personal and cannot be easily replicated or stolen. For example, while passwords can be hacked or forgotten, a person's fingerprint or iris pattern remains constant and exclusive to them. This significantly reduces the risk of unauthorized access to sensitive information or resources. Biometric security systems also employ advanced algorithms and encryption techniques to further safeguard the biometric data, ensuring its integrity and protection from potential breaches. As a result, biometric authentication offers a robust and reliable security solution in various domains, including physical access control, digital identity verification, and financial transactions.

- Convenience: Biometric security systems provide a high level of convenience for users by eliminating the need to remember and enter passwords or PINs. Traditional authentication methods often require users to create and remember complex passwords, which can be challenging and lead to security vulnerabilities if users resort to using weak passwords or reusing them across multiple accounts. Biometric authentication simplifies this process by using an individual's unique biological traits, such as fingerprints, facial features, or iris patterns, to authenticate their identity. Users simply need to present their biometric data to the system, which then compares it to the stored template for verification. This streamlined process saves time and effort for users, eliminating the frustration of forgetting, or mistyping passwords. Additionally, biometric authentication is particularly beneficial for individuals with disabilities or impairments who may have difficulty using traditional authentication methods. The inherent ease and speed of biometric systems make them a convenient and user-friendly option for secure authentication in various applications, ranging from unlocking smartphones to accessing secure facilities.

- Accuracy: Biometric security systems are renowned for their exceptional accuracy, providing reliable identification with a low false positive rate (FPR). False positives occur when the system incorrectly matches an individual's biometric data to another person's template, leading to a potential security breach. Biometric systems undergo rigorous testing and optimization to minimize the occurrence of false positives and enhance accuracy. Advanced algorithms and machine learning techniques are employed to precisely analyze and compare biometric data, ensuring a high level of precision in matching individuals' unique characteristics. The use of multiple biometric modalities, such as combining fingerprint and iris recognition, further enhances accuracy by reducing the likelihood of false positives and false negatives. This high accuracy enables biometric security systems to effectively distinguish between authorized individuals and impostors, providing robust protection in various domains, including access control, financial transactions, and border security. The reliability and precision of biometric systems make them a trusted and preferred choice for organizations seeking heightened security measures.

- Disadvantages of biometric security are as follows:
  - High implementation costs: While biometric security systems offer numerous advantages, one significant challenge is the associated high implementation costs. The costs stem from several factors, including the need for specialized hardware and software, infrastructure upgrades, and system integration. Biometric systems require the installation of appropriate sensors or scanners to capture biometric data accurately, along with the necessary computing equipment to process and store the data securely. Additionally, organizations must invest in robust algorithms and software solutions capable of efficiently analyzing and matching biometric templates. Furthermore, large-scale implementation across multiple locations or departments may require substantial financial resources for deployment and maintenance. The costs of training personnel, ensuring regulatory compliance, and addressing potential system vulnerabilities add to the overall expenses. While the initial investment can be significant, it is essential to consider the long-term benefits and the potential return on investment in terms of enhanced security and operational efficiency. Organizations must carefully evaluate their requirements and conduct a cost–benefit analysis before committing to the implementation of biometric security systems.
  - Privacy concerns: Despite the advantages of biometric security systems, they also raise valid concerns regarding privacy and data protection. Biometric data, which includes unique physical or behavioral characteristics, is highly personal and sensitive in nature. Storing and managing biometric data requires robust security measures to prevent unauthorized access, hacking, or data breaches. Individuals may worry about the potential misuse of their biometric information if it falls into the wrong hands. Moreover, there are concerns about the possibility of biometric data being used for surveillance purposes, leading to infringements on privacy rights. It is crucial for organizations and regulatory bodies to establish clear guidelines and strict protocols to ensure the responsible and ethical use of biometric data. Implementing strong encryption techniques, access controls, and data anonymization methods can help address privacy concerns and foster public trust in biometric security systems. Transparency in data handling practices, informed consent procedures, and compliance with applicable privacy laws are essential to protect individuals' rights and maintain their confidence in the technology.
  - False negatives: While biometric security systems generally offer high accuracy, they are not infallible and may occasionally produce false negative results. False negatives occur when the system fails to recognize an authorized individual, denying them access despite their valid credentials. This can be a concern in high-security environments where a missed identification could lead to inconvenience, delays, or potential security breaches. Factors, such as environmental conditions, variations in biometric samples, or system limitations, can contribute to false negatives. To mitigate this risk, system designers and operators strive to optimize the performance of

Table 3.1   Comparison of several types of biometric technologies used in security

Biometric	Fingerprint	Facial	Iris	Voice	DNA
Barriers to universality	Worn ridge or finger impairment	None	Visual impairment	Speech impairment	Genetic barriers
Distinctiveness	High	Low	High	Low	High
Permanence	High	Medium	High	Low	High
Collectability	Medium	High	Medium	Medium	Low
Performance	High	Low	High	Low	High
Acceptability	Medium	High	Low	High	Low
Potential for circumvention	Low	High	Low	High	Low

biometric algorithms, enhance sensor technology, and implement robust calibration and training processes. Ongoing system monitoring, periodic recalibration, and user feedback mechanisms can help identify and rectify false negatives, ensuring the system's reliability and minimizing the chances of authorized individuals being denied access.

We can conclude that biometric security is a technology that uses unique biological characteristics to verify the identity of an individual. There are several types of biometric technologies used in security, each with its own advantages and disadvantages. While biometric security is generally considered to be more secure than traditional methods of authentication, it can be expensive to implement, and there are concerns about privacy and false negatives. Summary of the comparison of several types of the previous biometric technologies used in security is shown in Table 3.1.

3.3   Performance evaluation metrics

In order to evaluate the performance of biometric security systems, several metrics are used to measure the accuracy and efficiency of the system. This section will discuss some of the most commonly used performance evaluation metrics in biometric security [32].

- False acceptance rate (FAR):
  The FAR is a metric that measures the rate at which an unauthorized individual is incorrectly accepted by the system. This occurs when the biometric system incorrectly matches the biometric data of an unauthorized individual with that of an authorized individual in the system. A high FAR can result in compromised security, as unauthorized individuals may be able to gain access to secure areas or perform secure transactions. FAR can be computed as the following:

$$FAR = \frac{FP}{FP + TN} \times 100 \qquad (3.1)$$

where *FP* is the number of false positive and *TN* is the number of true negative.

- False rejection rate (FRR):
  The FRR is a metric that measures the rate at which an authorized individual is incorrectly rejected by the system. This occurs when the biometric system fails to match the biometric data of an authorized individual with that of the same individual in the system. A high FRR can result in frustration for authorized individuals who are denied access to secure areas or transactions, which can be computed as the following:

$$FRR = \frac{FN}{FN + TP} \times 100 \tag{3.2}$$

where *FN* is the number of false negative and *TP* is the number of true positive.

- Receiver-operating characteristic (ROC) curve:
  The ROC curve is a graphical representation of the performance of a biometric system. The ROC curve plots the true positive rate (TPR) against the FPR for different thresholds. The TPR represents the rate at which the system correctly identifies an authorized individual, while the FPR represents the rate at which the system incorrectly identifies an unauthorized individual. A higher TPR and a lower FPR indicate a more accurate biometric system as shown in Figure 3.2.

From Figure 3.2, TPR, which is also called sensitivity, recall, and hit rate, is defined as

$$TPR = \frac{TP}{TP + FN} \times 100 \tag{3.3}$$

and FPR is defined as

$$FPR = \frac{FP}{FP + TN} \tag{3.4}$$

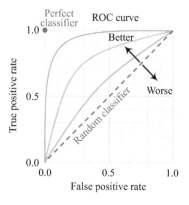

Figure 3.2   The ROC space for a "better" and "worse" classifier

Also, there are some other metrics that are used to evaluate the performance of the biometric system as in the following:

- Specificity, selectivity, or true negative rate (TNR) are defined as

$$TNR = \frac{TN}{TN + FP} \qquad (3.5)$$

- Precision or positive predictive value is defined as

$$PPV = \frac{TP}{TP + FP} \qquad (3.6)$$

- $F1$-score, which is the harmonic mean of precision and sensitivity, is defined as

$$F1 - score = 2 \times \frac{PPV \times TPR}{PPV + TPR} \qquad (3.7)$$

- phi coefficient (φ or $r\varphi$) or Matthew's correlation coefficient (MCC) is defined as

$$MCC = \frac{TP \times TN - FP \times FN}{\sqrt{(TP + FP)(TP + FN)(TN + FP)(TN + FN)}} \qquad (3.8)$$

- Equal error rate (EER):

The EER is a metric that represents the point at which the FAR and FRR are equal. This is the point at which the biometric system is considered to have the most balanced performance, as it minimizes both the FARs and FRRs. EER is also called crossover error rate (CER), which describes the overall accuracy of a biometric system as shown in Figure 3.3.

- Failure to enroll (FTE) rate:
  The FTE rate is a metric that measures the rate at which the biometric system fails to enroll an individual into the system. This can occur when the biometric

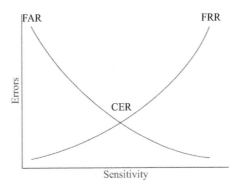

Figure 3.3   Crossover error rate (CER)

data of an individual is of poor quality, or when there are technical issues with the system. A high FTE can result in delays in the enrollment process and can impact the overall efficiency of the biometric system.

- Failure to acquire (FTA) rate:
  The FTA rate is a metric that measures the rate at which the biometric system fails to acquire the biometric data of an individual. This can occur when the individual's biometric data is not captured properly or when there are technical issues with the system. A high FTA can result in delays in the authentication process and can impact the overall efficiency of the biometric system.

Appendix A shows an example of Python code to calculate three commonly used biometric metrics, FPR, false negative rate (FNR), and EER, using a hypothetical dataset. Appendix B shows an example of the Python code to calculate the ROC curve and other related metrics, such as TPR, FPR, and area under the curve (AUC).

3.4   Biometric performance evaluation methods

In order to evaluate the performance of biometric security systems, several methods have been developed [33]. These methods involve the use of test and evaluation standards [34], verification and identification performance metrics [35], performance testing procedures [36], and performance testing protocols [37].

3.4.1   Test and evaluation standards

Test and evaluation standards provide a framework for evaluating the performance of biometric security systems [34]. These standards specify the types of tests to be conducted, the performance metrics to be used, and the procedures for conducting the tests. The most commonly used test and evaluation standards for biometric security systems are the National Institute of Standards and Technology (NIST) [38] and the International Organization for Standardization (ISO) [39].

3.4.2   Verification and identification performance metrics

Verification and identification performance metrics are used to evaluate the accuracy and efficiency of biometric security systems [35]. Verification performance metrics are used to evaluate the accuracy of the system in verifying the identity of an individual, while identification performance metrics are used to evaluate the accuracy of the system in identifying an individual from a large database. The most commonly used verification performance metric is the FAR, whereas the most commonly used identification performance metric is the false match rate.

3.4.3   Performance testing procedures

Performance testing procedures involve the use of various tests to evaluate the performance of biometric security systems [36]. These tests include the use of synthetic datasets, live datasets, and standardized test protocols. Synthetic datasets are created using computer-generated biometric data and are used to evaluate the performance of the system under controlled conditions. Live datasets are collected from actual users and are used to evaluate the performance of the system under realistic conditions. Standardized test protocols are used to ensure that the testing procedures are consistent across different testing environments [40].

3.4.4   Performance testing protocols

Performance testing protocols are used to ensure that the performance testing procedures are consistent across different testing environments [37]. These protocols specify the procedures for collecting and analyzing biometric data, the performance metrics to be used, and the procedures for conducting the tests. The most commonly used performance testing protocols for biometric security systems are the NIST Biometric Evaluation Framework and the ISO/IEC 19795-1:2006 Information technology—Biometric performance testing and reporting—Part 1: Principles and framework [41].

In conclusion, the evaluation of biometric security systems involves the use of test and evaluation standards, verification and identification performance metrics, performance testing procedures, and performance testing protocols. These methods are essential for ensuring the accuracy and efficiency of biometric security systems and for providing a framework for comparing different biometric systems. The use of standardized methods for evaluating biometric security systems is critical for ensuring that these systems are reliable and effective in protecting against unauthorized access.

3.5   Biometric system performance analysis

Biometric systems are used for a wide range of applications, such as access control [42–45], identity verification [46–50], and authentication [51–55]. The performance of biometric systems is typically evaluated using performance metrics, performance analysis techniques, and accuracy, speed, and robustness testing.

3.5.1   Performance metrics for biometric systems

The most commonly used performance metrics for biometric systems are FAR, FRR, ROC curve, EER, FTE rate, and FTA rate. These metrics are used to evaluate the accuracy, speed, and robustness of biometric systems.

3.5.2   Performance analysis techniques

There are several techniques used for analyzing the performance of biometric systems. Some of the commonly used techniques include statistical analysis [56], data visualization [57], and machine learning techniques [58–60]. Statistical analysis is used to determine the correlation between the performance metrics and the factors that affect the performance of the system. Data visualization is used to represent the performance metrics in a graphical format, which makes it easier to understand the results. Machine learning techniques are used to develop models that can predict the performance of the system under different conditions.

3.5.3   Accuracy, speed, and robustness testing

Biometric systems undergo rigorous testing to assess their performance in terms of accuracy, speed, and robustness. Accuracy testing aims to evaluate the system's ability to correctly identify or verify the identity of individuals by comparing the biometric data captured with the stored templates. This testing involves measuring metrics such as the FPR and FNR to ensure that the system achieves high accuracy.

Speed testing is crucial, especially for real-time applications, as it measures the processing time required for the system to perform identification or verification tasks. Evaluating the system's speed helps determine its efficiency and responsiveness in handling biometric data in a timely manner.

Robustness testing assesses the system's performance under various challenging conditions that can impact its accuracy and reliability. This includes testing the system's resilience to changes in lighting conditions, variations in the appearance of users (e.g., facial hair and glasses), and environmental factors (e.g., noise and temperature). Robustness testing ensures that the system remains effective and dependable in different real-world scenarios.

These testing procedures involve capturing biometric samples under controlled conditions, simulating different scenarios, and analyzing the system's performance against predefined benchmarks. By subjecting the system to rigorous accuracy, speed, and robustness testing, developers and researchers can fine-tune algorithms, optimize hardware components, and enhance system configurations to deliver biometric solutions that are accurate, efficient, and reliable in a wide range of practical applications.

The accuracy can be calculated as

$$Accuracy = \frac{TP + TN}{TP + TN + FP + FN} \tag{3.9}$$

In summary, the performance analysis of biometric systems involves the use of performance metrics, performance analysis techniques, and accuracy, speed, and robustness testing. The evaluation of biometric systems is critical for ensuring that they are accurate, efficient, and robust and can be used for a wide range of applications. By using performance analysis techniques, it is possible to identify the factors that affect the performance of the system and to develop strategies for improving the performance of biometric systems.

3.6   Biometric security evaluation

Biometric systems are increasingly being used for various security applications, but they are not immune to vulnerabilities and attacks [61]. Therefore, it is crucial to evaluate the security of biometric systems to identify vulnerabilities, threats, and potential attacks. This evaluation involves identifying and analyzing the vulnerabilities [62], developing threat models [63], and designing countermeasures and mitigation techniques to prevent or minimize the impact of attacks [64].

3.6.1   Biometric system vulnerabilities

Biometric systems, while offering enhanced security, are not immune to potential vulnerabilities and attacks. Various types of attacks can exploit weaknesses in the system and compromise its security. Spoofing attacks pose a significant threat, where an attacker presents a fabricated or synthetic biometric sample to deceive the system into granting unauthorized access. This can involve presenting a replica fingerprint, a facial image, or a voice recording that mimics the characteristics of a legitimate user [65].

Replay attacks involve capturing and replaying previously recorded biometric data to the system, tricking it into recognizing the replayed data as a legitimate input. This can be achieved by capturing biometric samples during a legitimate authentication process and later replaying them to bypass the system's security measures [66].

Impersonation attacks occur when an attacker successfully uses another person's biometric data to gain access to the system. This can happen through the acquisition of stolen biometric information or by creating forged biometric data that closely matches the target individual's traits [67].

To mitigate these vulnerabilities, biometric systems employ various countermeasures and anti-spoofing techniques. These may include liveness detection mechanisms, which assess the vitality of the presented biometric sample to differentiate between live individuals and fake representations, such as photographs or masks. Additionally, system designers incorporate robust encryption algorithms, secure storage methods, and strict access control policies to safeguard the biometric data and prevent unauthorized access or tampering.

Continued research and advancements in biometric technology aim to enhance the security of biometric systems by developing more sophisticated anti-spoofing methods, improving detection capabilities, and integrating multifactor authentication (MFA) approaches. By addressing these vulnerabilities, biometric systems can maintain their effectiveness as reliable and secure solutions for identity verification and access control in various domains, including government, finance, and personal devices.

3.6.2   Threat models and attacks

Threat models are essential tools in assessing the security of biometric systems, providing a systematic approach to identify and evaluate potential threats and vulnerabilities. By considering both internal and external factors, threat models help organizations understand the risks associated with their biometric systems and develop appropriate security measures to mitigate those risks.

Internal threats involve individuals within the organization who have authorized access to the biometric system. This can include employees, administrators, or contractors who may misuse their privileges or intentionally compromise the system's security. Internal threats can range from unauthorized data access or manipulation to insider attacks aimed at stealing or altering biometric data. By identifying and understanding these internal threats, organizations can implement strict access controls, monitoring mechanisms, and employee training programs to minimize the risk of insider attacks.

External threats encompass a wide range of potential attackers who are not affiliated with the organization. These may include hackers, cybercriminals, or individuals attempting to gain unauthorized access to the biometric system. External threats can target system vulnerabilities, exploit weaknesses in communication channels, or employ various attack techniques to bypass authentication mechanisms. By analyzing external threats, organizations can implement strong authentication protocols, encryption mechanisms, and intrusion detection systems to protect against external attacks.

Once the threats have been identified, organizations need to conduct a comprehensive analysis of potential attacks that could be used to exploit vulnerabilities in the biometric system. This analysis involves examining different attack vectors, such as spoofing attacks where adversaries present fake biometric samples, replay attacks where captured biometric data is replayed to the system, or impersonation attacks where an individual uses someone else's biometric data to gain unauthorized access. By understanding these potential attack scenarios, organizations can implement countermeasures such as liveness detection techniques, robust anti-spoofing algorithms, and MFA to enhance the security of their biometric systems.

Threat modeling is an ongoing process that should be regularly updated to adapt to evolving security risks and new attack vectors. It helps organizations proactively identify and address potential vulnerabilities in their biometric systems, ensuring the integrity, confidentiality, and availability of biometric data and maintaining the trust of users and stakeholders. Through a thorough understanding of threats, vulnerabilities, and attack vectors, organizations can establish comprehensive security strategies that safeguard their biometric systems in today's ever-evolving threat landscape.

3.6.3   *Countermeasures and mitigation techniques*

Countermeasures and mitigation techniques play a critical role in enhancing the security of biometric systems and mitigating potential attacks. These techniques encompass a range of measures designed to prevent unauthorized access and protect the integrity of biometric data.

Data encryption is a fundamental countermeasure that ensures the confidentiality of biometric data. By encrypting data both in transit and at rest, organizations can prevent unauthorized interception or access to sensitive biometric information. Encryption techniques, such as symmetric or asymmetric encryption algorithms, are employed to safeguard data integrity and maintain privacy.

MFA is another effective countermeasure used in conjunction with biometric authentication. MFA combines biometric identification with additional authentication factors, such as passwords, tokens, or smart cards. By requiring multiple factors for authentication, the system adds an extra layer of security, reducing the risk of unauthorized access even if one factor is compromised.

Biometric template protection focuses on securing the stored biometric templates. Encryption and hashing techniques are applied to the templates, rendering them unreadable and protecting against unauthorized access or tampering. This ensures that even if the templates are compromised, they cannot be used to reconstruct the original biometric data.

Liveness detection techniques are employed to differentiate between live individuals and fraudulent attempts to deceive the system, such as using a photograph or a synthetic replica. Sensors, such as infrared or thermal cameras, can be utilized to detect vital signs or physical attributes that indicate the presence of a living person. Liveness detection helps prevent spoofing attacks and enhances the system's resistance against fraudulent attempts.

Continuous authentication is a proactive approach that continuously monitors the user's behavior throughout the authentication process. By analyzing user patterns, keystrokes, or mouse movements, the system can detect anomalies or deviations from normal behavior, signaling a potential security threat. Continuous authentication adds an extra layer of security by constantly verifying the user's identity during an active session.

Implementing these countermeasures and mitigation techniques is crucial for maintaining the security and integrity of biometric systems. By employing data encryption, MFA, biometric template protection, liveness detection, and continuous authentication, organizations can significantly enhance the overall security posture of their biometric systems, mitigating the risk of unauthorized access and ensuring the trustworthiness of their authentication mechanisms.

In conclusion, the evaluation of biometric security involves identifying and analyzing vulnerabilities, developing threat models, and designing countermeasures and mitigation techniques to prevent or minimize the impact of attacks. By using these techniques, it is possible to ensure that biometric systems are secure and can be used for various security applications with confidence.

3.7 Biometric security performance evaluation tools

Biometric security performance evaluation tools are essential for testing and evaluating the performance and security of biometric systems. These tools can be categorized into open-source and proprietary tools and are used for various purposes, such as performance testing, analysis, evaluation, and security evaluation and assessment.

3.7.1 Open-source and proprietary tools

Open-source tools and proprietary tools represent two distinct approaches to software development and distribution, each with its own advantages and considerations.

Open-source tools refer to software tools, the source code of which is made freely available to the public, allowing anyone to view, modify, distribute, and use the software. This open nature fosters collaboration, innovation, and community-driven development. Open-source tools are often developed and maintained by a community of contributors, and they benefit from peer review and continuous improvement. These tools are typically distributed under open-source licenses, such as the GNU General Public License (GPL) or the Apache License.

Proprietary tools, on the other hand, are commercial software tools that are owned and licensed by a specific company or organization. The source code of proprietary tools is typically not available to the public and is tightly controlled by the software vendor. Proprietary tools often require users to purchase licenses or subscriptions to use the software, and they come with support and maintenance services provided by the vendor.

When it comes to cost, open-source tools are generally less expensive than proprietary tools. Since open-source tools are freely available, organizations can save on licensing fees and reduce their upfront expenses. Moreover, the open nature of the software allows customization and flexibility to adapt the tool to specific needs without incurring additional costs. However, it is important to consider that while open-source tools may be free to use, organizations may still incur costs related to training, support, and integration.

In terms of functionalities, proprietary tools often offer a wide range of features and comprehensive support. Since these tools are developed by specific companies, they tend to have dedicated teams working on product enhancements, bug fixes, and customer support. Proprietary tools may also provide specialized functionalities tailored to specific industries or use cases. On the other hand, open-source tools may have a more limited feature set, depending on the scope of community contributions and development resources available.

The choice between open-source and proprietary tools depends on various factors, including budget, specific requirements, available expertise, and desired level of support. Organizations seeking cost-effective solutions, flexibility, and the ability to customize may opt for open-source tools. Conversely, organizations that prioritize comprehensive support, extensive features, and vendor-backed maintenance may opt for proprietary tools. Ultimately, it is important to carefully evaluate the specific needs and considerations of the organization when choosing between open-source and proprietary tools.

3.7.2   Tools for performance testing, analysis, and evaluation

Tools for performance testing, analysis, and evaluation play a crucial role in assessing the effectiveness and reliability of biometric systems. These tools provide standardized methodologies and metrics for benchmarking the performance of biometric algorithms and systems. Here are some commonly used tools in the field:

- NIST Biometric Image Software (NBIS): Developed by the NIST, NBIS is a collection of software tools and libraries designed for the analysis and processing of biometric images. It provides functionality for image quality assessment, fingerprint feature extraction, and biometric performance evaluation.

- BioAPI: BioAPI is a standardized framework that facilitates interoperability and compatibility among different biometric systems. It defines a common programming interface for biometric devices and enables the development of biometric applications that can work with multiple devices and algorithms.
- OpenBR: OpenBR is an open-source biometric recognition platform that offers a wide range of tools and algorithms for biometric analysis and recognition. It provides modules for face recognition, fingerprint identification, iris recognition, and other biometric modalities. OpenBR supports performance evaluation and benchmarking against standard datasets. Appendix C shows an example code snippet related to the evaluation of biometric systems using open-source tools.
- FVC-onGoing: FVC-onGoing is an ongoing benchmarking evaluation campaign for fingerprint recognition systems. It provides a standardized evaluation framework and datasets for assessing the performance of fingerprint recognition algorithms. The campaign includes different evaluation scenarios, such as verification and identification tasks, and tracks advancements in fingerprint recognition technology.

These tools enable researchers, developers, and evaluators to conduct comprehensive performance testing and analysis of biometric systems. They offer standardized evaluation protocols, reference datasets, and performance metrics, such as accuracy, speed, and robustness. By using these tools, the performance of biometric systems can be assessed, compared, and improved over time, fostering advancements in the field and ensuring the deployment of reliable and efficient biometric solutions.

3.7.3 Tools for security evaluation and assessment

Tools for security evaluation and assessment are essential for identifying and mitigating vulnerabilities in biometric systems, ensuring their robustness against potential attacks. Here are some commonly used tools in this domain:

- Biometric evaluation framework (BEF): The BEF is a comprehensive framework developed by the NIST to evaluate the security and performance of biometric systems. It includes tools and resources for assessing the vulnerability of biometric systems to various types of attacks, including spoofing, replay, and impersonation attacks.
- Open biometrics initiative (OBI): The OBI is an open-source initiative that provides a set of tools and resources for the evaluation and analysis of biometric systems' security. It offers a platform for sharing attack scenarios, datasets, and evaluation methodologies, enabling researchers and practitioners to assess the security of biometric systems and develop countermeasures.
- Biometric security and privacy analysis (BSPA) tool: The BSPA tool is a software tool designed for analyzing the security and privacy aspects of biometric systems. It provides capabilities for simulating attacks, evaluating system vulnerabilities, and assessing the potential impact of attacks on the overall security of the system. The BSPA tool helps in identifying potential weaknesses and implementing appropriate countermeasures.

These tools aid in assessing the security of biometric systems by simulating real-world attack scenarios, evaluating system vulnerabilities, and measuring the effectiveness of security countermeasures. They contribute to the development of robust and secure biometric systems by identifying and addressing potential threats and vulnerabilities. By utilizing these tools, organizations can enhance the overall security posture of their biometric systems and ensure the protection of sensitive biometric data.

In conclusion, biometric security performance evaluation tools are critical for testing and evaluating the performance and security of biometric systems. These tools include open-source and proprietary tools and are used for performance testing, analysis, evaluation, and security evaluation and assessment. By using these tools, it is possible to ensure that biometric systems are secure and perform optimally for various security applications.

3.8   Case studies

Case studies are an effective way to understand the real-world application of biometric security performance evaluation. They provide insight into the performance and security of biometric systems in different settings and highlight the best practices and lessons learned from the evaluation process.

3.8.1   Case studies of biometric security performance evaluation

Case studies of biometric security performance evaluation focus on evaluating the performance and security of biometric systems in various settings. These case studies may involve evaluating biometric systems in controlled laboratory environments or in real-world applications, such as border control, law enforcement, or financial institutions. The case studies may evaluate various biometric technologies, such as fingerprint, face recognition, iris recognition, or voice recognition, and may use different performance evaluation metrics, such as the FAR, FRR, or the EER.

3.8.2   Best practices in biometric security performance evaluation

Best practices in biometric security performance evaluation involve following a standardized process for evaluating the performance and security of biometric systems. These best practices may include using established evaluation protocols, benchmarking against standard datasets, and using performance evaluation metrics that are relevant to the application of the biometric system. Best practices may also involve using a combination of evaluation techniques, such as simulation, testing, and analysis, to ensure that the biometric system performs optimally under different conditions.

3.8.3   *Lessons learned from biometric security performance evaluation*

Lessons learned from biometric security performance evaluation include identifying common vulnerabilities and threats to biometric systems, understanding the limitations of biometric technologies, and the importance of regular maintenance and updates to biometric systems. Lessons learned may also include the need for user education and training, the importance of data privacy and protection, and the need for continuous monitoring and evaluation of biometric systems to ensure optimal performance and security.

In conclusion, case studies of biometric security performance evaluation, best practices, and lessons learned provide valuable insights into the performance and security of biometric systems. By following established evaluation protocols, benchmarking against standard datasets, and using relevant performance evaluation metrics, it is possible to ensure that biometric systems perform optimally and provide effective security solutions for various applications.

3.9   Conclusion

The evaluation of biometric security performance is crucial in ensuring the effectiveness and reliability of biometric systems in various applications. This chapter has provided an overview of biometric security, the metrics used for performance evaluation, and the methods and tools available for evaluating the performance and security of biometric systems. In summary, biometric security performance evaluation requires a combination of testing, analysis, and simulation to assess the accuracy, speed, and robustness of the system. The metrics used for evaluation, such as the FAR, FRR, ROC curve, EER, FTE, and FTA, provide a standardized framework for measuring the performance of biometric systems.

The implications for future research in biometric security performance evaluation include the need for more standardized evaluation protocols and benchmark datasets, as well as the development of new metrics to evaluate the security and privacy of biometric systems. There is also a need for research into the performance and security of emerging biometric technologies, such as gait recognition, ear recognition, and brainwave recognition. Recommendations for biometric security performance evaluation include the adoption of standardized evaluation protocols, the use of relevant performance evaluation metrics, and the regular monitoring and evaluation of biometric systems to ensure optimal performance and security. The development of open-source tools and platforms for biometric security performance evaluation can also facilitate the widespread adoption of best practices and ensure that biometric systems are secure, reliable, and effective. Finally, biometric security performance evaluation is a critical aspect of ensuring the effectiveness and reliability of biometric systems in various applications. By following established evaluation protocols, using relevant performance evaluation metrics, and regularly monitoring and evaluating biometric systems, it is possible to ensure that biometric systems are secure and provide effective security solutions for different applications.

Appendix A

Example of code to calculate three commonly used biometric metrics using Python:

```python
# Assume we have a dataset with ground truth labels and
predicted labels
ground_truth = [1, 0, 0, 1, 1, 0, 1, 0, 0, 1] # True labels (1
for match, 0 for non-match)
predicted_labels = [1, 0, 1, 1, 0, 0, 1, 0, 0, 0] # Predicted
labels

# Calculate False Positive Rate (FPR)
false_positives = sum([(p == 1 and g == 0) for p, g in zip
(predicted_labels, ground_truth)])
true_negatives = sum([(p == 0 and g == 0) for p, g in zip
(predicted_labels, ground_truth)])
total_negatives = sum([g == 0 for g in ground_truth])
fpr = false_positives / total_negatives

# Calculate False Negative Rate (FNR)
false_negatives = sum([(p == 0 and g == 1) for p, g in zip
(predicted_labels, ground_truth)])
true_positives = sum([(p == 1 and g == 1) for p, g in zip
(predicted_labels, ground_truth)])
total_positives = sum([g == 1 for g in ground_truth])
fnr = false_negatives / total_positives

# Calculate Equal Error Rate (EER)
scores_match = [0.8, 0.6, 0.4, 0.7, 0.9] # Matching scores
for genuine (match) samples
scores_non_match = [0.3, 0.2, 0.6, 0.1, 0.5] # Matching
scores for impostor (non-match) samples
thresholds = sorted(scores_match + scores_non_match) #
Sort all matching scores
min_distance = float('inf')
eer = 1.0
for threshold in thresholds:
        fnr_threshold = sum([s >= threshold for s in scores_
match]) / len(scores_match)
        fpr_threshold = sum([s >= threshold for s in scor-
es_non_match]) / len(scores_non_match)
```

```
    distance = abs(fnr_threshold - fpr_threshold)
    if distance < min_distance:
        min_distance = distance
        eer = max(fnr_threshold, fpr_threshold)
```

```
# Print the calculated metrics
print("False Positive Rate (FPR):", fpr)
print("False Negative Rate (FNR):", fnr)
print("Equal Error Rate (EER):", eer)
```

Appendix B

Example of Python code to calculate the ROC curve and other related metrics, such as TPR, FPR, and AUC:

```
import numpy as np
import matplotlib.pyplot as plt
from sklearn.metrics import roc_curve, roc_auc_score

# Assume we have a dataset with ground truth labels and
matching scores
ground_truth = [1, 1, 0, 0, 1, 0, 1, 0, 0, 1] # True labels (1
for match, 0 for non-match)
matching_scores = [0.8, 0.6, 0.4, 0.7, 0.9, 0.3, 0.6, 0.1,
0.5, 0.7] # Matching scores

# Calculate the False Positive Rate (FPR) and True Positive
Rate (TPR) using the roc_curve function
fpr, tpr, thresholds = roc_curve(ground_truth,
matching_scores)

# Calculate the Area Under the Curve (AUC)
auc = roc_auc_score(ground_truth, matching_scores)

# Plot the ROC curve
plt.plot(fpr, tpr, label='ROC Curve (AUC = {:.2f})'.format
(auc))
plt.plot([0, 1], [0, 1], 'k--') # Plot the random classi-
fier curve
plt.xlabel('False Positive Rate (FPR)')
plt.ylabel('True Positive Rate (TPR)')
```

```
plt.title('Receiver    Operating    Characteristic    (ROC)
Curve')
plt.legend(loc='lower right')
plt.grid(True)
plt.show()

# Print the calculated metrics
print("False Positive Rate (FPR):", fpr)
print("True Positive Rate (TPR):", tpr)
print("Thresholds:", thresholds)
print("Area Under the Curve (AUC):", auc)
```

This code utilizes the roc_curve function from the sklearn.metrics module to calculate the FPR, TPR, and thresholds for the ROC curve. It also uses the roc_auc_score function to calculate the AUC. The resulting metrics are then plotted on an ROC curve using Matplotlib.

Note that this code assumes you have the necessary packages (NumPy, matplotlib, scikit-learn) installed. Additionally, make sure to replace the ground_truth and matching_scores list with your own data to calculate the metrics for your specific application.

Appendix C

Example code snippet related to the evaluation of biometric systems using open-source tools:

```
from openbr import *
from sklearn.metrics import accuracy_score, precision_
score, recall_score, f1_score

# Initialize OpenBR
context = Context()

# Load the templates and predictions
templates = [Template("path_to_template_1"), Template
("path_to_template_2")]
predictions = [Template("path_to_prediction_1"),
Template("path_to_prediction_2")]

# Perform matching and calculate scores
scores = []
```

```
for i, prediction in enumerate(predictions):
        comparison = Comparison()
        comparison.reference = templates[i]
        comparison.probe = prediction
        algorithm = context.algorithm("FaceRecognition")
        algorithm.compare(comparison)
        scores.append(comparison.score)

# Calculate evaluation metrics
labels = [0, 1] # Example ground truth labels
predictions = [1 if score < threshold else 0 for score in
scores] # Example thresholding
accuracy = accuracy_score(labels, predictions)
precision = precision_score(labels, predictions)
recall = recall_score(labels, predictions)
f1 = f1_score(labels, predictions)

# Print the results
print("Accuracy:", accuracy)
print("Precision:", precision)
print("Recall:", recall)
print("F1-score:", f1)
```

Note that this code snippet uses the OpenBR library for biometric analysis. You would need to install OpenBR and its Python bindings to run this code. This example demonstrates the evaluation of facial recognition systems by comparing templates and predictions using the OpenBR framework. You would need to replace the file paths with the actual paths to your templates and predictions.

Remember to customize the code according to your specific requirements and the type of biometric system you are evaluating.

References

[1] Maguire, M. (2009). The birth of biometric security. *Anthropology Today*, 25(2), 9–14.
[2] Ali, A., Baghel, V. S., and Prakash, S. (2022). A novel technique for fingerprint template security in biometric authentication systems. *The Visual Computer*, 1–15.
[3] Hammad, M. and Wang, K. (2017, April). Fingerprint classification based on a Q-Gaussian multiclass support vector machine. In *Proceedings of the 2017*

International Conference on Biometrics Engineering and Application (pp. 39–44).

[4]   Hammad, M., Iliyasu, A. M., Elgendy, I. A., and Abd El-Latif, A. A. (2022). End-to-end data authentication deep learning model for securing IoT configurations. *Human-centric Computing and Information Sciences*, 12(4).

[5]   Sakr, A. S., Pławiak, P., Tadeusiewicz, R., and Hammad, M. (2022). Cancelable ECG biometric based on combination of deep transfer learning with DNA and amino acid approaches for human authentication. *Information Sciences*, 585, 127–143.

[6]   Hammad, M., Ibrahim, M., and Hadhoud, M. M. (2016). A novel biometric based on ECG signals and images for human authentication. *International Arab Journal of Information Technology*, 13(6A), 959–964.

[7]   Prakash, A. J., Patro, K. K., Hammad, M., Tadeusiewicz, R., and Pławiak, P. (2022). BAED: A secured biometric authentication system using ECG signal based on deep learning techniques. *Biocybernetics and Biomedical Engineering*, 42(4), 1081–1093.

[8]   Abd El-Rahiem, B. and Hammad, M. (2022). A multi-fusion IoT authentication system based on internal deep fusion of ECG signals. In *Security and Privacy Preserving for IoT and 5G Networks: Techniques, Challenges, and New Directions*, Springer, pp. 53–79.

[9]   Wang, Y., Shi, D., and Zhou, W. (2022). Convolutional neural network approach based on multimodal biometric system with fusion of face and finger vein features. *Sensors*, 22(16), 6039.

[10] Dong, X., Miao, Z., Ma, L., *et al.* (2023). Reconstruct face from features based on genetic algorithm using GAN generator as a distribution constraint. *Computers & Security*, 125, 103026.

[11] Sengupta, A. and Chaurasia, R. (2022). Secured convolutional layer IP core in convolutional neural network using facial biometric. *IEEE Transactions on Consumer Electronics*, 68(3), 291–306.

[12] Jadhav, S. B., Deshmukh, N. K., and Humbe, V. T. (2022). HDL-PI: Hybrid DeepLearning technique for person identification using multimodal finger print, iris and face biometric features. *Multimedia Tools and Applications*, 1–26.

[13] Rafiq, S. and Selwal, A. (2022). Block-XOR based cancellable template protection scheme for multi-instance iris biometric system. *Multimedia Tools and Applications*, 81(16), 23217–23235.

[14] Harikrishnan, D., Sunilkumar, N., Shelby, J., Kishor, N., and Remya, G. (2023). An effective authentication scheme for a secured IRIS recognition system based on a novel encoding technique. *Measurement: Sensors*, 25, 100626.

[15] Abdellatef, E., Soliman, R. F., Omran, E. M., *et al.* (2022). Cancelable face and iris recognition system based on deep learning. *Optical and Quantum Electronics*, 54(11), 702.

[16] Zhang, R., Yan, Z., Wang, X., and Deng, R. H. (2023). LiVoAuth: Liveness detection in voiceprint authentication with random challenges and detection modes. *IEEE Transactions on Industrial Informatics*, 19(6), 7676–7688.

[17] Jiang, P., Wang, Q., Lin, X., *et al.* (2022). Securing liveness detection for voice authentication via pop noises. *IEEE Transactions on Dependable and Secure Computing*, 20(2), 1702–1718.

[18] Yanping, C. and Linlin, C. (2022). Research on face-voiceprint correspondence learning with Aux-output supervised convolution neural network. *Pattern Recognition and Image Analysis*, 32(2), 448–455.

[19] Hammad, M., Liu, Y., and Wang, K. (2018). Multimodal biometric authentication systems using convolution neural network based on different level fusion of ECG and fingerprint. *IEEE Access*, 7, 26527–26542.

[20] Venkatraman, S. and Delpachitra, I. (2008). Biometrics in banking security: A case study. *Information Management & Computer Security*, 16(4), 415–430.

[21] Hammad, M., Meshoul, S., Dziwiński, P., Pławiak, P., and Elgendy, I. A. (2022). Efficient lightweight multimodel deep fusion based on ECG for arrhythmia classification. *Sensors*, 22(23), 9347.

[22] Hammad, M., Bakrey, M., Bakhiet, A., Tadeusiewicz, R., Abd El-Latif, A. A., and Pławiak, P. (2022). A novel end-to-end deep learning approach for cancer detection based on microscopic medical images. *Biocybernetics and Biomedical Engineering*, 42(3), 737–748.

[23] Hammad, M., Tawalbeh, L. A., Iliyasu, A. M., *et al.* (2022). Efficient multimodal deep-learning-based COVID-19 diagnostic system for noisy and corrupted images. *Journal of King Saud University-Science*, 34(3), 101898.

[24] Saber, S., Amin, K., Pławiak, P., Tadeusiewicz, R., and Hammad, M. (2022). Graph convolutional network with triplet attention learning for person re-identification. *Information Sciences*, 617, 331–345.

[25] Saber, S., Amin, K. M., and Adel Hammad, M. (2021). An efficient person re-identification method based on deep transfer learning techniques. *IJCI. International Journal of Computers and Information*, 8(2), 94–99.

[26] Zureik, E. and Hindle, K. (2004). Governance, security and technology: The case of biometrics. *Studies in Political Economy*, 73(1), 113–137.

[27] Amoore, L. (2006). Biometric borders: Governing mobilities in the war on terror. *Political Geography*, 25(3), 336–351.

[28] Matyas Jr, S. M. and Stapleton, J. (2000). A biometric standard for information management and security. *Computers & Security*, 19(5), 428–441.

[29] Hammad, M., Pławiak, P., Wang, K., and Acharya, U. R. (2021). ResNet—Attention model for human authentication using ECG signals. *Expert Systems*, 38(6), e12547.

[30] Hammad, M., Zhang, S., and Wang, K. (2019). A novel two-dimensional ECG feature extraction and classification algorithm based on convolution neural network for human authentication. *Future Generation Computer Systems*, 101, 180–196.

[31] Hammad, M. and Wang, K. (2019). Parallel score fusion of ECG and fingerprint for human authentication based on convolution neural network. *Computers & Security*, 81, 107–122.

[32] Katsanis, S. H., Claes, P., Doerr, M., *et al.* (2021). US adult perspectives on facial images, DNA, and other biometrics. *IEEE Transactions on Technology and Society*, 3(1), 9–15.

[33] Gomez-Barrero, M., Galbally, J., Rathgeb, C., and Busch, C. (2017). General framework to evaluate unlinkability in biometric template protection systems. *IEEE Transactions on Information Forensics and Security*, 13(6), 1406–1420.

[34] Kukula, E. P., Sutton, M. J., and Elliott, S. J. (2010). The human–biometric-sensor interaction evaluation method: Biometric performance and usability measurements. *IEEE Transactions on Instrumentation and Measurement*, 59(4), 784–791.

[35] Crosswhite, N., Byrne, J., Stauffer, C., Parkhi, O., Cao, Q., and Zisserman, A. (2018). Template adaptation for face verification and identification. *Image and Vision Computing*, 79, 35–48.

[36] Duta, N. (2009). A survey of biometric technology based on hand shape. *Pattern Recognition*, 42(11), 2797–2806.

[37] Gunasinghe, H. and Bertino, E. (2017). PrivBioMTAuth: Privacy preserving biometrics-based and user centric protocol for user authentication from mobile phones. *IEEE Transactions on Information Forensics and Security*, 13(4), 1042–1057.

[38] Garris, M. D., Watson, C. I., McCabe, R., and Wilson, C. L. (2001). *User's Guide to NIST Fingerprint Image Software (NFIS)*. National Institute of Standards and Technology: United States.

[39] Murphy, C. N. and Yates, J. (2009). *The International Organization for Standardization (ISO): Global Governance Through Voluntary Consensus*. Milton Park: Routledge.

[40] Mansfield, T., Kelly, G., Chandler, D., and Kane, J. (2001). Biometric product testing final report. *Contract*, 92(4009), 309.

[41] Wayman, J. L., Possolo, A., and Mansfield, A. J. (2010, March). Fundamental issues in biometric performance testing: A modern statistical and philosophical framework for uncertainty assessment. In *Presentation to IBPC Conference, NIST*.

[42] Mittal, Y., Varshney, A., Aggarwal, P., Matani, K., and Mittal, V. K. (2015, December). Fingerprint biometric based access control and classroom attendance management system. In *2015 Annual IEEE India Conference (INDICON)* (pp. 1–6). IEEE.

[43] Ye, S., Luo, Y., Zhao, J., and Cheung, S. C. (2009). Anonymous biometric access control. *EURASIP Journal on Information Security*, 2009(1), 1–17.

[44] Dargan, S. and Kumar, M. (2020). A comprehensive survey on the biometric recognition systems based on physiological and behavioral modalities. *Expert Systems with Applications*, 143, 113114.

[45] Abdulrahman, S. A. and Alhayani, B. (2023). A comprehensive survey on the biometric systems based on physiological and behavioural characteristics. *Materials Today: Proceedings*, 80, 2642–2646. https://doi.org/10.1016/j.matpr.2021.07.005.

[46] Jain, A., Hong, L., and Pankanti, S. (2000). Biometric identification. *Communications of the ACM*, 43(2), 90–98.

[47] Zhang, W. Z., Elgendy, I. A., Hammad, M., *et al.* (2020). Secure and optimized load balancing for multitier IoT and edge-cloud computing systems. *IEEE Internet of Things Journal*, 8(10), 8119–8132.

[48] Unar, J. A., Seng, W. C., and Abbasi, A. (2014). A review of biometric technology along with trends and prospects. *Pattern Recognition*, 47(8), 2673–2688.

[49] de Luis-García, R., Alberola-Lopez, C., Aghzout, O., and Ruiz-Alzola, J. (2003). Biometric identification systems. *Signal Processing*, 83(12), 2539–2557.

[50] Sedik, A., Hammad, M., Abd El-Latif, A. A., *et al.* (2021). Deep learning modalities for biometric alteration detection in 5G networks-based secure smart cities. *IEEE Access*, 9, 94780–94788.

[51] Hammad, M., Luo, G., and Wang, K. (2019). Cancelable biometric authentication system based on ECG. *Multimedia Tools and Applications*, 78, 1857–1887.

[52] Prakash, A. J., Patro, K. K., Samantray, S., Pławiak, P., and Hammad, M. (2023). A deep learning technique for biometric authentication using ECG beat template matching. *Information*, 14(2), 65.

[53] Upmanyu, M., Namboodiri, A. M., Srinathan, K., and Jawahar, C. V. (2010). Blind authentication: A secure crypto-biometric verification protocol. *IEEE Transactions on Information Forensics and Security*, 5(2), 255–268.

[54] Cabana, A., Charrier, C., and Louis, A. (2019). Mono and multi-modal biometric systems assessment by a common black box testing framework. *Future Generation Computer Systems*, 101, 293–303.

[55] Ross, A. and Jain, A. (2003). Information fusion in biometrics. *Pattern Recognition Letters*, 24(13), 2115–2125.

[56] Bookstein, F. L. (1996). Biometrics, biomathematics and the morphometric synthesis. *Bulletin of Mathematical Biology*, 58(2), 313–365.

[57] Dantcheva, A., Elia, P., and Ross, A. (2015). What else does your biometric data reveal? A survey on soft biometrics. *IEEE Transactions on Information Forensics and Security*, 11(3), 441–467.

[58] Bibi, K., Naz, S., and Rehman, A. (2020). Biometric signature authentication using machine learning techniques: Current trends, challenges and opportunities. *Multimedia Tools and Applications*, 79(1–2), 289–340.

[59] Biggio, B., Russu, P., Didaci, L., and Roli, F. (2015). Adversarial biometric recognition: A review on biometric system security from the adversarial machine-learning perspective. *IEEE Signal Processing Magazine*, 32(5), 31–41.

[60] Kim, S. K., Yeun, C. Y., Damiani, E., and Lo, N. W. (2019). A machine learning framework for biometric authentication using electrocardiogram. *IEEE Access*, 7, 94858–94868.

[61] Galbally, J., McCool, C., Fierrez, J., Marcel, S., and Ortega-Garcia, J. (2010). On the vulnerability of face verification systems to hill-climbing attacks. *Pattern Recognition*, 43(3), 1027–1038.

[62]   Apostolakis, G. E. and Lemon, D. M. (2005). A screening methodology for the identification and ranking of infrastructure vulnerabilities due to terrorism. *Risk Analysis: An International Journal*, 25(2), 361–376.

[63]   Ali, G., Ally Dida, M., and Elikana Sam, A. (2020). Two-factor authentication scheme for mobile money: A review of threat models and countermeasures. *Future Internet*, 12(10), 160.

[64]   Chung, C. J., Khatkar, P., Xing, T., Lee, J., and Huang, D. (2013). NICE: Network intrusion detection and countermeasure selection in virtual network systems. *IEEE Transactions on Dependable and Secure Computing*, 10(4), 198–211.

[65]   Roberts, C. (2007). Biometric attack vectors and defences. *Computers & Security*, 26(1), 14–25.

[66]   Smith, D. F., Wiliem, A., and Lovell, B. C. (2015). Face recognition on consumer devices: Reflections on replay attacks. *IEEE Transactions on Information Forensics and Security*, 10(4), 736–745.

[67]   Hadid, A., Evans, N., Marcel, S., and Fierrez, J. (2015). Biometrics systems under spoofing attack: An evaluation methodology and lessons learned. *IEEE Signal Processing Magazine*, 32(5), 20–30.

Chapter 4

Leveraging generative adversarial networks and federated learning for enhanced cybersecurity: a concise review

Mohamed Hammad[1,2], Basma Abd El-Rahiem[3] and Ahmed A. Abd El-Latif[1,3]

The rise of cyber threats in recent years has made cybersecurity a critical concern for individuals, organizations, and governments worldwide. Machine learning has proven to be a powerful tool in security mechanisms, providing more effective and efficient detection and response capabilities to cyber threats. Deep learning, a subset of machine learning, has also shown promising results in various fields, including cybersecurity. This chapter explores the use of advanced technologies such as generative adversarial networks (GANs) and federated learning (FL) in cybersecurity to provide more effective and efficient detection and response capabilities to cyber threats while preserving data privacy. GANs can be used to generate synthetic data for training machine learning models and simulate cyber-attacks for training and testing cybersecurity defenses. FL enables devices or parties to collaborate and train a machine learning model without sharing their data with a central server, thereby mitigating the risks of data breaches and misuse while also enhancing model accuracy. The goal of using GANs and FL in cybersecurity is to develop novel approaches that leverage the power of artificial intelligence and machine learning to improve threat detection and response while also addressing the growing concerns around data privacy and security, ultimately contributing to a safer and more secure digital world.

4.1 Introduction

In recent years, cybersecurity has become a critical concern for individuals, organizations, and governments worldwide [1]. It means keeping computer systems and

[1]EIAS Data Science Lab, College of Computer and Information Sciences, Prince Sultan University, Saudi Arabia
[2]Department of Information Technology, Faculty of Computers and Information, Menoufia University, Egypt
[3]Department of Mathematics and Computer Science, Faculty of Science, Menoufia University, Egypt

networks safe from cyber threats like theft, damage, and unauthorized access [1]. The threat landscape is always changing, and new attack vectors appear all the time [2]. This makes it hard for organizations to stay ahead of attackers when it comes to cybersecurity, which is the use of different technologies, processes, and practices to protect computer systems and networks from attacks and unauthorized access [3]. One of these technologies is machine learning, which has been shown to be an effective way to use artificial intelligence to improve security by making it easier to find and stop cyber threats [4]. Machine learning algorithms can look at a huge amount of data and find patterns that humans might miss. Machine learning algorithms can be used in cybersecurity to find and stop attacks, find oddities in network traffic, and analyze threat intelligence data [5]. Deep learning is a subset of machine learning that uses artificial neural networks to learn from large amounts of data. Deep learning models can learn complex patterns and representations from raw data [6]. This has led to breakthroughs in many fields, such as computer vision [7,8], natural language processing [9,10], and pattern recognition [11–16]. Deep learning algorithms can be used in cybersecurity to look at network traffic and find outliers, malware, and security events [17–20].

The main motivation of this chapter is to address the challenges of cybersecurity, which has become an increasingly pressing issue in recent years. With the rise of cyber threats such as data breaches, phishing attacks, and malware infections, there is an urgent need to develop new approaches to protect computer systems and networks from unauthorized access, theft, damage, or other cyber threats. One of the primary goals of this topic is to explore the use of advanced technologies such as generative adversarial networks (GANs) and federated learning (FL) to provide more effective and efficient detection and response capabilities to cyber threats while preserving data privacy.

GANs are a type of deep learning model that is made up of two neural networks: a generator network and a discriminator network [21,22]. The generator network generates new data (e.g., images), while the discriminator network tries to distinguish between real and generated data. GANs can be used to generate realistic and diverse images, which have various applications in image synthesis, image translation, and image enhancement. In cybersecurity, GANs can be used to generate synthetic data for training machine learning models and simulate cyber-attacks for training and testing cybersecurity defenses [23,24]. GANs can be used to improve image security by generating images that are difficult to distinguish from real images, thus making it more challenging for hackers to launch attacks. Figure 4.1 shows a graphical representation and structure of GAN.

In Figure 4.1, we can see that the graphical representation and structure of a GAN consists of two main components: a generator and a discriminator network. The generator network takes a random noise vector as input and produces a new data point, typically an image, that is intended to be similar to real data points from the training set. The generator's goal is to produce realistic-looking data points that can detect the discriminator network. The discriminator network, on the other hand, takes either a real or generated data point as input and outputs a probability value indicating whether the input is real or fake. The discriminator's goal is to accurately

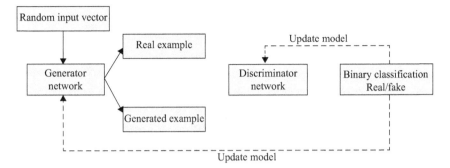

Figure 4.1   Graphical representation and structure of GAN

distinguish between real and generated data points. The training process of GANs involves training the generator and discriminator networks simultaneously in a two-player minimax game. The generator network aims to generate realistic-looking data points to deceive the discriminator network, while the discriminator network aims to accurately distinguish between real and generated data points. As the training progresses, the generator network learns to produce more realistic-looking data points that can deceive the discriminator network, and the discriminator network learns to become better at distinguishing between real and generated data points. Ideally, the training process should result in a generator network that can produce data points that are indistinguishable from real data points.

FL, on the other hand, is a machine learning technique that allows multiple devices or parties to collaborate and train a machine learning model without sharing their data with a central server [25–27]. In traditional machine learning, all the data is collected by a central server, which then trains a model and sends it to all the devices or parties. But this method raises privacy concerns because the central server has access to all the data, and there is a chance that data could be leaked or used in a bad way. FL gets around these privacy concerns by spreading the model-training process to each device or party. This way, each device or party can keep its own data on its own device or on its own device. The global model is kept up to date by the central server, which collects the model updates from each device or party. The global model becomes more accurate as it trains on a more diverse set of data from multiple devices or parties. FL has many advantages over traditional machine learning methods, such as more privacy, better accuracy, and more efficiency. By enabling devices or parties to maintain their data privacy, FL mitigates the risks of data breaches and misuse while also reducing the need to transfer large amounts of data to a central server [28–30]. Moreover, FL's ability to train on a more diverse set of data from multiple devices or parties enhances model accuracy, making it an attractive option for a variety of applications in which privacy and accuracy are critical. In cybersecurity, FL can be used to train machine learning models on data from multiple sources without sharing sensitive data with a central server. The overall architecture of FL can be represented graphically as a

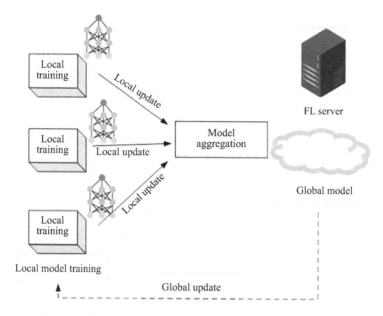

Figure 4.2   Graphical representation and structure of FL

distributed network of devices and a central server, as shown in Figure 4.2. The devices are connected to the central server through communication channels, and each device performs local training on its data. The central server coordinates the model training process by initializing the global model and aggregating the model updates from the devices to update the global model. The global model is then distributed to the devices, and the process repeats until convergence.

In the figure, we can see that the graphical representation of FL can be divided into *three* main components: the central server, the devices/parties, and the communication channels between them. At the center of the FL, architecture is the central server, which is responsible for coordinating the model training process. The server initializes the global model and distributes it to the devices/parties. The server then collects the model updates from the devices/parties and aggregates them to update the global model. The server repeats this process until the global model converges to a satisfactory level of accuracy. The second component of FL is the devices/parties that participate in the model training. These devices can be smartphones, laptops, or Internet of Things (IoT) devices, and they are responsible for performing the local model training on their respective data. Each device maintains its data privacy by keeping its data locally and only sharing model updates with the central server. The third component of FL is the communication channels that enable the exchange of information between the central server and the devices/parties. These channels can be wireless or wired and can use a variety of protocols to ensure secure and reliable data transfer. The communication channels allow the central server to distribute the initial model to the devices/parties, collect model updates, and send the updated global model back to the devices/parties.

The goal of using GANs and FL in cybersecurity is to develop novel approaches that leverage the power of artificial intelligence and machine learning to improve threat detection and response while also addressing the growing concerns around data privacy and security [31,32]. Ultimately, the aim is to provide a more secure and private computing environment for individuals, businesses, and organizations. By exploring the use of GANs and FL in cybersecurity, we can develop new and innovative ways to protect computer systems and networks from cyber threats, ultimately contributing to a safer and more secure digital world.

4.2   Mathematical formulation

GANs are a type of deep learning model that is made up of two neural networks: a generator and a discriminator. The generator network takes in a random noise vector Z and makes a fake data point $G(Z)$ that tries to look like how real data points are distributed. On the other hand, the discriminator network takes as input a data point X and outputs a probability $D(X)$ that shows whether the input is real or made up. The goal of the generator network is to make fake data that looks exactly like real data. The goal of the discriminator network is to correctly tell whether a given data point is real or fake.

The loss function of GANs can be formulated as a minimax game between the generator and the discriminator networks [33]. Let G be the generator network and D be discriminator network. The objective of the generator network is to minimize the following loss function:

$$L\_G = \log(1 - D(G(Z))) \tag{4.1}$$

where Z is a random noise vector sampled from a prior distribution. The objective of the discriminator network is to maximize the following loss function:

$$L\_D = \log(D(X)) + \log(1 - D(G(Z))) \tag{4.2}$$

where X is a real data point sampled from the true data distribution. Therefore, the overall objective of the GANs can be formulated as

$$\min\_G \max\_D L(G, D) = E[X \sim P\_data(X)][\log(D(X))] \\ + E[Z \sim P\_z(Z)][\log(1 - D(G(Z)))] \tag{4.3}$$

where $P\_data(X)$ is the distribution of the real data X, and $P\_z(Z)$ is the distribution of the random noise input Z. The first term in the objective function represents the expectation of the log-probability that D assigns to real data X, and the second term represents the expectation of the log-probability that D assigns to the fake data generated by G from the random noise Z. The generator G tries to minimize this objective function, while the discriminator D tries to maximize it. The equilibrium of this minimax game is reached when the generator generates data that is indistinguishable from real data, and the discriminator assigns a probability of 0.5 to both the real and the fake data.

FL is a machine learning technique that lets multiple devices or parties work together to train a machine learning model without sharing their data with a central server. In FL, each device or party maintains its own local model parameters and trains the model using its own data. The local model parameters are then aggregated to update the global model parameters, which are distributed to all devices or parties.

The objective function of FL can be formulated as

$$\min_w f(w) = E_i[F_i(w)] \tag{4.4}$$

where $F_i(w)$ is the local loss function of the ith device or party, and w is the global model parameters. The goal is to minimize the average of the local loss functions over all devices or parties.

The update of the global model parameters in FL can be formulated as

$$w_t + 1 = w_t - \eta \times \left(\nabla(1/n) \times \sum (i = 1)^{F_i(w_t)} \right) \tag{4.5}$$

where w_t is the current global model parameters, η is the learning rate, n is the number of devices or parties, and $\nabla(1/n)$ represents the averaging operator over all devices or parties. The gradient of the global loss function is approximated using the local gradients of each device or party.

During the aggregation process, FL also uses secure aggregation protocols to protect the privacy of the local model parameters. These protocols make sure that the global model parameters are updated without letting each device or party's local model parameters slip.

4.3 GAN and federated learning for image security

Image security means keeping digital photos safe from being stolen, changed, or accessed by people who should not be able to. Techniques for protecting images from cyber threats can include encryption, watermarking, steganography, and other methods. In the last few years, GAN and FL have been getting a lot of attention in the field of image security. In this section, we will talk about how GAN and FL can be used to improve image security.

4.3.1 GAN for image security

GANs, or generative adversarial networks, have emerged as a powerful tool in the field of image security, contributing to tasks such as image editing, synthesis, restoration, and fraud detection. One of the primary applications of GANs in image security is generating realistic images that resemble the original dataset. By learning the underlying distribution of a set of images, GANs can generate new images that possess similar characteristics, enabling their use in various domains like gaming, art, and film production. GANs have proven instrumental in creating visually appealing and immersive environments by generating synthetic images that are indistinguishable from the real ones [22,34].

Furthermore, GANs offer capabilities for image editing, allowing for the alteration of various attributes within an image. By manipulating the generator network of a GAN, it becomes possible to modify attributes such as style, color, and texture. This application finds relevance in domains like fashion and design, where GANs can assist in creating diverse visual styles and exploring novel design possibilities.

GANs also excel in image restoration tasks, particularly in the restoration of old or damaged images. By training a GAN on a dataset of high-quality images, the network learns the distribution of pristine images, enabling it to restore degraded or damaged images by leveraging its learned knowledge. This capability is particularly valuable in archival and restoration projects, where GANs can contribute to the preservation and enhancement of historical or deteriorated images.

Moreover, GANs have demonstrated efficacy in the realm of image fraud detection. By training a GAN to differentiate between real and fake images, the network can learn to identify the subtle differences between manipulated or forged images and authentic ones. This application is crucial in combating image-based fraud, such as photo tampering or the dissemination of misleading visual content. GANs offer the potential to automate the detection process, aiding in the identification of deceptive or fraudulent images [34].

Overall, GANs have revolutionized image security by providing advanced capabilities in generating realistic images, facilitating image editing and restoration, and enhancing fraud detection. Their ability to learn and replicate complex visual distributions has opened up new possibilities across various industries, advancing the fields of art, entertainment, design, forensics, and preservation.

4.3.2 Federated learning for image security

FL has emerged as a promising approach in the field of image security, offering notable applications that address privacy concerns and enable collaborative image analysis. One significant application of FL in image security revolves around privacy-preserving image analysis. By adopting this approach, the image data remains stored on local devices, and the analysis is performed locally without transmitting the sensitive data to a centralized server [35]. This decentralized approach enhances privacy and confidentiality, making it particularly valuable in contexts like medical imaging, where preserving patient data privacy is paramount.

FL also offers benefits in the realm of image classification. In this scenario, the image data is distributed across multiple devices, and the model is trained collaboratively [36]. Through iterative updates, the model aggregates individual device-level contributions to improve its accuracy and robustness. This distributed approach becomes advantageous when dealing with large-scale image datasets that cannot be stored on a single device. By leveraging FL, devices can collectively contribute to the training process while maintaining the privacy of their local data.

Additionally, FL has demonstrated potential in the detection of malicious images. By training an FL model to distinguish between malicious and benign images, the model can learn to identify patterns and features that differentiate harmful content. This application is crucial in combating the proliferation of malicious or inappropriate visual content, such as detecting and filtering out explicit or offensive images from online platforms or preventing the distribution of harmful visual material.

4.3.3   Combining GANs with FL

GAN and FL can be used together in the following ways to improve image security:

- First, GANs can be used to generate synthetic images that are similar to the original images but with added noise or distortion. These synthetic images can then be used to train the FL model.
- In the FL approach, instead of collecting all the images from the users and training a central model, the users' devices train their own models using their local data. These models are then aggregated to create a global model without transferring the actual data. This approach provides better privacy and security, as the users' data remains on their devices.
- To incorporate the GAN-generated synthetic images into FL, each user's local model can be trained using a combination of their own data and the GAN-generated images. This approach helps to prevent overfitting on a user's specific data, as well as improving the diversity of the training data.
- Furthermore, the GAN-generated images can be used to create a more robust model that is resistant to adversarial attacks. Adversarial attacks involve adding small perturbations to the input images to fool the model into making incorrect predictions. By training on synthetic images that have been specifically designed to be robust to such attacks, the FL model can be made more secure.
- In addition, GAN is used to generate synthetic images that can be used to augment the training data in an FL system. This approach can help address the problem of limited training data, which can be a major bottleneck in image classification tasks. For example, in an FL system for detecting images of fraudulent credit cards, the limited availability of real-world fraudulent credit card images could hinder the effectiveness of the model. In this case, GAN can be used to generate synthetic images of fraudulent credit cards, which can be added to the training dataset in the FL system to improve the model's performance.
- Another way to use GANs and FL together for image security is to employ federated GANs, which use GANs in a distributed manner across multiple devices to generate synthetic data. In this approach, each device generates synthetic data using its local GAN model, and the generated data is then shared and aggregated across the devices to improve the overall performance of the GAN model. This can be particularly useful in scenarios where the data is highly sensitive and cannot be shared across devices, such as medical imaging data.
- Finally, the combination of GAN and FL techniques can lead to better image security, by improving the privacy of the user data, increasing the diversity of

the training data, and creating a more robust model that is resistant to adversarial attacks.

4.4 GAN and federated learning for cybersecurity

GAN and FL can also be utilized for cybersecurity applications [37–39]. In this context, the goal is to detect and prevent potential security breaches, such as malware or other cyber-attacks.

In the case of GANs, they can be used to generate synthetic data that mimics the behavior of malicious software or network traffic. This synthetic data can then be used to train machine learning models for detecting and preventing these types of security breaches. GANs can also be used to generate adversarial examples, which are modified versions of legitimate data that are designed to fool machine learning models. By training machine learning models to detect these adversarial examples, GANs can help improve the robustness and security of these models. On the other hand, FL can be used for collaborative training of machine learning models across multiple devices or networks while maintaining data privacy. This is particularly important in the context of cybersecurity, where sensitive data, such as user profiles, login credentials, or financial information, must be protected. By using FL, each device or network can train its own local model using its own data and then send only the updated model parameters to a central server for aggregation. This way, the sensitive data is never shared or exposed, and the global model can still benefit from the collective knowledge of all devices or networks.

When used together, GANs and FL can make machine learning models for cybersecurity applications even safer. For example, GAN-generated synthetic data can be used for training machine learning models using FL, without risking the privacy of real user data. GANs can also be used to detect and prevent adversarial attacks during FL by generating adversarial examples and testing the robustness of the trained models against these attacks.

The applications of GANs and FL in cybersecurity are numerous [40–44], and as the field continues to evolve, new and innovative ways to leverage these technologies are emerging. Let us explore some of the most promising applications of GANs and FL in cybersecurity.

- *Malware detection* [40]: GANs have proven to be instrumental in the domain of malware detection. They can generate synthetic malware samples that contribute to training machine learning models for enhanced detection capabilities. By incorporating a diverse range of malware samples, including those generated synthetically through GANs, the models become more resilient and accurate in identifying new variants of malware. Furthermore, FL can be leveraged for training malware detection models in a decentralized fashion, fostering improved privacy and mitigating the potential risks associated with data breaches. Through the collaborative nature of FL, the privacy of sensitive data is preserved, allowing for the development of robust malware detection systems with increased accuracy and reduced dependence on centralized data repositories.

- **Intrusion detection** [41]: GANs have emerged as valuable tools in the context of intrusion detection. They can generate realistic network traffic data that aids in training intrusion detection systems. By incorporating synthetic data into the training process, the accuracy of the intrusion detection system can be enhanced, as it learns from a more diverse range of data, including uncommon attack scenarios. Additionally, FL can be leveraged to train intrusion detection models in a distributed manner, offering benefits such as improved system scalability and reduced vulnerability to data breaches. Through the collaborative nature of FL, multiple devices contribute their local data to collectively train the intrusion detection models, ensuring the preservation of data privacy and promoting the development of robust and efficient intrusion detection systems.
- **Vulnerability detection** [42]: GANs have proven to be effective in the domain of vulnerability detection. They can generate synthetic inputs that serve as test cases for assessing software vulnerabilities. By subjecting software to synthetic inputs produced by GANs, developers can proactively identify and address potential vulnerabilities, mitigating the risk of exploitation by malicious actors. Furthermore, FL can be employed to train vulnerability detection models in a decentralized fashion. This approach ensures that sensitive data remains on local devices, enhancing privacy and minimizing the potential for data breaches. By collaboratively aggregating the insights gained from multiple devices, FL enables the development of robust vulnerability detection models while preserving the security of sensitive information.
- **Password cracking** [43]: GANs have demonstrated their utility in the realm of password cracking. They can generate synthetic passwords that serve as training samples for password-cracking algorithms. By training these algorithms on a diverse range of passwords, including synthetic ones generated by GANs, their accuracy and efficiency in password cracking can be enhanced. Additionally, FL can be leveraged to train password-cracking models in a decentralized manner, thereby bolstering privacy and diminishing the likelihood of data breaches. FL enables the collaborative aggregation of insights from various devices, empowering the development of robust password-cracking models while safeguarding sensitive data on local devices.
- **Cyber threat intelligence** [44]: GANs can be used to generate synthetic cyber threat intelligence reports that can be used to train machine learning models for threat intelligence analysis. By training the models on a diverse set of threat intelligence reports, including the synthetic ones generated by GANs, the models can become more accurate in detecting and responding to cyber threats. FL can also be used to train threat intelligence models in a decentralized manner, which can help improve the scalability of the system and reduce the risk of data breaches.

To cogenerate and FL for cybersecurity, one possible approach is to use GANs to generate synthetic data that can be used to train machine learning models and use FL to train the models in a decentralized manner, while preserving the privacy of the data. Another approach is to use GANs to generate synthetic inputs that can be used to test software for vulnerabilities and use FL to train vulnerability detection models in a decentralized manner. Appendix A shows a Python code of GAN for image generation and FL for image classification and for malware detection using both techniques.

4.5 Evaluation and performance analysis

Effective evaluation and performance analysis of GANs, FL, and their combined approach are critical in the realm of cybersecurity. Accurately assessing the capabilities, limitations, and comparative effectiveness of these techniques not only helps us understand their potential impact but also enables us to make informed decisions when developing robust cybersecurity solutions. In this section, we delve into the intricacies of evaluating and analyzing the performance of GANs, FL, and the combined approach in the context of cybersecurity.

- **Metrics and benchmarks for cybersecurity**: Evaluating the effectiveness of GANs, FL, and their combined approach in the context of cybersecurity requires well-defined metrics and benchmarks. Metrics can include accuracy, precision, recall, $F1$-score, area under the ROC curve, and other domain-specific measures. Additionally, benchmarks provide reference points for comparing different models and approaches. Common benchmarks in cybersecurity may include publicly available datasets, simulated attack scenarios, or proprietary datasets representative of real-world cyber threats.
- **Experimental setup and datasets**: To conduct a rigorous evaluation, it is crucial to establish a well-defined experimental setup. This includes selecting appropriate datasets that encompass a wide range of cyber threats and attack types. The datasets should capture both known and emerging threats to ensure the evaluation reflects real-world scenarios. Additionally, the experimental setup should consider factors, such as data preprocessing, feature engineering, hyperparameter tuning, and model selection, to ensure fair comparisons between different techniques.
- **Performance evaluation of GANs, FL, and combined approach**: The performance evaluation should assess the individual efficacy of GANs and FL in addressing cybersecurity challenges. For GANs, key evaluation aspects include the quality and diversity of generated samples, discrimination ability, and resilience to adversarial attacks. In FL, the evaluation should consider metrics such as accuracy, convergence speed, privacy preservation, and communication overhead. Furthermore, evaluating the combined approach requires assessing the synergistic effects and improvements achieved by integrating GANs and FL.
- **Comparative analysis and results**: To gain insights into the strengths and weaknesses of different techniques, a comparative analysis is essential. This analysis can involve comparing GANs, FL, and their combined approach against traditional cybersecurity methods or other state-of-the-art approaches.

The evaluation should consider multiple dimensions, including detection accuracy, false positive rates, robustness against adversarial attacks, computational efficiency, and scalability. Presenting comprehensive and statistically sound results enables researchers and practitioners to identify the most effective approach for specific cybersecurity use cases.

The evaluation and performance analysis of GANs, FL, and their combined approach provide valuable insights into their efficacy in addressing cybersecurity challenges. By employing well-defined metrics, benchmarks, and experimental setups, we were able to assess the strengths and limitations of these techniques. The comparative analysis revealed intriguing patterns and trends, highlighting the potential of GANs, FL, and their integration for enhancing cybersecurity. The findings from this evaluation not only contribute to our understanding of these techniques but also serve as a foundation for future research and development in the field. With continued evaluation and analysis, we can advance toward more effective and robust cybersecurity solutions.

4.6   Open challenges in leveraging GANs and FL for cybersecurity

Despite the promising potential of leveraging GANs and FL for enhanced cybersecurity, several open challenges need to be addressed to ensure their effective application. While these techniques offer intriguing opportunities to bolster cybersecurity measures, they also bring forth a set of complex challenges that demand careful consideration. The integration of GANs and FL methodologies in real-world scenarios requires overcoming obstacles such as data privacy concerns, model robustness, and adversarial attacks. Additionally, the scalability and efficiency of FL algorithms need to be further optimized to handle large-scale cybersecurity systems. Understanding these open challenges is crucial for researchers and practitioners to navigate the path toward successful implementation and maximize the effectiveness of GANs and FL in the realm of cybersecurity.

These challenges are as follows:

- **Data privacy and security**: One of the primary challenges in leveraging GANs and FL for cybersecurity is ensuring data privacy and security. GANs and FL involve sharing sensitive data across multiple entities, which raises concerns about data breaches and unauthorized access. Developing robust privacy-preserving techniques, secure communication protocols, and encryption mechanisms is crucial to address these challenges.
- **Data heterogeneity and distribution**: GANs and FL often encounter challenges related to the heterogeneity and distribution of data across different sources or entities. The variations in data characteristics, quality, and imbalance can impact the performance and generalization of models. Developing effective techniques to handle data heterogeneity, domain adaptation, and data distribution shifts is essential for achieving reliable and robust cybersecurity solutions.

- **Model interpretability and explainability**: GANs, and to some extent FL, can be complex and black-box models, making it challenging to interpret and explain their decisions and behaviors. In cybersecurity, interpretability and explainability are crucial for understanding vulnerabilities, attack patterns, and adversarial behavior. Researchers need to explore techniques for enhancing the interpretability and explainability of GANs and FL models in the cybersecurity domain.
- **Adversarial attacks and countermeasures**: GANs and FL models are susceptible to adversarial attacks, where malicious entities attempt to manipulate or exploit the models' vulnerabilities. Adversarial attacks can compromise the integrity, confidentiality, and availability of cybersecurity systems. Developing robust adversarial defense mechanisms, including adversarial training, robust optimization, and detection techniques, is critical for ensuring the reliability and resilience of GANs and FL in cybersecurity applications.
- **Scalability and resource constraints**: GANs and FL often require significant computational resources, memory, and communication bandwidth. Scalability becomes a challenge when dealing with large-scale cybersecurity datasets and distributed learning across numerous entities. Efficient techniques for model compression, distributed optimization, and resource allocation need to be explored to address the scalability and resource constraints associated with GANs and FL for cybersecurity.

As the field of cybersecurity continues to evolve, it is evident that leveraging GANs and FL holds immense promise. However, to fully harness their potential, it is imperative to address the open challenges discussed in this section. By tackling issues such as data privacy, model robustness, adversarial attacks, scalability, and efficiency, researchers and practitioners can pave the way for secure and effective implementations of GANs and FL in cybersecurity systems. By remaining vigilant and actively addressing these challenges, we can forge a path toward a safer and more resilient digital landscape, ensuring that GANs and FL become valuable tools for enhancing cybersecurity.

4.7   Conclusion and future directions

The increasing number of cybersecurity threats has made it necessary to explore advanced technologies that can effectively and efficiently detect and respond to cyber threats while preserving data privacy. Machine learning and deep learning algorithms have proven to be powerful tools in security mechanisms, particularly in detecting and preventing attacks, identifying anomalies in network traffic, and analyzing threat intelligence data. This chapter has explored the potential of GANs and FL in cybersecurity to develop new approaches that leverage the power of artificial intelligence and machine learning. GANs can be used to generate synthetic data for training machine learning models and simulate cyber-attacks for training and testing cybersecurity defenses. On the other hand, FL enables multiple devices or parties to collaborate and train a machine learning model without sharing their data with a central server, mitigating the risks of data breaches and misuse while also enhancing model accuracy. Ultimately, these technologies can contribute to a safer and more secure digital world by addressing the growing concerns around data privacy and security. The combination of GANs and FL in cybersecurity has the potential to enhance model accuracy while maintaining data privacy, making it a promising approach for developing robust cybersecurity solutions.

Using advanced technologies like GANs and FL in cybersecurity has shown promising results in improving threat detection and response while addressing growing concerns about data privacy and security. In the future, there are several directions that this chapter could explore to further advance the application of these technologies in cybersecurity.

One direction is to explore the use of GANs for generating realistic and diverse network traffic for testing and evaluating cybersecurity defenses. This can help organizations identify and address weaknesses in their security mechanisms and improve their preparedness for cyber-attacks. GANs can be trained to generate network traffic that resembles legitimate traffic, as well as traffic generated by different types of cyber-attacks. By using synthetic data generated by GANs, organizations can conduct more comprehensive and realistic testing of their cybersecurity defenses.

Another direction is to investigate the use of FL for training machine learning models for detecting and preventing cyber-attacks in decentralized environments. In decentralized environments such as the IoT and edge computing, there are numerous devices and nodes that generate data and communicate with each other. FL can enable these devices to collaborate and train a machine learning model without sharing their data with a central server, thereby mitigating the risks of data breaches and misuse while also enhancing model accuracy. By using FL, organizations can develop more efficient and effective cybersecurity mechanisms for decentralized environments.

A third direction is to explore the use of GANs and FL for developing adaptive and resilient cybersecurity defenses. Cyber attackers are constantly evolving their tactics and techniques, and cybersecurity defenses need to adapt and evolve in response. GANs and FL can be used to train machine learning models that can adapt to new attack patterns and learn from past attacks. By using these technologies, organizations can develop cybersecurity mechanisms that are more resilient and can respond more effectively to new and emerging cyber threats.

Advancements in GAN-based image encryption have enabled the generation of encrypted images that can only be decrypted using a specific key. However, these techniques are vulnerable to attacks, and future research can explore more advanced GAN architectures for image encryption that are more robust and can withstand different types of attacks. GAN-based image steganography is another promising area where GANs can be used to hide secret information within an image. Future research can explore the use of GANs for high-capacity and secure image steganography that can protect the integrity of secret information.

FL is a distributed machine learning approach that allows multiple devices to collaborate to train a model without sharing their data. This approach can be used for secure image sharing, where images are stored locally on devices and only shared with other devices in a privacy-preserving manner. This can be a promising area of research for developing secure image sharing techniques that can protect user privacy.

With the increasing amount of image data being generated, privacy-preserving image analysis has become a crucial research area. FL can be used to develop privacy-preserving image analysis techniques that allow image data to be analyzed without compromising user privacy. This approach can be used in various applications such as medical imaging and surveillance, where the privacy of the image data is paramount.

Image search engines need to ensure that the images they index are secure and not malicious. Future research can explore the use of GANs and FL for secure image search by filtering out malicious images and preventing them from being indexed. This can be a promising area of research for developing techniques that can protect users from malicious content while searching for images.

GANs and FL have great potential for advancing image security. Future research can explore the abovementioned directions to develop more robust and secure image security techniques.

Appendix A

GANs for image generation:

```
# GAN model for image generation
import tensorflow as tf


# Define generator and discriminator models
generator = tf.keras.models.Sequential([...]) #
Generator model
discriminator = tf.keras.models.Sequential([...]) #
Discriminator model

# Compile discriminator
discriminator.compile(loss='binary_crossentropy',
optimizer='adam')

# Combine generator and discriminator
gan = tf.keras.models.Sequential([generator,
discriminator])
gan.compile(loss='binary_crossentropy',
optimizer='adam')
```

```
# Train GAN model
for epoch in range(num_epochs):
        # Generate fake images
        fake_images = generator.predict(noise)

        # Train discriminator on real and fake images
        discriminator_loss_real  =  discriminator.train_
on_batch(real_images, real_labels)
        discriminator_loss_fake  =  discriminator.train_
on_batch(fake_images, fake_labels)
        discriminator_loss = (discriminator_loss_real +
discriminator_loss_fake) / 2

        # Train generator using combined model
        generator_loss = gan.train_on_batch(noise, real_
labels)
```

Federated learning (FL) for image classification:

```
# FL model for image classification
import tensorflow as tf
import tensorflow_federated as tff

# Define model architecture
model = tf.keras.models.Sequential([...]) # Model for
image classification

# Define federated learning algorithm
iterative_process = tff.learning.build_federated_aver-
aging_process(model)

# Train the federated model
for round_num in range(num_rounds):
        state, metrics = iterative_process.next(state,
federated_train_data)

# Evaluate the federated model
evaluation = tff.learning.build_federated_evaluation
(model)
test_metrics = evaluation(state.model,
federated_test_data)
```

GANs for malware detection:

```
# GAN model for generating synthetic malware samples
import tensorflow as tf

# Define generator model
generator = tf.keras.models.Sequential([...]) #
Generator model

# Compile generator
generator.compile(loss='binary_crossentropy',
optimizer='adam')

# Generate synthetic malware samples
synthetic_samples = generator.predict(noise)
# Train machine learning model for malware detection using
synthetic and real samples
model = tf.keras.models.Sequential([...]) #
Malware detection model
model.fit([real_samples, synthetic_samples],
labels, epochs=num_epochs)
```

FL for malware detection:

```
# FL model for malware detection
import tensorflow as tf
import tensorflow_federated as tff

# Define model architecture
model = tf.keras.models.Sequential([...]) #
Model for malware detection

# Define federated learning algorithm
iterative_process = tff.learning.build_federated_aver-
aging_process(model)

# Train the federated model
for round_num in range(num_rounds):
        state, metrics = iterative_process.next(state,
federated_train_data)
```

```
# Evaluate the federated model
evaluation = tff.learning.build_federated_evaluation
(model)
test_metrics = evaluation(state.model,
federated_test_data)
```

GANs for intrusion detection:

```
# GAN model for generating realistic network traffic data
import tensorflow as tf

# Define generator model
generator = tf.keras.models.Sequential([...]) #
Generator model

# Compile generator
generator.compile(loss='binary_crossentropy',
optimizer='adam')

# Generate synthetic network traffic data
synthetic_data = generator.predict(noise)

# Train intrusion detection model using real and synthetic
data
model = tf.keras.models.Sequential([...]) #
Intrusion detection model
model.fit([real_data, synthetic_data], labels,
epochs=num_epochs)
```

FL for intrusion detection:

```
# FL model for intrusion detection
import tensorflow as tf
import tensorflow_federated as tff

# Define model architecture
model = tf.keras.models.Sequential([...]) #
Model for intrusion detection

# Define federated learning algorithm
iterative_process = tff.learning.build_federated_
averaging_process(model)
```

```
# Train the federated model
for round_num in range(num_rounds):
state, metrics = iterative_process.next(state,
federated_train_data)

# Evaluate the federated model
evaluation = tff.learning.build_federated_evaluation
(model)
test_metrics = evaluation(state.model,
federated_test_data)
```

GANs for vulnerability detection:

```
# GAN model for generating synthetic inputs for
vulnerability testing
import tensorflow as tf

# Define generator model
generator = tf.keras.models.Sequential([...]) #
Generator model

# Compile generator
generator.compile(loss='binary_crossentropy',
optimizer='adam')

# Generate synthetic inputs for vulnerability testing
synthetic_inputs = generator.predict(noise)

# Test software with synthetic inputs for vulnerability
detection
for input in synthetic_inputs:
vulnerability_test(input)
```

FL for vulnerability detection:

```
# FL model for vulnerability detection
import tensorflow as tf
import tensorflow_federated as tff

# Define model architecture
model = tf.keras.models.Sequential([...]) #
Model for vulnerability detection
```

```
# Define federated learning algorithm
iterative_process = tff.learning.build_federated_aver-
aging_process(model)

# Train the federated model
for round_num in range(num_rounds):
state, metrics = iterative_process.next(state,
federated_train_data)

# Evaluate the federated model
evaluation = tff.learning.build_federated_evaluation
(model)
test_metrics = evaluation(state.model,
federated_test_data)
```

Note that these code snippets provide a high-level overview of the implementation and may require additional modifications based on your specific use case and data format.

References

[1]   Albahar, M. (2019). Cyber attacks and terrorism: A twenty-first century conundrum. *Science and Engineering Ethics*, 25, 993–1006.
[2]   Choo, K. K. R. (2011). The cyber threat landscape: Challenges and future research directions. *Computers & Security*, 30(8), 719–731.
[3]   Cole, E. (2011). *Network security bible*. New York: Wiley.
[4]   Dai, D. and Boroomand, S. (2021). A review of artificial intelligence to enhance the security of big data systems: State-of-art, methodologies, applications, and challenges. *Archives of Computational Methods in Engineering*, 29, 1291–1309.
[5]   Surden, H. (2014). Machine learning and law. *Washington Law Review*, 89, 87.
[6]   LeCun, Y., Bengio, Y., and Hinton, G. (2015). Deep learning. *Nature*, 521 (7553), 436–444.
[7]   Voulodimos, A., Doulamis, N., Doulamis, A., and Protopapadakis, E. (2018). Deep learning for computer vision: A brief review. *Computational Intelligence and Neuroscience*, 2018.
[8]   Chai, J., Zeng, H., Li, A., and Ngai, E. W. (2021). Deep learning in computer vision: A critical review of emerging techniques and application scenarios. *Machine Learning with Applications*, 6, 100134.
[9]   Socher, R., Bengio, Y., and Manning, C. D. (2012). Deep learning for NLP (without magic). In *Tutorial Abstracts of ACL 2012* (pp. 5–5), Association for Computational Linguistics, USA.

[10]   Kamath, U., Liu, J., and Whitaker, J. (2019). *Deep learning for NLP and speech recognition* (Vol. 84). Cham: Springer.

[11]   Hammad, M., Iliyasu, A. M., Elgendy, I. A., and Abd El-Latif, A. A. (2022). End-to-end data authentication deep learning model for securing IoT configurations. *Human-centric Computing and Information Sciences*, 12(4).

[12]   Sakr, A. S., Pławiak, P., Tadeusiewicz, R., and Hammad, M. (2022). Cancelable ECG biometric based on combination of deep transfer learning with DNA and amino acid approaches for human authentication. *Information Sciences*, 585, 127–143.

[13]   Prakash, A. J., Patro, K. K., Hammad, M., Tadeusiewicz, R., and Pławiak, P. (2022). BAED: A secured biometric authentication system using ECG signal based on deep learning techniques. *Biocybernetics and Biomedical Engineering*, 42(4), 1081–1093.

[14]   Saber, S., Amin, K., Pławiak, P., Tadeusiewicz, R., and Hammad, M. (2022). Graph convolutional network with triplet attention learning for person re-identification. *Information Sciences*, 617, 331–345.

[15]   Abd El-Rahiem, B. and Hammad, M. (2022). A multi-fusion IoT authentication system based on internal deep fusion of ECG signals. In *Security and Privacy Preserving for IoT and 5G Networks: Techniques, Challenges, and New Directions*, Springer (pp. 53–79).

[16]   Hammad, M., Zhang, S., and Wang, K. (2019). A novel two-dimensional ECG feature extraction and classification algorithm based on convolution neural network for human authentication. *Future Generation Computer Systems*, 101, 180–196.

[17]   Sarker, I. H. (2021). Deep cybersecurity: A comprehensive overview from neural network and deep learning perspective. *SN Computer Science*, 2(3), 154.

[18]   Sedik, A., Hammad, M., Abd El-Latif, A. A., *et al.* (2021). Deep learning modalities for biometric alteration detection in 5G networks-based secure smart cities. *IEEE Access*, 9, 94780–94788.

[19]   Vinayakumar, R., Alazab, M., Soman, K. P., Poornachandran, P., Al-Nemrat, A., and Venkatraman, S. (2019). Deep learning approach for intelligent intrusion detection system. *IEEE Access*, 7, 41525–41550.

[20]   Alazab, M. and Tang, M. (Eds.) (eds.) . (2019). *Deep learning applications for cyber security*. Berlin: Springer.

[21]   Durgadevi, M. (2021, July). Generative adversarial network (GAN): A general review on different variants of GAN and applications. In *2021 Sixth International Conference on Communication and Electronics Systems (ICCES)* (pp. 1–8). Piscataway, NJ: IEEE.

[22]   Porkodi, S. P., Sarada, V., Maik, V., and Gurushankar, K. (2022). Generic image application using GANs (generative adversarial networks): A review. *Evolving Systems*, 1–15.

[23]   Navidan, H., Moshiri, P. F., Nabati, M., *et al.* (2021). Generative adversarial networks (GANs) in networking: A comprehensive survey and evaluation. *Computer Networks*, 194, 108149.

[24] Andresini, G., Appice, A., De Rose, L., and Malerba, D. (2021). GAN augmentation to deal with imbalance in imaging-based intrusion detection. *Future Generation Computer Systems*, 123, 108–127.

[25] Xue, X., Mao, H., Li, Q., Huang, F., and Abd El-Latif, A. A. (2022). An energy efficient specializing DAG federated learning based on event-triggered communication. *Mathematics,* 10(22), 4388; https://doi.org/ 10.3390/math10224388.

[26] Xu, M., Peng, J., Gupta, B. B., *et al.* (2021). Multi-agent federated reinforcement learning for secure incentive mechanism in intelligent cyber-physical systems. *IEEE Internet of Things Journal*; 10.1109/ JIOT.2021.3081626

[27] Liu, Y., Peng, J., Kang, J., Iliyasu, A. M., Niyato, D., and Abd El-Latif, A. A. (2020). A secure federated learning framework for 5G networks. *IEEE Wireless Communications,* 27(4), 24–31.

[28] Moshawrab, M., Adda, M., Bouzouane, A., Ibrahim, H., and Raad, A. (2023). Reviewing federated machine learning and its use in diseases prediction. *Sensors*, 23(4), 2112.

[29] Li, Q., Wen, Z., Wu, Z., *et al.* (2021). A survey on federated learning systems: Vision, hype and reality for data privacy and protection. *IEEE Transactions on Knowledge and Data Engineering*, 35, 3347–3366.

[30] Liu, Y., James, J. Q., Kang, J., Niyato, D., and Zhang, S. (2020). Privacy-preserving traffic flow prediction: A federated learning approach. *IEEE Internet of Things Journal*, 7(8), 7751–7763.

[31] Mothukuri, V., Parizi, R. M., Pouriyeh, S., Huang, Y., Dehghantanha, A., and Srivastava, G. (2021). A survey on security and privacy of federated learning. *Future Generation Computer Systems*, 115, 619–640.

[32] Macas, M., Wu, C., and Fuertes, W. (2022). A survey on deep learning for cybersecurity: Progress, challenges, and opportunities. *Computer Networks*, 212, 109032.

[33] Ma, J., Yu, W., Chen, C., Liang, P., Guo, X., and Jiang, J. (2020). Pan-GAN: An unsupervised pan-sharpening method for remote sensing image fusion. *Information Fusion*, 62, 110–120.

[34] Li, W. (2021, July). Image synthesis and editing with generative adversarial networks (GANs): A review. In *2021 Fifth World Conference on Smart Trends in Systems Security and Sustainability (WorldS4)* (pp. 65–70). Piscataway, NJ: IEEE.

[35] Alazab, M., Priya, S., M, P., Reddy, P. K., Gadekallu, T. R., and Pham, Q. V. (2021). Federated learning for cybersecurity: Concepts, challenges, and future directions. *IEEE Transactions on Industrial Informatics*, 18(5), 3501–3509.

[36] Rieke, N., Hancox, J., Li, W., *et al.* (2020). The future of digital health with federated learning. *NPJ Digital Medicine*, 3(1), 119.

[37] Loukas, G., Vuong, T., Heartfield, R., Sakellari, G., Yoon, Y., and Gan, D. (2017). Cloud-based cyber-physical intrusion detection for vehicles using deep learning. *IEEE Access*, 6, 3491–3508.

[38] Ghimire, B. and Rawat, D. B. (2022). Recent advances on federated learning for cybersecurity and cybersecurity for federated learning for internet of things. *IEEE Internet of Things Journal*, 9(11), 8229–8249.

[39] Ferrag, M. A., Friha, O., Maglaras, L., Janicke, H., and Shu, L. (2021). Federated deep learning for cyber security in the internet of things: Concepts, applications, and experimental analysis. *IEEE Access*, 9, 138509–138542.

[40] Singh, A., Dutta, D., and Saha, A. (2019, July). MIGAN: Malware image synthesis using GANs. *Proceedings of the AAAI Conference on Artificial Intelligence*, 33(01), 10033–10034.

[41] Seo, E., Song, H. M., and Kim, H. K. (2018, August). GIDS: GAN based intrusion detection system for in-vehicle network. In *2018 16th Annual Conference on Privacy, Security and Trust (PST)* (pp. 1–6). IEEE.

[42] Yi, S., Sagduyu, Y. E., Davaslioglu, K., and Levy R. (2018). Vulnerability detection and analysis in adversarial deep learning. In *Guide to vulnerability analysis for computer networks and systems: An artificial intelligence approach*, Springer (pp. 211–234).

[43] Nam, S., Jeon, S., Kim, H., and Moon, J. (2020). Recurrent GANs password cracker for IoT password security enhancement. *Sensors*, 20(11), 3106.

[44] Arora, A. and Shantanu. (2022). A review on application of GANs in cybersecurity domain. *IETE Technical Review*, 39(2), 433–441.

Chapter 5

A survey on face recognition methods with federated leaning

Huiting Sun[1], Jialiang Peng[2,3] and Zhaogong Zhang[1]

Face recognition technology is a hot issue that today's neural networks need to continue to study in depth. With the development of deep neural networks, face recognition technology has achieved great results even in some datasets, and the computer's ability to recognize faces has exceeded human eye observations. However, with the widespread use of face recognition technology, the problem of privacy protection of face information has emerged. This chapter analyzes and summarizes the development status and technical achievements of face recognition technology under the federal learning framework. First of all, the definition status and development status of federated learning and traditional face recognition technology are introduced. Then the analysis summarizes the relevant achievements of face recognition technology based on the federated learning framework that have been proposed so far. Finally, we will analyze the possible problems and prospects for future development.

5.1 Introduction

In recent years, the advancement and extensive research in deep neural networks have propelled face recognition technology to new heights. Deep neural networks have demonstrated remarkable capabilities in accurately identifying and verifying faces, often surpassing human observation abilities. However, with the increasing adoption of face recognition technology, concerns regarding the privacy protection of face information have emerged as a critical challenge. Traditional face recognition methods heavily rely on large-scale datasets for training deep neural networks. However, face information is inherently personal and private, and utilizing such data during model training poses the risk of privacy breaches. In some instances, malicious individuals exploit various means to unlawfully access and acquire users' face information. This situation raises significant concerns regarding

[1]School of Computer and Science and Technology Software, Heilongjiang University, China
[2]School of Data Science and Technology, Heilongjiang University, China
[3]Institute for Cryptology and Network Security, Heilongjiang University, China

data privacy and the ethical implications associated with the utilization of personal biometric information.

Recognizing the need for data protection, the European Union introduced the General Data Protection Regulation (GDPR) in 2018. This regulation restricts businesses from indiscriminately using personal information and requires enterprises to conduct thorough risk assessments on the necessity and security of biometric features such as faces, gaits, fingerprints, irises, and voiceprint recognition for personal identity authentication. The GDPR aims to prevent the excessive collection and utilization of personal biometric data and ensures that individuals provide informed consent before their data is collected. In the era of big data, where our daily interactions involve mobile phones and cloud services, our personal information becomes increasingly exposed to the Internet. Criminal elements exploit technical means to illicitly obtain user information for illicit purposes, resulting in compromised data security. Consequently, safeguarding user data privacy remains a pressing challenge that requires urgent attention. Moreover, the lack of data sharing between edge devices gives rise to the problem of data fortresses. Different users with distinct devices create isolated data silos that cannot be securely shared. This data fragmentation hinders the development of machine learning models on edge devices, limiting their ability to achieve global optimal solutions and local personalization based solely on existing datasets [1–4].

To address these challenges and provide a solution that preserves privacy and enhances data security, Google introduced federated learning technology in 2016. Federated learning adopts a distributed learning approach, where the model and training parameters remain on the edge device. Only the model parameters are uploaded and updated with a central server, ensuring the privacy and security of the edge device. The application of federated learning in face recognition technology presents a promising approach to protect the privacy of face images on edge devices.

However, despite the potential benefits, there have been relatively few studies investigating the application of federated learning to face recognition. Consequently, this article aims to comprehensively analyze and summarize the existing literature on face recognition methods within the federated learning framework. The article will describe the problem areas that can be effectively addressed by each method and the underlying technologies employed. Additionally, this study will explore the intersection of federated learning with other privacy-enhancing technologies such as privacy computing and differential privacy. Finally, the article will discuss the application prospects and identify research areas that hold promise for the future development of face recognition based on federated learning.

By examining the current landscape of face recognition technology and its integration with federated learning, this survey contributes to the advancement of privacy-preserving face recognition methods. It sheds light on the potential of federated learning in safeguarding data privacy, addressing data fortresses, and enabling collaborative learning across edge devices. The insights gained from this research will aid in the identification of future research directions and promote the development of secure and privacy-aware face recognition systems.

5.2   Federated learning

5.2.1   Concept and definition of federated learning

With the continuous updating of computer technology, the continuous improvement of algorithms, and the increasing number of layers of deep neural networks, deep learning technology has achieved great success in the field of artificial intelligence [5–7]. In the field of image recognition, visual algorithms implemented through convolutional neural networks (CNNs) have long surpassed humans. However, the success of deep learning is based on a large amount of data, and the value of data is mainly reflected in the fact that it is used as a "fuel" to provide a large number of sample training data for artificial intelligence models to help improve the effectiveness of the model. However, with the rapid development of the mobile Internet, the scale of data has become more and more large and complex, and the value of data is no longer limited to training data but serves enterprises in the form of assets and brings economic benefits to enterprises. Because data has the attributes of an asset, governments, businesses, and even individuals are paying more and more attention to data. However, due to the competition between each other, it is difficult to share the data of all parties, resulting in the state of the data on the plate, which affects the development of artificial intelligence that relies heavily on data. In order to meet the growing requirements of algorithm design, some large institutions will open source some large data, but this large data is also limited, it cannot cover all the possibility data in a certain direction, and the amount of data of the size of ImageNet is difficult or even impossible to achieve by manually annotating and crowdsourcing uploads. This is mainly due to the fact that the data available in real life is either small in scale or lacks important information (such as lack of label information or lack of some feature values). As a result, it is often very difficult to obtain training data in large quantities and of high quality.

At the same time, due to people's increasing concern about user privacy and data security, users have begun to pay more attention to whether the use of personal privacy information is approved by themselves. Multiple cases have proven that it has become impossible to disclose user personal data. A series of legal provisions such as the GDPR proposed by the European Union in 2018 put forward strict constraints and controls on the collection and processing of data.

Because of the previous problems, we need a method where the data does not leave the local but can be trained globally. Federal learning is here! The core idea emphasized by federated learning is that data does not move the model, and data is available and invisible. This ensures that the data is local and the participants work together to build the training model. The training principle of federated learning is shown in Figure 5.1. Therefore, in general, the definition of federated learning is as follows: "Federated learning is a distributed training method that uses datasets scattered in various participants, fuses data information through privacy protection technology, and collaboratively builds a global model."

5.2.2 Classification of federated learning

The application scenarios of federated learning encompass a diverse range of distributed environments, each with unique data distributions. These data distributions can be classified into three distinct categories: (1) data distributions with a large number of common features but a small number of common labels, (2) data distributions with a large number of common labels but a small number of common features, and (3) data distributions without any common features or labels. To address these varying data distributions, federated learning has evolved into three subcategories: horizontal federated learning, vertical federated learning, and federated transfer learning [8].

5.2.2.1 Horizontal federated learning

Horizontal federated learning, as depicted in Figure 5.2, is a form of federated learning where multiple participants collaborate to train a shared learning model. In this context, the participants have overlapping data features, which means that their individual datasets contain similar characteristics despite potentially having different user groups. An example scenario could involve two banks operating in

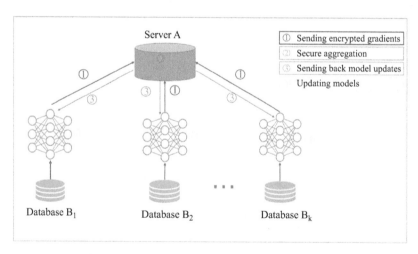

Figure 5.1   Federated learning flowchart [8]

	ID	X1	X2	X3	Y
	U1				
clientA	U2				
	U3				
	U4				
clientB	U5				
	U6				

Figure 5.2   Horizontal federated learning [8]

different regions, with a small overlap in their user base but similar data characteristics due to their similar business models.

The primary goal of horizontal federated learning is to leverage the combined data from multiple participants to enhance the learning model's performance. By pooling their data together, the participants increase the overall amount of available data for training the model. In the given example, the two banks can collaborate through horizontal federated learning to create a more comprehensive learning model that can better serve their customers' needs.

The key advantage of horizontal federated learning is that it allows participants to jointly establish a learning model without directly sharing sensitive customer data. Instead, the model is trained locally on each participant's data, and only the model updates are exchanged and aggregated. This approach helps address privacy concerns and data security issues, making it suitable for scenarios where data privacy is crucial, such as in the financial industry.

The term "sample division federated learning" is often used interchangeably with horizontal federated learning because the participants divide their data into samples and collectively train the model. The focus is on sharing and utilizing the overlapping data characteristics to improve the model's performance rather than sharing the entire datasets.

By leveraging horizontal federated learning, organizations with similar data characteristics can collaborate and benefit from each other's data without compromising individual data privacy. This approach allows for more accurate and personalized recommendations for financial products, as the combined knowledge from multiple sources enhances the understanding of customer preferences and behaviors.

5.2.2.2   Vertical federated learning

Vertical federated learning, as illustrated in Figure 5.3, is a form of federated learning where participants collaborate by aligning their data samples while having different data characteristics. In this context, the participants share overlapping data samples, typically derived from a common user base, but each participant's data possesses unique characteristics due to their diverse services or domains.

An example scenario could involve a collaboration between a bank and an e-commerce company that serves different services but shares a significant portion of their customer base. In such cases, vertical federated learning enables the participants to jointly analyze their respective data feature spaces to develop a more

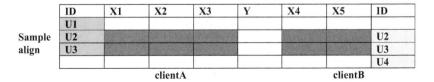

Figure 5.3   Vertical federated learning [8]

accurate machine learning model. Specifically, they can leverage the relationship between the user's assets (e.g., financial information from the bank) and the user's purchase behavior (e.g., transaction history from the e-commerce company) to make predictions or judgments, such as estimating the user's likelihood of purchasing a particular item.

The objective of vertical federated learning is to leverage the complementary information from different data sources to enhance the predictive capabilities of the learning model. By aligning their data samples based on a common set of users, the participants can establish connections between different data characteristics and derive meaningful insights that can improve the accuracy and effectiveness of their predictive models.

Vertical federated learning offers several advantages in scenarios where data characteristics differ between participants. It allows organizations with different service offerings or domains to collaborate and benefit from the shared user base without directly sharing sensitive data. Instead, the participants securely exchange only the necessary information for model training and aggregate the results to generate a comprehensive model.

The term "overlapping data samples" refers to the common user data points that exist between the participants' datasets. While the data characteristics may differ, the overlapping data samples provide an opportunity to bridge the information gap and derive valuable insights. By utilizing vertical federated learning, the bank and e-commerce company in the given example can leverage the alignment of their overlapping data samples to gain a deeper understanding of the relationship between user assets and purchase behavior. This knowledge can be used to make more accurate predictions and inform decision-making processes.

5.2.2.3   Federated transfer learning

Federated transfer learning, as depicted in Figure 5.4, is a technique employed when there is limited overlap between data samples and data features among participants. In this context, there are two distinct parties involved: the source domain and the target domain. The objective is to learn the feature distribution within the source domain and transfer the learned feature information from the source domain to the target domain.

Consider a scenario where two organizations have different datasets that exhibit little overlap in terms of both data samples and data characteristics. One organization can be designated as the source domain, which possesses a well-established dataset with abundant labeled data and a learned feature distribution.

ID	X1	X2	X3	Y	X4	X5	ID
U1							
U2							
							U3
							U4

clientA   clientB

Figure 5.4   Federated transfer learning [8]

The other organization can be considered the target domain, with a limited dataset and insufficient labeled data. The aim is to leverage the knowledge acquired from the source domain to enhance the learning process in the target domain.

Federated transfer learning allows the transfer of feature information learned from the source domain to the target domain, enabling the target domain to benefit from the knowledge and insights derived from the source domain's data. By leveraging the feature distribution learned in the source domain, the target domain can improve its model's performance, generalize better, and enhance its predictive capabilities.

The process of federated transfer learning involves extracting relevant features from the source domain's dataset and adapting them to the target domain. This adaptation aims to align the feature distributions between the two domains, allowing the target domain to leverage the knowledge gained from the source domain's data without directly sharing sensitive or proprietary information.

The primary advantage of federated transfer learning is its ability to address the limitations imposed by limited data overlap and feature divergence among participants. By utilizing the source domain's feature distribution, the target domain can leverage existing knowledge to improve its own learning process. This approach is particularly valuable when data acquisition in the target domain is challenging, expensive, or time-consuming.

By categorizing federated learning into these three distinct approaches, researchers and practitioners can design and develop tailored algorithms and strategies to address the specific challenges associated with each data distribution scenario. Horizontal federated learning focuses on leveraging shared data features, vertical federated learning emphasizes the alignment of common labels, and federated transfer learning enables knowledge transfer between domains with minimal overlap. Understanding these categories facilitates the selection of appropriate techniques and methodologies to deploy federated learning in various real-world applications. Furthermore, this categorization paves the way for future advancements and innovations in federated learning research, opening possibilities for addressing more complex and diverse data distribution scenarios.

5.3 Face recognition

5.3.1 The concept of face recognition

Face recognition, also known as facial recognition, is a biometric recognition technology that automatically identifies individuals based on their facial features. It has become a widely used and researched field in computer vision and pattern recognition [9–11]. The process of face recognition involves capturing face images or video streams using a camera or similar device. The captured images are then analyzed to detect and track faces present in the scene. This detection and tracking process may utilize various techniques, such as face detection algorithms that identify the facial region within an image or video frame. Once the faces are detected and tracked, a series of operations are performed on the detected face images to extract relevant information and make identification or verification decisions.

The technical pipeline of face recognition typically includes several stages. First, image acquisition is performed using a camera or other imaging device to capture face images or video streams. This step can be accomplished using common cameras, making face image acquisition a simple and accessible process that does not require specialized equipment. The image acquisition process is fast and can be completed within seconds, allowing for efficient face data collection.

Next, feature localization is conducted to identify specific facial landmarks or regions of interest within the captured face images. These landmarks may include points such as the position of the eyes, nose, mouth, and other distinctive facial characteristics. Feature localization aims to extract relevant facial information that is essential for subsequent identification or verification processes.

After feature localization, identity confirmation and search take place. In this stage, the extracted facial features are compared to a database of known faces or templates to determine the identity of the individual. The comparison is typically based on statistical or geometric features extracted from the face, such as the relative positions of facial landmarks or the statistical distributions of pixel intensities in specific regions. By comparing the extracted features with the stored templates, the system can identify or verify the person's identity.

Overall, face recognition technology offers several advantages compared to other biometric recognition methods. It provides a simple and fast means of collecting biometric data, as face images can be acquired using common cameras without the need for complex or specialized equipment. The noncontact nature of face recognition makes it particularly convenient and suitable for various applications. Furthermore, face recognition supports concurrent processing, allowing for multiple individuals to be recognized simultaneously, making it suitable for scenarios with high-throughput requirements. During the COVID-19 pandemic, face recognition technology has gained even more significance as it enables touchless interactions and reduces the risk of viral transmission. Users can benefit from the convenience, noncontact operation, concurrency, and inherent human characteristics offered by face recognition systems.

With AlexNet [12] winning the ImageNet [13] Challenge in 2012, CNNs have shown great power in image classification, with a feature+ classifier significantly superior to the artificially designed feature and classifier through convolutional kernels. In the process of face recognition, the CNN is used to learn a large number of face pictures, and then the input images are extracted to extract feature vectors that are useful for distinguishing different people, replacing artificially designed features. Therefore, deep learning technology plays an important role in various fields, greatly improving SOTA for many tasks. By 2014, Facebook's DeepFace [14] had for the first time achieved the same accuracy as humans on the LFW [15] dataset (DeepFace: 97.35% vs. Human: 97.53%) [14]. In the following years, with the advent of SphereFace [16], ArcFace [17], and CosFace [18], deep learning-based facial recognition technology has reached SOTA.

5.3.2   Face recognition database

In the early stages of face recognition technology, face databases were relatively small due to limited computational capabilities and the complexity of collecting and annotating large-scale datasets. For instance, the Yale Face Dataset [19], created by Yale University, consisted of images from 15 individuals, each exhibiting 11 different expressions, gestures, and lighting conditions. In total, the dataset comprised 165 pictures, each with a size of 100×100 pixels. The dataset was relatively small, and the images contained relatively simple information.

However, as face recognition algorithms advanced and computer performance improved, the size and complexity of face recognition databases grew significantly. Presently, there exist numerous large-scale face recognition databases, and this article focuses on a subset of these databases, as outlined in Table 5.1.

Large-scale face recognition databases are instrumental in training and evaluating robust face recognition models. These databases encompass diverse populations, varied facial appearances, and complex environmental conditions, enabling researchers to develop and validate face recognition algorithms that perform well in real-world scenarios.

Table 5.1 provides an overview of selected large-scale face recognition databases used in research and development. These databases typically contain tens of thousands to millions of images collected from numerous individuals. They encompass various demographics, including different ethnicities, ages, genders, and facial characteristics, ensuring a comprehensive representation of the human population.

Table 5.1   Popular face recognition databases

Databases	Detailed information	Scope of application
WebFace	10k+ people, about 500k images	Unrestricted scenarios
FaceScrub	530 people, about 100k images	Unrestricted scenarios
YouTubeFace	1,595 people, 3,425 videos	Unrestricted scenarios
LFW	5k+ people, over 10k images	Evaluate the performance of the face verification algorithm
Mulipie	337 people with different postures, expressions, lighting face images, a total of 750k+ face images	Restricted scenarios face recognition
MegaFace	690k people with 1,000k face images	Evaluate the performance of the face recognition and verification algorithm
IJB-A(B/C)		Face recognition and verification
CASIA-FACEV5	2,500 Asian faces of 500 people	Face recognition and verification
Pubfig	200 people with 58k+ face images	Unrestricted scenarios face recognition
CelebFaces	200k face with 40+ face attributes	Face attributes recognition

The availability of large-scale face recognition databases has facilitated significant advancements in face recognition technology. Researchers can now leverage these extensive datasets to train deep learning models, such as CNNs, which can learn intricate facial features and patterns, enabling more accurate and robust face recognition systems.

Moreover, large-scale face recognition databases allow researchers to investigate challenging scenarios, such as pose variations, occlusions, and lighting conditions. By including diverse and complex data, these databases enable the development of face recognition algorithms that can handle real-world challenges and provide reliable performance across a wide range of conditions.

5.3.3   Face recognition technology process

The face recognition system mainly includes four components, namely: face detection (make box position), face image preprocessing (face alignment), face image feature extraction, and matching and recognition.

5.3.3.1   Face image acquisition

Face image acquisition involves the collection of various types of face images using camera lenses. These images can include both still images and dynamic images, capturing the face from different positions and with different expressions. When a user is within the shooting range of the acquisition device, such as a camera or a video camera, the device automatically searches for and captures an image of the user's face. This process can be facilitated through face detection algorithms, which are capable of identifying and localizing faces within an image or video stream.

The acquisition device may employ various techniques to ensure optimal image quality and capture the desired facial information. For instance, the device may adjust camera settings, such as focus, exposure, and white balance, to ensure clear and well-lit face images. Additionally, the device may use facial tracking algorithms to track the movement of the user's face, enabling the acquisition of dynamic images or images from different perspectives. By collecting face images under different conditions, such as different positions and expressions, a more comprehensive representation of the individual's face can be obtained. This variability in the acquired face images helps to enhance the robustness and accuracy of subsequent face recognition algorithms, allowing for improved performance in real-world scenarios.

It is important to note that the acquisition of face images should comply with ethical and legal considerations, respecting privacy and obtaining consent from individuals involved. Privacy protection measures and adherence to data protection regulations, such as obtaining informed consent and securely handling the collected face images, should be implemented to ensure the responsible use of biometric data.

Face detection is an essential preprocessing step in practical face recognition systems. It involves accurately identifying the position and size of faces within an image. By locating the faces, further analysis and processing can be performed on the detected regions to extract relevant facial features and enable subsequent recognition tasks. In face detection, various pattern features are used to identify and distinguish faces from the background or other objects within an image. These features encompass a range of characteristics, including histogram features, color features, template features, structural features, and Haar features [20]. Each of these features provides valuable information that can aid in detecting faces.

Histogram features capture the distribution of pixel intensities within a face image, representing its unique color or grayscale profile. Color features focus on color variations and patterns within the face, allowing for discrimination based on skin tone, hair color, or other visual attributes. Template features involve comparing local image regions to predefined templates or models of faces, assessing the similarity or matching scores. Structural features analyze the spatial relationships and geometric arrangements of facial components, such as the eyes, nose, and mouth. Haar features, popularized by the Viola–Jones algorithm, are rectangular pattern descriptors that efficiently capture variations in facial appearance.

Face detection algorithms use these diverse features to identify potential face regions within an image. This typically involves applying machine learning techniques, such as classifiers or detectors trained on labeled datasets. These models are trained to differentiate between facial and non-facial patterns based on the extracted features. Once a potential face region is detected, further processing steps can be employed to refine the detection, align the face, or extract more detailed facial features. These subsequent steps may involve techniques such as face alignment, pose estimation, or landmark localization to ensure accurate positioning and alignment of the detected face region. By accurately detecting and localizing faces in an image, face detection facilitates subsequent operations in face recognition, such as feature extraction, identity confirmation, and matching. It enables the extraction of relevant facial information and sets the stage for subsequent stages of the face recognition pipeline. Efficient and reliable face detection algorithms contribute to the overall accuracy and performance of face recognition systems.

The mainstream face detection method uses the Adaboost [21] learning algorithm based on the previous features. This algorithm is a classification method, which combines some of the weaker classification methods to combine new and strong classification methods. In the process of face detection, the Adaboost algorithm is used to select some rectangular features that can best represent the face (weak classifier), the weak classifier is constructed as a strong classifier according to the weighted voting method, and then several strong classifiers trained are connected in series to form a cascading structure of cascading classifiers, which effectively improves the detection speed of the classifier.

5.3.3.2 Face image preprocessing

Face image preprocessing: Image preprocessing for faces is based on the results of face detection, which processes the image and ultimately serves the process of feature extraction. Due to the limitations of various conditions and random interference, the original image obtained by the system is often not directly used, and it must be preprocessed in the early stage of image processing such as grayscale

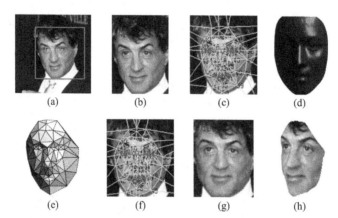

Figure 5.5   *DeepFace uses the local binary pattern (LBP)+SVR method to detect the six reference points of the face, as shown in (a), and then fits the transformation (scaling, rotation) of a reference point. Pan to crop the image as shown in (b). After positioning 67 datum points on the image and performing triangulation, part (c) is obtained. Get an average 3D face model (front face) (d) with a 3D face library USF Human-ID, learn the mapping between a 3D face model and the original 2D face P, and visualize the triangular blocks, as shown in (e). Through the relevant mapping, the reference point in the original 2D face is converted into the reference point generated by the 3D model, and the reference point is obtained as shown in (f). The final positive face is (g). A new view generated by 3D model (but not used in the Deepface) (h) [14].*

correction and noise filtering. For face images, the pretreatment process mainly includes light compensation, grayscale transformation, histogram equalization, normalization, geometric correction, filtering, and sharpening of the face image.

For example, in terms of face alignment, such as DeepFace, the pioneering work of face recognition is used as an example, as shown in Figure 5.5. In the DeepFace, the experimental results show the accuracy rate on the LFW is 87.9% without the face alignment step, whereas the accuracy rate on the LFW reaches 97.35% with the face alignment step. It also underlines the importance of face alignment.

5.3.3.3   Face image feature extraction

Face image feature extraction: The features that can be used by the face recognition system are usually divided into visual features, pixel statistical features, face image transformation coefficient features, face image algebraic features, and so on. Face feature extraction is performed on certain features of a face. Face feature extraction, also known as face representation, is the process of modeling features on faces. The methods of facial feature extraction are summarized into two categories: one is a knowledge-based representation method; the other is a characterization method based on algebraic features or statistical learning. Knowledge-based

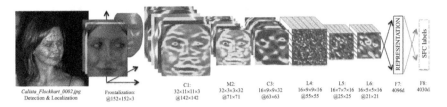

Figure 5.6   Feature extraction [14]

characterization methods are mainly based on the shape description of face organs and the distance characteristics between them to obtain feature data that are helpful for face classification, and their feature components usually include Euclidean distance, curvature, and angle between feature points. The human face is composed of parts such as eyes, nose, mouth, and chin, and the geometric description of these parts and the structural relationship between them can be used as important features to identify the face, which are called geometric features. Knowledge-based face representation mainly includes methods based on geometric features and template-matching methods.

Nowadays, the mainstream face feature extraction uses a deep neural network to extract the face information, input a face image, and convert the image into a vector through the neural network. Let us continue using DeepFace as an example, as shown in Figure 5.6. It uses eight layers of networks: the convolutional layer of C1 and C3, the maximum pooling layer of M2, the local convolutional layer of L4, L5, and L6, the F7 and F8 are fully connected layers, in which the output of the F7 layer is extracted as a face feature, and the feature of the F8 layer is input to SoftMax as a classification.

5.3.3.4   Face image matching and recognition

Face image matching and recognition are crucial stages in the face recognition process, enabling the system to identify and verify individuals based on their facial features. Once the features have been extracted from a given face image, the system proceeds with matching these features against the feature templates stored in its database. This matching process involves comparing the extracted features with the stored templates and assessing their level of similarity.

To facilitate the matching process, a threshold is set, serving as a criterion for determining the required level of similarity for a successful match. If the similarity between the extracted features and the stored template exceeds this threshold, the match is considered positive, and the system outputs the corresponding result. Face recognition entails comparing the features of the face to be recognized with the feature templates stored in the database. By evaluating the degree of similarity, the system can infer the identity information associated with the face. The recognition process can be categorized into two main types: confirmation and identification.

Confirmation, also referred to as verification, involves a one-to-one image comparison. In this scenario, the system compares the features of the target face with the features of a specific individual stored in the database. The goal is to confirm whether the target face matches the stored template for the given individual.

Identification, on the other hand, is a one-to-many image matching and comparison process. Here, the system matches the features of the target face with multiple feature templates stored in the database. The objective is to identify the most likely identity of the target face by comparing its features with a range of possibilities in the database.

Both confirmation and identification processes rely on the comparison of facial features and the assessment of their similarity. Feature extraction techniques, such as deep neural networks, are commonly used to extract discriminative features from face images. Various similarity measurement algorithms, such as Euclidean distance or cosine similarity, are then applied to quantify the similarity between the extracted features and the stored templates.

The accuracy and reliability of face recognition systems depend on the effectiveness of feature extraction methods, the choice of similarity measurement algorithms, and the quality and diversity of the stored templates in the database. Advancements in these areas, along with the development of large-scale face databases and deep learning techniques, have significantly improved the performance of face recognition systems, enabling them to achieve impressive results even surpassing human-level accuracy in some cases.

5.3.4   Advantages and limitations of different face recognition approaches

Face recognition approaches can be broadly categorized into traditional methods and deep learning-based techniques. Each approach offers unique advantages and limitations, which are important to consider when selecting the most suitable method for a specific application.

5.3.4.1   Traditional face recognition methods

Traditional face recognition methods typically rely on handcrafted features and statistical models. These approaches have been extensively studied and developed over the years and offer several advantages:

Advantages:

- Robustness to variations: Traditional methods often incorporate techniques to handle variations in lighting conditions, pose changes, and facial expressions. They can handle limited variations in the face and still achieve reasonable recognition accuracy.
- Efficiency: Traditional algorithms can be computationally efficient, making them suitable for real-time applications.
- Interpretability: These methods provide interpretable results as they are based on explicitly defined features and models. It is easier to understand and analyze the underlying mechanisms of traditional face recognition algorithms.

However, traditional face recognition approaches also have certain limitations:

Limitations:

- Feature engineering: Handcrafting effective features for face recognition can be challenging and time-consuming. The performance of these methods heavily relies on the quality and relevance of the selected features.
- Limited adaptability: Traditional methods may struggle with handling complex variations, such as non-frontal poses, extreme lighting conditions, or occlusions. They may exhibit reduced accuracy when faced with significant variations in the face images.
- Scalability: Scaling traditional face recognition systems to handle large-scale datasets or extensive databases can be difficult due to computational and memory limitations.

5.3.4.2   Deep learning-based face recognition techniques

Deep learning has revolutionized the field of face recognition by automatically learning discriminative features from raw data. CNNs and other deep learning architectures have demonstrated exceptional performance in various computer vision tasks, including face recognition. These techniques offer several advantages:

Advantages:

- End-to-end learning: Deep learning models can learn discriminative features directly from raw images, eliminating the need for manual feature engineering. This ability enables the models to adapt and generalize well to complex variations in face images.
- High accuracy: Deep learning-based face recognition approaches have achieved remarkable accuracy on benchmark datasets, surpassing the performance of traditional methods in many cases.
- Scalability: Deep learning models can handle large-scale datasets and databases effectively, making them suitable for applications with a vast number of individuals.

However, deep learning-based face recognition techniques also come with their own set of limitations:

Limitations:

- Data requirements: Deep learning models typically require large amounts of labeled training data to achieve optimal performance. Acquiring and annotating such datasets can be time-consuming and resource intensive.
- Computationally intensive: Training and inference of deep learning models can be computationally demanding, requiring powerful hardware resources, especially for real-time applications.
- Lack of interpretability: Deep learning models often function as black boxes, making it challenging to interpret the learned representations and understand the decision-making process.

Understanding the advantages and limitations of different face recognition approaches is crucial in selecting the most suitable method for a given application. Traditional methods offer robustness and efficiency but may require manual feature engineering and struggle with complex variations. On the other hand, deep learning-based techniques provide end-to-end learning, high accuracy, and scalability but have data and computational requirements. It is essential to consider the specific needs, constraints, and trade-offs among interpretability, performance, and resource demands when deciding on a face recognition approach. The continuous advancements in face recognition technology, particularly in the field of deep learning, hold great promise for improving the accuracy and reliability of face recognition systems in various domains, further enhancing security and convenience.

5.4 The current development of FedFR technology

Federated learning has achieved significant results in many downstream tasks because it solves the problem of data silos. Especially in the healthcare industry, medical data is highly sensitive and is often collected and resided in different medical institutions. In fact, face information is highly private for everyone, especially the flooding of various face-brushing systems today, resulting in face information becoming more important and needing to be more protected.

To get a more generalized face recognition model, we often need a lot of data to train it or change its loss function. For example, SphereFace2 [22] is modified as follows: the original SoftMax loss leads to the competition of inter-classes, and then the scores between classes will be suppressed. As the training uses multi-classification, it is necessary to clarify the class to which each sample belongs. Therefore, it modifies the two-classification loss function from the following perspectives: positive and negative sample balance, difficult sample mining, angular margin, and the use of multiple two classifications instead of the multiple classifications during training.

In fact, based on the previous situation, face recognition technology based on federal learning is proposed. Each edge device trains its own data locally and then sends the trained model to a cloud server, which receives the model parameters of all devices and aggregates the model FedAvg [23]. The general process of the FedAvg algorithm: within each Communication Round, the E devices involved in the update iterate over E epochs on the local stochastic gradient descent (SGD) and then upload the model to the server side for aggregation.

However, our goal in introducing federated learning is to solve the problem of the scale of face database and the types of face. The introduction of federated learning allows more data to participate in model training, but in fact, after the introduction of federated learning, there will always be some malicious users using some means such as GAN [24] and so on, stealing model parameters or user information, so the information of the participants has the risk of leakage. Moreover, the participants join the federated learning; for each user, after participating in the training, the participants provide data for the central server that enhanced the generalization of the central server model, but for the participant model, the final global optimal model may not be the participant optimal model update. So, considering the previous several issues, this article mainly summarizes the existing face recognition development based on federated learning in the following aspects: FedFR with privacy protection and personalized FedFR.

5.4.1   FedFR with privacy protection

While federated learning has been introduced to protect users' face information, it has also led to new problems, namely, that malicious attackers, such as Melis [25] train binary classifiers on gradient information to infer which participant the data record belongs to, which leads to the disclosure of the user's private information. Zhu *et al.* [26] proposed a DLG algorithm aimed at training fuzzy gradients by generating fuzzy features and labels, so as to narrow the gap between the fuzzy gradient and the real gradient by continuously optimizing the fuzzy features, thereby reconstructing user data. Geiping *et al.* [27] performed an optimization attack on the gradient cosine similarity of the data to reconstruct high-resolution images.

Then people naturally think that uploading the real information of the user with the reconfigurable will led to the exposure of the user's private information then upload the model update parameters with disturbances. Therefore, Meng *et al.* [28] proposed that in the process of model update, because in order to protect the privacy of users, the class-embedding matrix is not shared among users, but the study shows that in the case of no sharing, the individual users will have features overlap during the model aggregation process. As shown in Figure 5.7, the left side represents the traditional federated learning framework. In the process of model aggregation, after mapping the user features to the hypersphere, it will be found that there is a feature overlap, which will lead to the accuracy of the model; so the authors propose to have a class-embedding matrix in de-privacy shared with other users, as shown on the right side of Figure 5.7. The server sends the user a class center matrix with noise disturbance of other users to solve the problem of feature overlap and not exposing user privacy. The differential privacy local clustering algorithm (DPLC) proposed by them proves that the complexity of the algorithm is low with a large number of formulas, and at the same time, the perturbation model with differential privacy protection is experimentally demonstrated to be available. Liu *et al.* proposed FedFV [29], similar methods to the DPLC, the premise of the article is that the server side is credible, when the model is trained. The user sends its own class center matrix to the server, and the server selects a part of the user's class-embedding matrix, performs averaging and normalization operations, and obtains the equivalent class vector matrix. When the equivalence vector matrix is sent to the client, it forms a categorical vector matrix with the client's categorical vector group as the weight of the classifier. Moreover, only the category vector of the user side is trained.

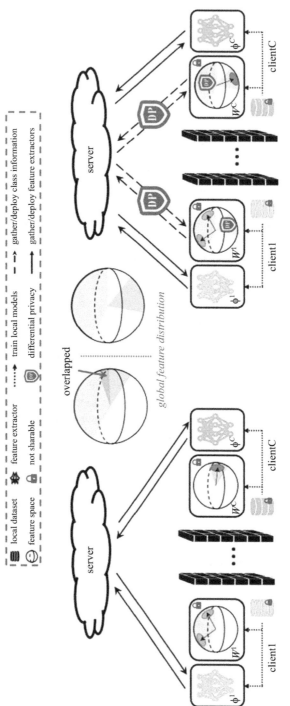

Figure 5.7 DPLC [28]

Similar to FedFV are FedAWS [30] and FedUV [31]. FedAws was proposed in the hope of being used in a specific scenario that has only one positive label, and protected user's embedding matrix. In FedAws [30], the server only sends the vector of the corresponding user in W to the user. Previously, a weight matrix of C*d was sent, but now only one of the rows is sent, and that line corresponds to the user's own row. In order to cope with specific scenarios, this algorithm adds a regular term while updating the parameters on the server side, which is a spread-out regularization. This regular term forces each row of W to have at least some distance from all other rows, which prevents the neural network from overfitting a class. FedUV [31] uses an error-correcting code mechanism, and as the number of training rounds increases, the negative loss in the loss function gradually becomes a redundant term, and the article proves that when the positive loss is small, whether the negative loss is discarded or not, the model accuracy is not affected. Niu *et al.* proposed FedGC [32], a federated learning framework for facial recognition, which also guaranteed higher privacy. It compensates for missing local optimization problems with face-specific SoftMax-based loss functions. From a new perspective of backpropagation, gradients are corrected, and cross-client gradients are introduced to ensure that the network is updated in the direction of standard SoftMax. At the same time, because the central model aggregates the model of all devices and is transmitted back to the central server, the updated model of the aggregated model is sent to each edge device, which will reduce the model performance of the edge device.

5.4.2   Personalized FedFR

Aggarwal *et al.* proposed FedFace [33], a framework for joint learning (FL) collaborative learning of facial recognition models, in a privacy-aware manner. The face information present on the client is shared with the server and other clients, and each client is a mobile device (one identity per client) that contains only the owner-related face image. Then the client uses their local database to train a local model and upload the model parameter update to the server, so that FedFace can use the face image training model provided on multiple clients, in a federated learning manner to increase the size of the dataset, so that the face recognition model performance becomes stronger. Experiments have shown that FedFace pre-trained on the CASIA-WebFace dataset has 2.36% better TAR performance than CosFace on IJB-A. Liu *et al.* [34] proposed an FL-based framework called FedFR, based on the previous FedFace, proposing more novel work. The author proposes a novel decoupling custom module to optimize the personality model for the corresponding customer. As shown in Figure 5.8, unlike the previous client-side training model sent to the server-side aggregation, the author uses the pretrained model in public dataset to send to each user. In order to solve the problem of overfitting caused by the small number of client datasets, the author chooses to distribute the public dataset to each client in his work. In addition, in order to adapt to the device hash rate of the client and improve the model performance of the client, the author set a threshold and selected only negative samples similar to the client to train with the local dataset. At the same time, the authors also proposed the idea of using

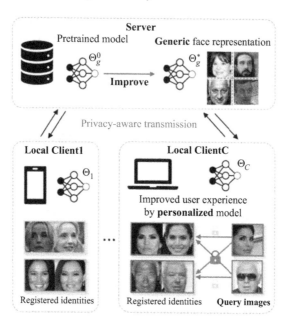

Figure 5.8   FedFR [34]

contrast learning (Simclr [35]), emphasizing the comparative experiment of mutual adjustment between the global model and the personalized model to improve the global model. And the authors of the article say that this is the first work to explore personalized face recognition in FL settings, and the proposed framework has been validated as superior to previous methods on several general and personalized face recognition benchmarks, with very good results in both face recognition and face verification. Zhuang *et al.* proposed FedFR [36], a federated learning-based unsupervised face recognition method with domain constraint loss, using the idea of transfer learning to address the generalization of models that have already performed well in deep neural networks, such as those used in fair faces in African faces. It improves the performance of the target domain by learning to iteratively aggregate knowledge in the source domain, while proposing an enhanced clustering algorithm that can solve the problem of edge devices without labels and finally gets a well-performed face recognition model in the target domain.

Bai *et al.* [37] proposed a framework also known as FedFace for innovative FL of facial recognition. Specifically, FedFace relies on two main innovative algorithms: partial joint momentum (PFM) and joint validation (FV). PFM applies the estimated equivalent global momentum locally to effectively approximate the centralized momentum SGD. FV repeatedly searches for better federated aggregation weights by testing the aggregation model on some private validation dataset, which can improve the generalization capability of the model. Ablation studies and extensive experiments have validated the effectiveness of the FedFace method and showed that it is comparable or even better in performance to the centralized baseline.

5.5   Hybrid approaches and ensemble methods

Face recognition technology plays a crucial role in various domains, including security systems, biometrics, and authentication. While traditional and deep learning-based face recognition methods have their own strengths and limitations, researchers and practitioners have been exploring the potential of hybrid approaches and ensemble methods to overcome these challenges and improve the overall performance of face recognition systems. This section provides an in-depth exploration of hybrid approaches and ensemble methods in the context of face recognition, highlighting their significance and how they can address the limitations of individual methods.

5.5.1   *Introduction to hybrid approaches in face recognition*

Hybrid approaches in face recognition aim to combine the strengths of traditional and deep learning-based techniques to enhance the accuracy and robustness of face recognition systems. Traditional face recognition methods, such as eigenfaces, fisherfaces, and LBP, have been widely used and have demonstrated good performance in certain scenarios. These methods often rely on handcrafted features and statistical classifiers to identify and match faces.

On the other hand, deep learning-based techniques, particularly CNNs, have revolutionized the field of face recognition by learning hierarchical representations directly from raw face images. CNNs can automatically extract discriminative features and have shown remarkable success in various face recognition tasks, including face detection, face verification, and face identification.

By combining traditional and deep learning-based techniques, hybrid approaches seek to leverage the complementary strengths of these two approaches. Traditional methods excel in handling variations in lighting conditions, pose, and expression, while deep learning models capture complex facial features and can generalize well to unseen faces. The integration of these approaches allows for more robust and accurate face recognition in real-world scenarios.

Hybrid approaches typically involve using traditional methods as a preprocessing step to extract low-level features from face images. These features are then fed into deep learning models, which learn high-level representations and perform classification or verification tasks. Alternatively, traditional methods can be used for post-processing, refining the results obtained from deep learning models.

The combination of traditional and deep learning-based techniques offers several advantages. First, it can enhance the discriminative power of face recognition models by incorporating both global and local features. Traditional methods capture global face characteristics, such as the overall shape and appearance, while deep learning models capture fine-grained features, such as facial landmarks and texture details.

Second, hybrid approaches can improve the robustness of face recognition systems by reducing sensitivity to variations in illumination, pose, and expression. Traditional methods are designed to handle such variations, while deep learning models learn robust representations that can generalize across different conditions.

Furthermore, hybrid approaches can address the challenges posed by limited training data. Deep learning models often require a large amount of labeled training data to achieve optimal performance. However, acquiring a massive dataset with labeled face images can be time-consuming and expensive. By using traditional methods to preprocess the data, hybrid approaches can reduce the data requirements for deep learning models, making face recognition more practical in scenarios where labeled data is limited.

5.5.2   Discussion of ensemble methods in face recognition

Ensemble methods in face recognition involve combining the predictions or decisions of multiple face recognition algorithms to improve overall performance. Instead of relying on a single algorithm, ensemble methods leverage the strengths of diverse algorithms to enhance accuracy, robustness, and generalization capabilities. These methods have gained significant attention in the face recognition community and have demonstrated promising results in various applications.

Ensemble methods can be broadly categorized into two types: *homogeneous* and *heterogeneous*.

- Homogeneous ensembles:
  Homogeneous ensembles consist of multiple instances of the same face recognition algorithm, trained on different subsets of the training data or with different parameter settings. Each individual algorithm, often referred to as a base classifier or base model, is trained independently and produces its own predictions. These predictions are then combined using techniques such as majority voting, weighted voting, or averaging to obtain the final ensemble prediction.

  The key idea behind homogeneous ensembles is that each base model may specialize in different aspects of face recognition, leading to diverse and complementary predictions. This diversity helps in capturing a wider range of variations in face images, improving the overall accuracy and robustness of the ensemble. Homogeneous ensembles also provide a mechanism to handle uncertainties and errors made by individual algorithms, reducing the risk of incorrect predictions.

- Heterogeneous ensembles:
  Heterogeneous ensembles, as the name suggests, combine different types of face recognition algorithms or models. These algorithms may employ distinct techniques, such as deep learning-based models, traditional methods, or

feature-based approaches. The ensemble can be formed by training each individual algorithm independently and combining their predictions, or by using a unified framework that integrates the different algorithms.

Heterogeneous ensembles exploit the complementary strengths of different algorithms. For example, deep learning models excel in capturing high-level features and handling complex variations, while traditional methods may be more effective in handling specific challenges like pose variations or occlusions. By combining these algorithms, the ensemble can benefit from their respective advantages and mitigate their individual limitations.

Ensemble methods offer several advantages in face recognition:

- Improved accuracy: Ensemble methods have the potential to achieve higher recognition accuracy compared to individual algorithms. The combination of diverse algorithms helps in capturing different aspects of face variations and reducing errors or biases present in individual models.
- Robustness to variations: Ensemble methods can enhance the robustness of face recognition systems by reducing sensitivity to variations in lighting conditions, pose, expression, and other factors. The ensemble's diverse predictions help in handling these variations more effectively.
- Generalization capabilities: Ensemble methods often exhibit better generalization capabilities, allowing them to perform well on unseen faces or in different environments. By combining the knowledge from multiple algorithms, ensembles can better capture the underlying patterns and variations in face images.
- Reducing bias and uncertainty: Ensemble methods provide a means to mitigate biases or errors inherent in individual algorithms. By combining the predictions, the ensemble can make more informed decisions and reduce the risk of incorrect classifications.

However, there are also challenges and considerations in using ensemble methods:

- Complexity and computational cost: Ensemble methods typically require training and maintaining multiple algorithms, which can be computationally expensive and resource intensive. The ensemble's decision-making process may also involve additional computational overhead.
- Diversity and independence: To achieve the full potential of ensemble methods, it is important to ensure diversity among the individual algorithms. The base models or classifiers should be sufficiently different and independent, as correlated or similar algorithms may not contribute significantly to the ensemble's performance.
- Ensemble size and selection: Determining the optimal ensemble size and selecting the appropriate algorithms for the ensemble can be challenging. Including too few or too many algorithms may impact the ensemble's

performance. Careful selection and evaluation of the constituent algorithms are essential to maximize the performance of the ensemble.

- Training and integration: Ensemble methods require training and integrating multiple algorithms, which can be a complex task. Each algorithm may have its own training requirements, hyperparameters, and optimization techniques. Ensuring proper training and integration of the algorithms is crucial to achieve effective collaboration within the ensemble.
- Overfitting and underfitting: Ensemble methods, if not properly designed, can suffer from overfitting or underfitting issues. Overfitting occurs when the ensemble overly relies on the training data and fails to generalize well to unseen examples. Underfitting, on the other hand, happens when the ensemble is too simple or lacks the capacity to capture complex patterns in the data. Careful regularization techniques and model selection can help mitigate these issues.
- Ensemble combination techniques: The combination of predictions from individual algorithms is a critical step in ensemble methods. The choice of combination technique, such as voting, averaging, or weighted fusion, can impact the ensemble's performance. Selecting an appropriate combination strategy based on the characteristics of the algorithms and the specific application is essential.
- Scalability and deployment: Ensembles should be scalable and deployable in real-world scenarios. The computational resources required for ensemble training and inference should be feasible, especially in resource-constrained environments. Efficient implementation and optimization techniques are necessary to ensure practical usability.

Despite these challenges, ensemble methods have shown promising results in improving face recognition performance. They have been successfully applied in various domains, including surveillance systems, access control, and identity verification. Researchers continue to explore novel ensemble architectures, combination strategies, and training paradigms to further enhance the effectiveness of ensemble methods in face recognition.

5.6 Conclusion

In conclusion, this chapter presents a survey on face recognition methods with federated learning, addressing the challenges of privacy protection and data security in the era of face recognition technology. The development status and achievements of traditional face recognition technology and federated learning are introduced, highlighting the need for privacy-preserving approaches in face recognition. The chapter analyzes the advancements in face recognition under the federated learning framework, discussing the potential solutions and techniques employed in recent literature. It also emphasizes the importance of addressing data fortress and data privacy concerns in the distributed and decentralized setting of edge devices. The introduction of federated learning as a solution to protect the privacy of face images on edge devices is highlighted, and the chapter highlights the need for further research and exploration in this emerging field. By combining privacy computing, differential privacy, and other relevant technologies, the prospects and research hot spots of face recognition based on federated learning are discussed, offering insights into the future development and application of this technology. Overall, this chapter provides a comprehensive overview of face recognition methods within the federated learning framework, contributing to the advancement of privacy-preserving face recognition technology. Appendix A shows an example of Python code that demonstrates how federated learning can be applied to face recognition using a simple model. In addition, Appendix B also shows an example of Python code that demonstrates the implementation of a federated learning approach for face recognition using the PySyft library.

5.7   Future outlook

In fact, from the problems and current situations mentioned in the previous chapter, the introduction of face recognition methods for federated learning is the right development direction. Protections related to data privacy present challenges to traditional machine learning, and coincidentally federated learning can solve the problem of data silos. Moreover, with the development of new technologies, the use of federated learning combined with contrast learning, reinforcement learning, transfer learning, and other technologies can make based on federated learning + downstream tasks get good performance. The face recognition technology learned by the federated learning still needs to be improved in terms of privacy protection, because as the capabilities of attackers continue to improve, we hope to get a model with strong privacy and robustness. The problem that follows is that with the improvement of the privacy of the model, the added privacy protection is probably differential privacy, multiparty homomorphic encryption, mostly cryptographic protection, which greatly increases the amount of data transmitted by the model, reduces the efficiency of the model, and how to find an appropriate encryption method makes us study the direction in the future.

The process of federated learning and training models is a task that there are a large number of edge devices working together to learn together. However, the question that arises is how to get more edge devices to join this big, federated learning framework. That is to say, how to make users trust the central server, some people have proposed to use blockchain technology as an incentive mechanism, so how to establish a perfect incentive mechanism and distribution mechanism to encourage more participants to join [38]. All in all, there is still a lot of room for the face recognition method of federated learning to be explored, but there are also many breakthrough points in technical research and technological integration.

Appendix A

Python code that demonstrates how federated learning can be applied to face recognition using a simple model:

```python
import torch
import torch.nn as nn
import torch.optim as optim
from torchvision import datasets, transforms


# Define the face recognition model
class FaceRecognitionModel(nn.Module):
    def __init__(self):
        super(FaceRecognitionModel, self).__init__()
        self.conv1 = nn.Conv2d(1, 32, kernel_size=3,
            stride=1)
        self.conv2 = nn.Conv2d(32, 64, kernel_size=3,
            stride=1)
        self.fc1 = nn.Linear(64 * 12 * 12, 128)
        self.fc2 = nn.Linear(128, 10)
    def forward(self, x):
        x = self.conv1(x)
        x = nn.functional.relu(x)
        x = self.conv2(x)
        x = nn.functional.relu(x)
        x = x.view(-1, 64 * 12 * 12)
        x = self.fc1(x)
        x = nn.functional.relu(x)
        x = self.fc2(x)
        return x
# Define the federated learning setup
def federated_learning(dataset):
    # Define the device
    device = torch.device("cuda" if torch.cuda.is_a-
vailable() else "cpu")

    # Create the face recognition model
    model = FaceRecognitionModel().to(device)
```

```python
# Define the loss function and optimizer
criterion = nn.CrossEntropyLoss()
optimizer = optim.SGD(model.parameters(), lr=0.01)


# Training loop
for epoch in range(10):
        running_loss = 0.0
        for images, labels in dataset:
            # Move images and labels to the device
            images, labels = images.to(device),
                labels.to(device)

            # Zero the parameter gradients
            optimizer.zero_grad()

            # Forward pass
            outputs = model(images)
            loss = criterion(outputs, labels)

            # Backward pass and optimization
            loss.backward()
            optimizer.step()

            # Print statistics
            running_loss += loss.item()
        print(f"Epoch {epoch+1}: Loss = {running_loss
            / len(dataset)}")

# Load the face recognition dataset
transform = transforms.Compose([transforms.ToTensor(),
transforms.Normalize((0.5,), (0.5,))])
train_dataset = datasets.MNIST(root="./data",
train=True, download=True, transform=transform)
test_dataset = datasets.MNIST(root="./data",
 train=False, download=True, transform=transform)
```

```
# Perform federated learning on the train_dataset
federated_learning(train_dataset)

# Evaluate the trained model on the test_dataset
def evaluate_model(model, dataset):
    device = torch.device("cuda" if torch.cuda.is_
        available() else "cpu")
    model.eval()
    correct = 0
    total = 0
    with torch.no_grad():
        for images, labels in dataset:
            images, labels = images.to(device),
                labels.to(device)
            outputs = model(images)
            _, predicted = torch.max(outputs.data, 1)
            total += labels.size(0)
            correct += (predicted == labels).sum().
                item()
        accuracy = 100 * correct / total

        print(f"Test Accuracy: {accuracy}%")
        evaluate_model(model, test_dataset)
```

In this code, a simple face recognition model based on CNNs is defined. The FL setup is also defined, where the model is trained on the federated dataset using the stochastic gradient descent (SGD) optimizer. The code demonstrates the training loop and the evaluation of the trained model.

Appendix B

Python code that demonstrates the implementation of a federated learning approach for face recognition using the PySyft library:

```
import torch
import syft as sy
from torchvision import datasets, transforms
# Hook PyTorch to PySyft
hook = sy.TorchHook(torch)
```

```python
# Define the face recognition model
class FaceRecognitionModel(torch.nn.Module):
    def __init__(self):
        super(FaceRecognitionModel, self).__init__()
        self.fc1 = torch.nn.Linear(784, 256)
        self.fc2 = torch.nn.Linear(256, 128)
        self.fc3 = torch.nn.Linear(128, 10)

    def forward(self, x):
        x = torch.nn.functional.relu(self.fc1(x))
        x = torch.nn.functional.relu(self.fc2(x))
        x = self.fc3(x)
        return x

# Create a virtual worker representing the central server
server = sy.VirtualWorker(hook, id="server")

# Create virtual workers representing the distributed
clients
client1 = sy.VirtualWorker(hook, id="client1")
client2 = sy.VirtualWorker(hook, id="client2")
client3 = sy.VirtualWorker(hook, id="client3")

# Load the face recognition dataset
transform = transforms.Compose([transforms.ToTensor(),
transforms.Normalize((0.5,), (0.5,))])
train_dataset = datasets.MNIST(root="./data",
train=True, download=True, transform=transform)
test_dataset = datasets.MNIST(root="./data",
train=False, download=True, transform=transform)
# Split the dataset among the clients
train_dataset = train_dataset.federate((client1,
client2, client3))
test_dataset = test_dataset.federate((client1, client2,
client3))

# Define the federated learning setup
model = FaceRecognitionModel()
```

```python
model.send(server)
optimizer = torch.optim.SGD(model.parameters(), lr=0.01)

# Training loop
for epoch in range(10):
    model.train()
    for batch_idx, (data, target) in enumerate
        (train_dataset):
        model.send(data.location)
        optimizer.zero_grad()
        output = model(data)
        loss = torch.nn.functional.cross_entropy
            (output, target)
        loss.backward()
        optimizer.step()
        model.get()
        if batch_idx % 100 == 0:
            print(f"Epoch {epoch+1}, Batch {batch_
                idx}: Loss = {loss.item()}")
# Evaluation on the test dataset
model.eval()
test_loss = 0
correct = 0
with torch.no_grad():
    for data, target in test_dataset:
        data, target = data.to(server), target.to
            (server)
        output = model(data)
        test_loss += torch.nn.functional.cross_entropy
            (output, target, reduction='sum').item()
        pred = output.argmax(1)
        correct += pred.eq(target.view_as(pred)).sum
            ().item()

test_loss /= len(test_dataset)
accuracy = 100.0 * correct / len(test_dataset)
print(f"Test Loss: {test_loss:.4f}, Accuracy:
{accuracy:.2f}%")
```

In this code, the PySyft library is used to create virtual workers representing the central server and distributed clients. The face recognition model is defined, and the federated learning setup is established. The dataset is split among the clients using the federate() method. The model is trained in a federated manner, where each client performs training on its local dataset and communicates with the central server. The model and data are securely transferred among the workers using the send() and get() methods. Finally, the trained model is evaluated on the federated test dataset, and the test loss and accuracy are calculated. The code demonstrates how to perform federated learning using PySyft, where the model and data are securely exchanged between the server and clients.

It is important to note that the code provided is a simplified example for demonstration purposes. In real-world scenarios, additional considerations such as secure aggregation, differential privacy, and robustness against adversarial attacks should be taken into account for practical implementation.

Ensure that you have the PySyft library installed (pip install syft) and the necessary dependencies imported before running the code.

References

[1] McMahan, B., Moore, E., Ramage, D., Hampson, S., and y Arcas, B. A. (2017). "Communication-efficient learning of deep networks from decentralized data." In *Artificial intelligence and statistics* (pp. 1273–1282). PMLR.

[2] Muthanna, A., Shamilova, R., Ateya, A. A., Paramonov, A., and Hammoudeh, M. (2020). "A mobile edge computing/software-defined networking-enabled architecture for vehicular networks." *Internet Technology Letters*, 3(6), e109.

[3] Muthanna, A., Ateya, A. A., Khakimov, A., *et al.* (2019). "Secure IoT network structure based on distributed Fog computing, with SDN/blockchain."

[4] Ateya, A. A., Muthanna, A., Koucheryavy, A., Maleh, Y., and El-Latif, A. A. A. (2023). "Energy efficient offloading scheme for MEC-based augmented reality system." *Cluster Computing*, 26, 789–806.

[5] Hammad, M., Bakrey, M., Bakhiet, A., Tadeusiewicz, R., El-Latif, A. A. A., and Pławiak, P. (2022). "A novel end-to-end deep learning approach for cancer detection based on microscopic medical images." *Biocybernetics and Biomedical Engineering*, 42(3), 737–748.

[6] Hammad, M., Iliyasu, A. M., Elgendy, I. A., and El-Latif, A. A. A. (2022). "End-to-end data authentication deep learning model for securing IoT configurations." *Human-Centric Computing and Information Sciences*, 12(4).

[7] Artem, V., Ateya, A. A., Muthanna, A., and Koucheryavy, A. (2019). "Novel AI-based scheme for traffic detection and recognition in 5G based networks." In *Internet of Things, Smart Spaces, and Next Generation Networks and Systems: 19th International Conference, NEW2AN 2019, and 12th*

Conference, ruSMART 2019*, St. Petersburg, Russia, August 26–28, 2019, Proceedings 19 (pp. 243–255), Berlin: Springer International Publishing.

[8]   Yang, Q., Liu, Y., Chen, T., and Tong, Y. (2019). "Federated machine learning: Concept and applications." *ACM Transactions on Intelligent Systems and Technology,* 10(2), 1–19.

[9]   Zhao, W., Chellappa, R., Phillips, P. J., and Rosenfeld, A. (2003). "Face recognition: A literature survey." *ACM Computing Surveys (CSUR)*, 35(4), 399–458.

[10]   Tolba, A. S., El-Baz, A. H., and El-Harby, A. A. (2006). "Face recognition: A literature review." *International Journal of Signal Processing*, 2(2), 88–103.

[11]   He, X., Yan, S., Hu, Y., Niyogi, P., and Zhang, H. J. (2005). "Face recognition using Laplacian faces." *IEEE Transactions on Pattern Analysis and Machine Intelligence*, 27(3), 328–340.

[12]   Krizhevsky, A., Sutskever,I., and Hinton,G. (2012). "ImageNet classification with deep convolutional neural networks." *Advances in Neural Information Processing Systems,* 25(2).

[13]   Deng, J., Dong, W., Socher, R., Li, L. J., Li, K., and Fei-Fei, L. (2009). "ImageNet: A large-scale hierarchical image database." In *2009 IEEE Conference on Computer Vision and Pattern Recognition* (pp. 248–255). IEEE.

[14]   Taigman, Y., Yang, M., Ranzato, M. A., and Wolf, L. (2014). "DeepFace: Closing the gap to human-level performance in face verification." In *IEEE Conference on Computer Vision & Pattern Recognition* (pp. 1701–1708), IEEE Computer Society.

[15]   Huang, G. B., Mattar, M., Berg, T., and Learned-Miller, E. (2008). "Labeled faces in the wild: A database for studying face recognition in unconstrained environments." In *Workshop on Faces in 'Real-Life' Images: Detection, Alignment, and Recognition*.

[16]   Liu, W., Wen, Y., Yu, Z., Li, M., Raj, B., and Song, L. (2017). "SphereFace: Deep hypersphere embedding for face recognition." In *Proceedings of the IEEE Conference on Computer Vision and Pattern Recognition (CVPR)* (pp. 212–220), Piscataway, NJ: IEEE.

[17]   Deng, J., Guo, J., Xue N., and Zafeiriou, S. (2018). "ArcFace: Additive angular margin loss for deep face recognition." In *Proceedings of the IEEE/ CVF Conference on Computer Vision and Pattern Recognition* (pp. 4690–4699).

[18]   Wang, H., Wang, Y., Zhou, Z., *et al.* (2018). "CosFace: Large margin cosine loss for deep face recognition." In *2018 IEEE/CVF Conference on Computer Vision and Pattern Recognition* (pp. 5265–5274), Piscataway, NJ: IEEE.

[19]   Ravi, R. and Yadhukrishna, S. V. (2020, March). "A face expression recognition using CNN & LBP." In *2020 Fourth International Conference on Computing Methodologies and Communication (ICCMC)* (pp. 684–689), Piscataway, NJ: IEEE.

[20] Lienhart, R. and Maydt, J. (2002). "An extended set of Haar-like features for rapid object detection." In *Proceedings: International Conference on Image Processing*, Piscataway, NJ: IEEE.

[21] Ratsch, G. (2001). "Soft margins for AdaBoost." *Machine Learning,* 42(3), 287–320.

[22] Wen, Y., Liu, W., Weller, A., Raj, B., and Singh, R. (2021). "SphereFace2: Binary classification is all you need for deep face recognition." arXiv preprint arXiv:2108.01513.

[23] Li, X., Huang, K., Yang, W., Wang, S., and Zhang, Z. (2019). "On the Convergence of FedAvg on non-IID Data." arXiv preprint arXiv:1907.02189.

[24] Huang, H., Yu, P. S., and Wang, C. (2018). "An introduction to image synthesis with generative adversarial Nets." arXiv preprint arXiv:1803.04469.

[25] Melis, L., Song, C., De Cristofaro, E., and Shmatikov, V. (2019). "Exploiting unintended feature leakage in collaborative learning." In *2019 IEEE Symposium on Security and Privacy (SP)* (pp. 691–706), Piscataway, NJ: IEEE.

[26] Zhu, L., Liu, Z., and Han, S. (2019). "Deep leakage from gradients." *Advances in Neural Information Processing Systems*, 32.

[27] Geiping, J., Bauermeister, H., Dröge, H., and Moeller, M. (2020). "Inverting gradients – How easy is it to break privacy in federated learning?." *Advances in Neural Information Processing Systems*, 33, 16937–16947.

[28] Meng, Q., Zhou, F., Ren, H., Feng, T., Liu, G., and Lin, Y. (2022). "Improving federated learning face recognition via privacy-agnostic clusters." arXiv preprint arXiv:2201.12467.

[29] Liu, L., Zhang, Y., Gao, H., *et al.* (2022). "FedFV: Federated face verification via equivalent class embeddings." *Multimedia Systems,* 28(2), 1–11.

[30] Rawat, A. S., Yu, X., Menon, A. K., *et al.* (2020). "Federated learning with only positive labels." In *International Conference on Machine Learning, PMLR*.

[31] Hosseini, H, Park, H, Yun, S, Louizos, C., Soriaga, J., and Welling, M. (2021). "Federated learning of user verification models without sharing embeddings." In *International Conference on Machine Learning* (pp. 4328–4336), *PMLR*.

[32] Niu, Y., and Deng, W. (2022). "Federated learning for face recognition with gradient correction." In *Proceedings of the AAAI Conference on Artificial Intelligence*, 36(2), 1999–2007.

[33] Aggarwal, D., Zhou, J., and Jain, A. K. (2021). "FedFace: Collaborative learning of face recognition model." In *2021 IEEE International Joint Conference on Biometrics (IJCB)* (pp. 1–8). IEEE.

[34] Liu, C. T., Wang, C. Y., Chien, S. Y., and Lai, S. H. (2021). "FedFR: Joint optimization federated framework for generic and personalized face recognition." In *Proceedings of the AAAI Conference on Artificial Intelligence*, 36 (2), 1656–1664.

[35] Chen, T., Kornblith, S., Norouzi, M., and Hinton, G. (2020). "A simple framework for contrastive learning of visual representations." In *International Conference on Machine Learning* (pp. 1597–1607). PMLR.

[36] Zhuang, W., Gan, X., Wen, Y., Zhang, X., Zhang, S., and Yi, S. (2021). "Towards unsupervised domain adaptation for deep face recognition under privacy constraints via federated learning." arXiv preprint arXiv: 2105.07606.

[37] Bai, F., Wu, J., Shen, P., Li, S., and Zhou, S. (2021). "Federated face recognition." arXiv preprint arXiv:2105.02501.

[38] Nilsson, A., Smith, S., Ulm, G., Gustavsson, E., and Jirstrand, M. (2018). "A performance evaluation of federated learning algorithms." In *The Second Workshop*. In *Proceedings of the Second Workshop on Distributed Infrastructures for Deep Learning* (pp. 1–8).

Chapter 6

Artificial intelligence-based biometric authentication using ECG signal

Kiran Kumar Patro[1], Jaya Prakash Allam[2], Babji Prasad Chapa[3], P Lalitha Kumari[4] and Mohamed Hammad[5,6]

6.1 Introduction

An electrocardiogram (ECG) signal is used to measure problems with the way the heart works. These days, the ECG is used not only as a diagnostic tool in hospitals but also as a new biometric tool in highly secured systems. ECG signal is a live indicator, it may be used as a tool for aliveness detection, and it possesses several key qualities to assess its usage as a biometric system, including universality, uniqueness, permanence, collectability, and circumvention.

A reliable identification system is essential in recent times in communication and networking technologies, which have expanded human activities and made the former indispensable. Traditional biometric systems like fingerprints, irises, faces, and voices, among others, each play a unique part in an individual's recognition [1–4]. For example, facial recognition systems may be tricked by a photograph, fingerprints and voice can be reconstructed, or prerecording can be made of the same voice. Authentication in current security systems is done through passwords or pins, which are easily lost or stolen. Falsification is a problem with present identifying techniques, which may not be able to fulfil more stringent security requirements.

Research on ECGs as diagnostic tools in clinical settings has been particularly active during the last two decades. According to a few different concepts, ECG has recently been brought up as a potential contender for use in human identity recognition systems. Initial interest in ECG-based identification systems stems

[1]Department of ECE, Aditya Institute of Technology and Management, India
[2]Department of EC, National Institute of Technology Rourkela, India
[3]Department of ECE, GMR Institute of Technology, India
[4]Department of SCOPE, VIT-AP, India
[5]EIAS Data Science Lab, College of Computer and Information Sciences, Prince Sultan University, Saudi Arabia
[6]Department of Information Technology, Faculty of Computers and Information, Menoufia University, Egypt

from the fact that ECG satisfies the majority of criteria for biometrics in addition to detecting life. An individual's ECG is a very confidential and private document. Because of this, it is difficult to copy or counterfeit. This is a distinct benefit of ECG over other biometric technologies, as it requires the user to be present for the biometric to work. For developing ECG-based biometric authentication methods, this study presents a framework for the proper adoption and adjustment of machine learning (ML) approaches. Researchers and developers were working on ECG-based biometric authentication systems with the help of AI methods, which may find the suggested framework helpful in developing appropriate models.

6.1.1   Overview of biometrics

The word 'biometrics' comes from the Greek words 'bio', which means 'life', and 'metric ', which means 'to measure' [5]. Biometrics is a term for measuring things about people. Biometrics is a way to identify people based on physical or behavioural characteristics that are unique to each person. Physiological and behavioural characteristics are the two primary subcategories that may be used to classify biometric traits [5]. Physiological relationships are linked to body form. However, physiologically based biometrics include fingerprint recognition, face identification, DNA, ECG, hand-and-palm geometry, and iris recognition. Biometrics based on behaviour is linked to a person's behaviour. Typing rhythm, stride, and voice are all examples.

Collecting and storing features of an individual that may later be used for identifying that individual through the utilization of automated means is the process involved in biometric technology [6]. In the context of the larger topic of human identity, biometric authentication might be described as the 'automated' and 'real-time' subset. Identifying a human person relies on a wide range of distinguishing traits. For instance, friends, relatives, and co-workers rely on their voices and features to recognize one other.

The development of biometric applications might be accelerated and expanded if the recognition rate increases without human intervention. The use of biometrics in the Internet, banking, government authentication, and travel papers, in addition to the most precise-demanding domains, particularly law enforcement, military usage, and court applications, is hindered by this factor.

6.1.1.1   ECG as biometric

The electrocardiogram, often known as an ECG, is a transthoracic interpretation of the heart's electrical activity that is monitored using electrodes attached to the body in various sites. The ECG works by detecting and magnifying the minute electrical charges produced on the skin as a result of the depolarization of the heart muscles that occurs throughout each heartbeat cycle. Therefore, the properties of the ECG are impacted by the subject's sex, age, and bodily habitus, in addition to the heart's unique geometrical and physiological qualities. Because of this, the ECG is an interesting choice for use as an input to a biometrics system [7]. The typical ECG

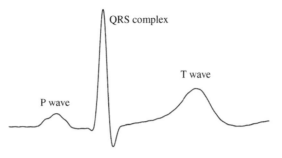

Figure 6.1   Typical ECG beat

beat shown in Figure 6.1 has three major portions: P wave, QRS complex, and T wave. P wave results from atrial depolarization, QRS complex from ventricular depolarization, and T wave from ventricular repolarization. The heart's beating produces electrical currents, which go not just through the heart itself but also throughout the rest of the body. Therefore, the shapes of ECG waveforms rely on the anatomy of the human heart and body. As a result, ECG may be thought of as a human biometric trait [7].

It is reasonable to believe that an ECG is a nearly unique human feature since the morphology and amplitudes of recorded cardiac complexes are regulated by a variety of individual characteristics, including the form and position of the heart, as well as the presence and type of diseases. ECG signal is a sign of life and can be used to determine if someone is still alive. The ECG signal is more universal than most other biometric characteristics. It is thought that everyone who is alive can make an ECG, so the universality property is almost certainly met. The heart rate variability is the most evident contributor to ECG variability [8,9]. At rest, the heart rate ranges between 60 and 80 beats per minute. The heart rate may reach 200 beats per minute under physical exercise, anxiety, or excitement. Certainly, such changes in heart rate affect the waveforms of the cardiac cycle since its length is decreased by two to three times. Increases in heart rate primarily result in a reduction in diastolic length, ventricular depolarization period, and R-wave amplitude. The heart rate does not greatly influence the length of the QRS complex, and this type of feature can be considered of primary interest to ECG biometrics [9].

An ECG record can be obtained by placing electrodes on a human body and having a sensor capture, amplify, and filter the electrical signal that is produced by the electrodes. These electrodes are arranged in particular configurations that are referred to as virtual vectors or leads. There are a total of 12 different lead configurations. The Lead-I test simply needs two electrodes to be attached to the patient's chest, arms, or fingers. Because of individual differences in heart size, position, gender, permeability, and the order in which the cardiac muscles are activated, an ECG produces a distinct signal for each person. Because of this property, an ECG may be used as a biometric.

6.2   Related works on AI-based ECG biometrics

In recent years, many approaches have been investigated for a biometric recognition system that uses an ECG [10–18]. Biel *et al.* [19] were the first to build an ECG-based biometric recognition system. Within this system, 12 features are proposed with specific hardware. This method was validated using 3-lead ECG data collected from 20 patients, while they were in the resting posture. The authors reported an overall identification rate of 95% for ECG biometric authentication. Tilendra *et al.* [20] proposed three levels of ECG-based biometric authentication. Pre-processing, ensemble-averaged beat creation, and similarity matching are the stages. The R-peak detector in the ensemble averaging stage is based on discrete cosine transform (DCT) and a Gaussian derivative filter. The results reveal that the ECG-biometric approach using the normalized cross-correlation measure produces consistent verification results under diverse noise situations and sample rates than the other four methods. This approach consistently produces 94.60% accurate identification results with the ECG-ID database from PhysioNet.

Using the multi-resolution analysis of discrete wavelet transform (DWT)-based characteristics, Dar *et al.* [21] proposed a biometric identification of the general population. The cardiac cycle was extracted, followed by DWT to recover the wavelet coefficients as the feature vector. Best first search is employed for feature reduction, whilst a single closest neighbour classifier is utilized for classification. The system is evaluated on three publicly accessible datasets, including MIT-BIH/Arrhythmia (MITDB), MIT-BIH/Normal Sinus Rhythm (NSRDB), and ECG-ID database (ECG-IDDB), which include all individuals in a combined and distinct way. The identification rate for the arrhythmic database was reported to be 93.1%, while the accuracy for the general population was 94.4%. Bashar *et al.* [22] came up with the idea of using multi-scale descriptors for ECG biometric authentication. This showed a new way to take geometrical features from ECG signals at different scales. Then, the refined ECG signal is split into several segments, and a feature matrix is made using a multi-scale pattern extraction technique. When the feature matrix is finally used with a simple minimum distance to the mean classifier that uses the 'leave-one-out' method, it gives a 91.67% accuracy rate for identification.

Zhang *et al.* [23] suggested a technique for biometric ECG identification using a classifier based on a hierarchical framework. The method's whole procedure, including pre-processing, feature extraction, and classification, is described. Cross-validation is used to improve performance while determining the classifier's parameters. Tested on the MIT-BIH NSRDB, the suggested technique yields exceptionally high recognition rates. The overall recorded heartbeat recognition rate is 97.98%. Kang *et al.* [24] developed feasible system architecture for biometric identification that is based on ECG data gathered from mobile or wearable devices. The cross-correlation of the templates extracted throughout the registration and authentication phases is an idea that the author recommends using. The strategy that has been presented has the potential to reduce the amount of time it takes to reach the desired false acceptance rate and false rejection rate.

Research on ECG biometrics may be split into two distinct categories, which are known as fiducial- and non-fiducial-based techniques. Most of the biometric system's performance is influenced by the type of features and its processing [15].

6.2.1   ECG biometrics based on fiducial features

Methods based on fiducial features utilize ECG signal characteristics such as P, Q, R, S, and T. Fiducial features extract amplitude, temporal, area, angle, and slope information from typical points. Singh [25] suggested fiducial-based features, including the distance between characteristic points of the same heartbeat, the distance between characteristic points of adjacent heartbeats, and the shape of the heartbeat. Then, Fisher discriminant analysis is used to create features that can be used to classify one heartbeat from another. Gahi *et al.* [26] came up with 24 amplitude and temporal features from an ECG signal. Relevant features are chosen for classification. The Mahalanobis classifier is utilized to help in the process of identification of a person.

Irvine *et al.* [27] suggested a technique of authentication that measures the minimal number of heartbeats necessary to authenticate an enrolled individual. The approach collects fiducial information from each pulse to calculate statistical features and sequentially make decisions. For Lead-I ECG, Venkatesh and Jayaraman [28] retrieved the QRS complex and the onset and offset of P, Q, S, and T waves. Dynamic time wrapping and Fisher's linear discriminant analysis (LDA) with the K-nearest neighbour (K-NN) classifier are used to classify ECG for biometric identification.

6.2.2   ECG biometrics based on non-fiducial features

Non-fiducial-point techniques are often holistic in nature, considering the whole ECG signal or isolated ECG pulse [29]. It is not recommended to use characteristic points for extracting feature sets when using methods that are based on non-fiducial features. Several of the available techniques for segmenting heartbeats use one or more characteristic points [30]. Some of the methods based on non-fiducial features require the detection of R-peaks for segmentation and alignment of the heartbeat [31–34].

A wavelet-based approach was presented by Zahra *et al.* [30] for ECG-based biometric identification. Feature selection approaches to expedite the classification process, techniques such as principal component analysis (PCA) and LDA are utilized. The experiments are conducted using the PhysioNet database and the PTB database from MIT-BIH. For the purpose of ECG biometrics, Odinaka *et al.* [31] suggested an innovative short-time frequency approach with robust feature selection. The selection of features is made only based on symmetric relative entropy, and an identification rate of 93.50% was successfully attained.

Wavelet decomposition was carried out after the features were collected from the filtered signals by Wan *et al.* [34]. The acquired wavelet coefficient structures are then used in a feed-forward neural network with three layers to achieve classification results. Li *et al.* [32] suggested cepstral and temporal ECG-based biometric identification. The Gaussian mixture modelling super vector kernel is employed for feature selection. The support vector machines (SVMs) classifier is utilized, and its accuracy is reported to be 98.30%.

6.2.3   ECG biometrics based on hybrid features

For identification, certain biometric approaches may employ both fiducial and non-fiducial traits. A hybrid feature set is created to improve recognition system performance by mixing fiducial and non-fiducial features [35–37]. Sriram *et al.* [35] developed accelerometer-based biometric recognition and offered patient authentication security in remote health monitoring. Fiducial and non-fiducial features frame the feature set. R–R distances, slopes, and R–R intervals are examples of fiducial characteristics. Normalized AC coefficients and spline interpolants are non-fiducial features. *K*-NN is used to classify the hybrid feature collection (*K*-NN).

Shen *et al.* [36] made use of a hybrid feature set, which included non-fiducial features to shrink the space and fiducial features for the purpose of classification. The identification model is developed through the use of template matching in conjunction with LDA distance classification. Experiments are carried out utilizing Lead-I ECG data for the general population.

6.2.4   ECG biometrics based on other approaches

Some state-of-the-art approaches [38] extract discriminative features by simply partitioning the ECG signal into several overlapping or non-overlapping signal segments without taking into account the fiducial points. Safie *et al.* [38] suggested a feature extraction approach for the generation of unique ECG feature vectors that they referred to as the pulse active ratio. Authors performed experiments on 112 people, completing 9800 ECG comparisons, and demonstrating a 10% improvement compared to standard temporal and amplitude feature extraction approaches that validated the suggested method. Zheng *et al.* [39] developed a superposition matrix to identify stable ECG signal characteristics under unconstrained conditions. Chu *et al.* [40] suggested a parallel multi-scale one-dimensional residual network to increase the generalization capacity of the recovered embedding characteristics.

In addition, the objective of dimensionality reduction [41] is extremely significant in the context of biometric systems and algorithms for pattern recognition. The DCT was utilized by Plataniotis *et al.* [42] to minimize the number of features recovered from windowed autocorrelation. Dimensionality reduction with LDA was shown to get superior results than dimensionality reduction with DCT in the study by Agrafioti and Hatzinakos [43]. Furthermore, Hejazi *et al.* [44] used LDA, PCA, and KPCA to reduce the number of dimensions, and they came to the conclusion that KPCA worked best.

However, the process of converting a raw ECG signal into a feature vector that can be used for classification takes meticulous engineering and a significant amount of specialized expertise from a trained professional. This constraint is solved by deep learning methods such as CNNs, which use several layers of representation and can capitalize on raw data to automatically identify the representations required for recognition [45]. Significant characteristics were recovered from one or more leads by Labati *et al.* [46] using a deep CNN. The deep-ECG can also acquire binary templates that can make it easier to deploy ECG biometric systems in combination with cryptography applications. da Silva Luz *et al.* explored the learning of feature representations for heart biometrics [12]. The authors focused their attention on the raw pulse signal and the heartbeat spectrogram. In addition, they presented ways for enhancing heartbeat data, which are highly significant for generalization in the context of deep learning approaches.

6.3   Materials and methods

The biometric system for identifying ECG records uses a classic method, which includes data acquisition, pre-processing, creation of input feature space (feature extraction), moving to reduced feature space (feature selection, optional), classifying the cardiac cycle, and identifying the ECG record. Figure 6.2 presents the comprehensive strategy for ECG-based biometric authentication.

The important data-processing processes are presented in the correct order inside the general system framework. Feed-forward connections represent the processed data that is transferred between stages. The output of one stage serves as the input for the next stage. Different processing methods may be used to implement each level. The comprehensive system structure outlines the potential approaches for use at each level of the system. These approaches are options for most steps; nevertheless, the data processing stage typically consists of multiple ways that complement one another. The step-by-step technique of the biometric authentication system is briefly outlined.

6.3.1   ECG database

The ECG signals were collected from a database [47] preserved online by the National Institute of Health, the National Institute of Biomedical Imaging and Bioengineering, and the National Institute of General Medical Sciences at http://www.physionet.org/physiobank/database/ecgiddb/.

In the Lead-I arrangement, Einthoven's triangle dictates that the negative electrode should be positioned on the right shoulder, and the positive electrode should be positioned on the left shoulder. Shoulder to shoulder is the path that this axis takes. The electrode on the left leg serves as the ground reference for the measurement shown in Figure 6.3.

The ECG-IDDB contains Lead-I ECG recordings from 90 distinct healthy people, each of which is 20 s long and was obtained on a particular day over 6 months. The database comprises 310 recordings from 46 female and 44 male participants aged 13–75. During 6 months, each individual's ECG records range between 2 and 20. The ECG signals were digitized at 500 Hz with 12-bit resolution over a nominal ±10 mV range. The raw ECG signal from the ECGID database is shown in Figure 6.4.

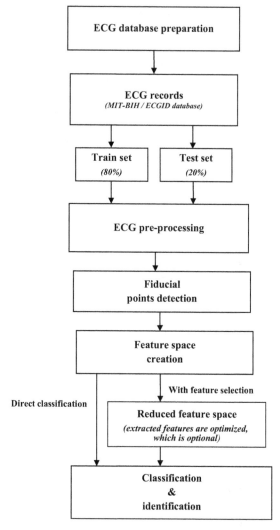

Figure 6.2   Methodology for ECG biometric authentication

6.3.2   ECG data pre-processing

The raw ECG has a lot of background noise and distortions that come from a variety of sources. Several frequency components may be utilized throughout the process of acquiring an ECG signal, which may result in interference during the signal recording process. This interference can contribute noise to the ECG signal. Because of this unwanted change in the signal, the original information included in the ECG signal may be altered, resulting in incorrect ECG data. Among these noises, interference from power lines and baseline drift is the most severe and can significantly impact ECG signal processing [48]. Baseline wander is undesirable

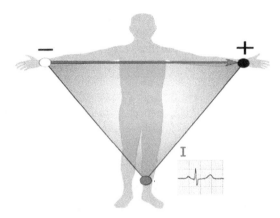

Figure 6.3   Lead-I ECG configuration [37]

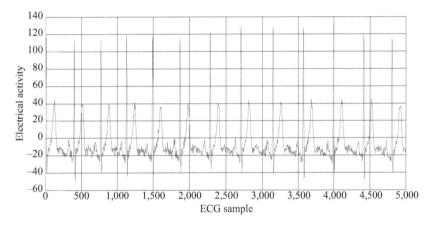

Figure 6.4   Raw ECG signal

ECG signal noise. Several noise sources create this noise, including body move-ments, breathing, perspiration, and faulty electrode connections. The magnitude of the wander frequently exceeds the amplitude of the QRS component, despite its spectral content falling below 1 Hz, between 0.15 and 0.3 Hz. Baseline drift in ECG takes the form of a sinusoidal component that is added as a frequency.

ECG signals are mostly affected by noise from the AC mains (power line interference) since the frequency of power line interference (50/60 Hz) is close to that of ECG. Improper grounding of the ECG equipment is the leading source of power line interference. It decreases the signal quality and impacts the minute details that might be crucial for signal processing, monitoring, and overall clinical diagnosis. Filtering methods must be used for each possible case in which a real ECG signal has been tampered up by adding unwanted noise. The right filter has to be chosen based on the type of noise that could be in the signal [48].

During this pre-processing step, the baseline drift is eliminated, and then the noise is filtered out using various techniques. The estimation of baseline wander is accomplished by utilizing a first-order zero phase low-pass filter with a cut-off frequency of 0.5 Hz. The baseline drift is then eliminated from the applied ECG signal shown in Figure 6.5.

The output signal is then sent through a band-pass filter with lower and higher cut-off frequencies of 5 and 40 Hz, respectively. Because power line interference has a frequency of 50 Hz, it may also be eliminated with the band pass filter as shown in Figure 6.6.

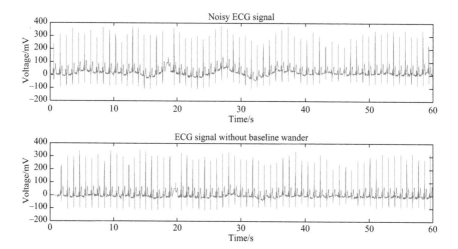

Figure 6.5   ECG signal with and without baseline wander noise

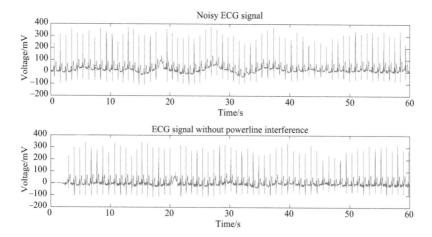

Figure 6.6   ECG signal with and without power line noise

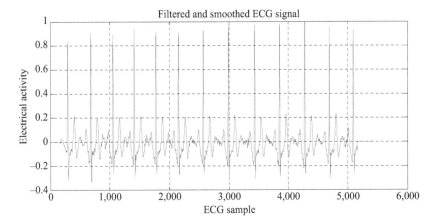

Figure 6.7   Smoothed ECG signal

The primary purpose of the filters is to clean the ECG signal by reducing the dominant noise sources of baseline wander and power line noise. After these noises have been reduced, a smoothing filter is added to the signal to eliminate the roughness they caused. This work employs a weighted moving average filter as a smoothing filter (Direct Form-II). Figure 6.7 depicts a smoothed ECG signal after de-noising.

6.3.3   ECG fiducial points detection

The ECG fiducial points (P, Q, R, S, and T) and the time intervals between them reveal crucial information about the heart's electrical activity [49]. The relationships between these points determine the characteristics of an ECG signal. Identifying the 'R' peak is the most crucial of the ECG's characteristic points for making a diagnosis. The remaining components (P, Q, S, and T) are found by using the position of the 'R' peak as a reference and tracing back and forth from that point [49].

6.3.3.1   R-peak detection

A common way to find the QRS complex is to look at the slope of the R wave. To get reliable results, we need to get other information from the signal, such as its amplitude, width, and QRS energy. The Pan–Tompkins algorithm [50] is a popular choice for locating R-peaks. This approach consists of three phases, which are as follows: differentiating, then squaring, and finally moving window integrating.

In the derivative stage, the information needed to determine the slope of the QRS is collected. The squaring procedure increases the slope of the frequency response curve of the derivative, which helps limit the number of false positives (FP) that can be generated by T waves that have greater spectral energies than is typical. The moving window integrator generates a signal that can provide information not only about the slope of the QRS complex but also about the width of the

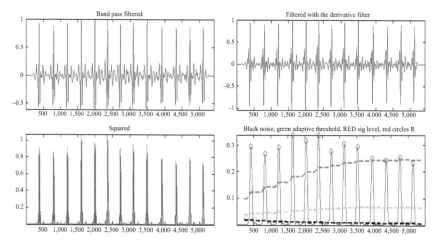

Figure 6.8   Step wise processes for detecting R-peak

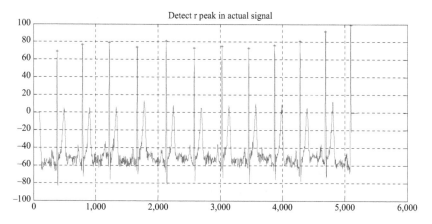

Figure 6.9   R-peak detection in ECG signal

complex. Figure 6.8 shows the whole process (stage-wise), along with the pre-processing step, and finally, R-peak detected ECG signal presented in Figure 6.9.

6.3.3.2   Time-domain analysis for other peaks detection

The Pan–Tompkins approach is used to detect only the R-peak, and then after additional peaks, P, Q, S, and T have been found using time-gap windows. The window length depends on the position of the R-peak (time domain). The typical ECG waveform is used to identify the P-peak relative to the R-peak; the P wave is positioned to the left of the R wave (i.e. before the R wave). P-peak is the point of the signal with the maximum amplitude within the defined range. Further, the left

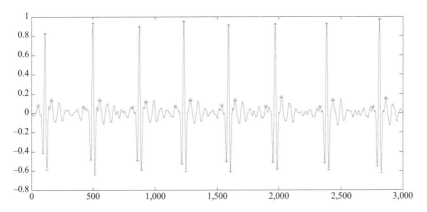

Figure 6.10   ECG fiducial points detection

side of the R wave is the Q wave (i.e. before the R wave). Q-peak is the point in the fixed range where the signal has the lowest amplitude.

The R wave's right side is represented by the S wave (i.e. after the R wave). In order to locate the S-peak, a time-domain window is constructed with a range that is determined by the location of the R-peak (Rloc). The S-peak is determined to be the amplitude value that is the lowest possible value within the window range. Furthermore, the T-wave follows the R-wave to its right (i.e. after the R wave). In order to locate the T-peak, a time-domain window is constructed with a range determined by the location of the R-peak. T-peak refers to the point where the amplitude reaches its highest value within the window range. All of the observed peaks for an ECG signal are presented in Figure 6.10 (zoomed version). A '*' denotes R-peaks', P-peaks are denoted by 'O', Q and S-peaks are denoted by '+', and T-peaks are denoted by 'Δ'.

6.3.4   ECG feature extraction

After locating all of the peaks of P, Q, R, S, and T in an ECG signal, it is observed that QRS area, ST, and especially QT intervals vary according to heart rate and physiology [51]. PQRST-fragment samples were collected for each ECG record since they are considered informative attributes for ECG signal processing. Out of all the PQRST-fragments, the finest cardiac impulses need to be identified to extract appropriate features for the biometric system. In this work, the top six finest PQRST-fragments are chosen based on the smallest deviation from the mean of the individual priorities [51,52]. The ECG signal was decomposed into its component pulses (PQRST) so that data from one pulse could be compared to another. Once the 'mean' PQRST-fragment was computed using Euclidean distance, the six closest PQRST fragments and the mean fragment were chosen for further study.

Each pulse was separated from the pulse's peak P to its peak T. However, a broken pulse cannot be used to compare their data since there is an inconsistency between the pulses. Prior to retrieving data from such pulses, their positions must

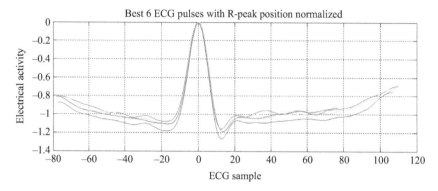

Figure 6.11   ECG fragments position normalization

Table 6.1   Extracted ECG features for biometric authentication

S. no.	Type of features	Features representation
1	Temporal (9)	P_x, Q_x, S_x, T_x, PQ, PT, QS, QT, ST
2	Amplitude (9)	P_y, Q_y, S_y, T_y, PQ, QR, RS, ST, QS
3	Slope (8)	PQ, QR, RS, ST, QS, PT, PS, QT
4	Distance (5)	QR, ST, PQ, RS, QS
5	Angle (5)	QRS_{angle}, PQR_{angle}, RQS_{angle}, RST_{angle}, RSQ_{angle}
6	Other features (11)	$(QT/QS)_{time}$, $(PT/QS)_{time}$, $(ST/QS)_{amp}$, $(RS/QR)_{amp}$, $(ST/QS)_{distance}$, $(RS/QR)_{distance}$, $(QRS)_{area}$, $(QRS_{area}/(RS)^2_{amp})$, $(QRS/RST)_{angle}$, (QRS_{angle}/QS_{time}), (RST_{angle}/QT_{time})

be normalized based on a common reference point. So, the R-peak of each of these fragments was assumed to be at the origin, and the P-, Q-, S-, and T-peaks were moved to new coordinates while keeping their original aspect ratios shown in Figure 6.11.

The extracted features from PQRST fragments are closely associated with temporal (x), amplitude (y), slope, distance, angel, and other mathematical features. All attributes were estimated relative to the point of R, which was the origin. A total of 47 features (feature space) were calculated from each PQRST fragment and reported in Table 6.1.

6.3.5   ECG feature optimization or selection (optional)

A large feature collection may contain irrelevant, correlated, or overfit features, which may cause the classification approach to provide inaccurate results. To improve the accuracy of the prediction, such features need to be pulled out from the dataset. Techniques for feature optimization or selection may limit the feature space based on appropriate individual frameworks. In order to improve both the accuracy of a classification and the efficiency with which it may be performed, it creates a smaller feature subset from a superset of the original features [53].

A search strategy that is used to generate new features while also incorporating assessment metrics is known as a feature selection algorithm. The acquired feature subsets are put through rigorous testing for every conceivable scenario to identify the one that results in the lowest error rate. An evaluation metric is the most important factor when developing a feature selection algorithm, which may be further subdivided into wrapper methods, filter methods, and embedding techniques [53].

6.3.6   ECG signal classification and identification

In most cases, the classification is accomplished through the use of ML methods. For an accurate evaluation of the classifier's performance in practical uses, the ML technique requires the selection of a suitable algorithm that is robust enough to represent complicated internal data interactions and dataset splitting. The concept of classification is one of the most important processes in artificial intelligence (AI) and ML. The classifier assigns categories to data based on the training set and the values contained in a classifying attribute. It then applies this information when assigning categories to new test data. The ECG signal can be biometrically classified by supplying its feature data to ML classification algorithms. ML algorithms vary in nature, are based on various ideas and mathematical frameworks, and are often utilized in various applications. These criteria should be considered while deciding on the best algorithm for ECG classification and identification [54].

6.4   Experimental results

Biometric identification of the ECG signal may be performed by feeding ECG feature data to the top ten AI-based ML algorithms. To process the data, the data-splitting step must be carefully done prior to the classification. The process of splitting datasets entails the partition of the datasets into two subsets: training and test. The samples from the training set are utilized in the process of fitting a classification model. In contrast, the samples from the test set are utilized in the process of providing an objective evaluation of the model's performance.

The MIT-BIH ECG-IDDB was utilized for training with 80% of the data and testing with 20%. This database was chosen because some of its subjects have more than one record. Three records are used for training, and other remaining ECG records are used for testing. This work uses promising classification algorithms such as logistic regression, liner regression, J48, decision tree, naïve Bayes, random tree, MLP-NN, *K*-NN, SVM, and random forest (RF) were chosen for ECG-based biometric authentication.

6.4.1   Performance metrics of the classifiers

When assessing the effectiveness of a classifier, there are several approaches to performance measurement that may be used. Applying the classifier to the test set yields four values that are used as the basis for all performance measurements when supervised learning is used. These four sets of figures are referred to respectively as true positives (TP), FP, true negatives (TN), and false negatives (FN). TP tests detect the condition when it is present. TN test results do not detect an absent condition. Further, a test result is considered FP if it detects the condition even when it is not present. A test result is considered to be FN if it fails to identify the presence of the condition despite the fact that the ailment is actually present. On the basis of classification outcomes, common performance measures have been defined in [16–18]:

$$\text{Accuracy } (\%) = \frac{\text{TP} + \text{TN}}{\text{TP} + \text{FP} + \text{TN} + \text{FN}} \times 100 \tag{6.1}$$

$$\text{Precision } (\%) \quad = \frac{\text{TP}}{\text{TP} + \text{FP}} \times 100 \tag{6.2}$$

$$\text{Recall } (\%) = \frac{\text{TP}}{\text{TP} + \text{FN}} \times 100 \tag{6.3}$$

$$F_{\text{Score}} \, (\%) = \frac{(2 \times \text{TP})}{(2 \times \text{TP}) + \text{FP} + \text{FN}} \times 100 \tag{6.4}$$

$$MCC = \frac{(\text{TP} \times \text{TN}) - (\text{FP} \times \text{FN})}{\sqrt{(\text{TP} + \text{FP})(\text{TP} + \text{FN})(\text{TN} + \text{FP})(\text{TN} + \text{FN})}} \tag{6.5}$$

In addition to these parameters, other essential classification metrics such as the area under the curve, the TP rate, the FP rate, kappa statistic, mean absolute error, the root mean square error, and the relative absolute error were also calculated in this work.

The AI-based ML classifiers in this work can be divided into classical, graphical, and ensemble models [55]. Classical type includes naive Bayes, logistic regression, and liner regression. The classifier such as SVM, RF, random tree, decision tree, J48, and *K*-NN comes under the ensemble model. On the other hand, graphical models include things like Bayesian networks and MLP-NN.

6.4.2   *Performance parameters for classical model classifiers*

The retrieved ECG features from the feature extraction phase are supplied to the classification phase in order to evaluate the performance of the AI-based classical model ML classifiers. In this work, classifiers such as naive Bayes, logistic regression, and linear regression are utilized for experimentation for the use of ECG biometrics. The performance of the suggested classifiers for ECG biometric application is evaluated using an open-source ECG-ID database that is publicly accessible. In the identification phase, the training dataset is simulated over the test data, including the ECG signal features of a person organized in the same sequence as the train data. During the simulation, the probability matrix, also known as the confusion matrix, is generated for each ECG signal and the complete target set.

Table 6.2   Performance metrics for classical model classifiers

Parameter	Classical model		
	Naive Bayes	**Logistic regression**	**Linear regression**
Accuracy (%)	88.321	90.510	91.240
Precision (%)	90.41	92.23	94.18
Recall (%)	88.35	90.50	91.22
***F*-Score (%)**	88.42	90.91	90.94
MCC	0.883	0.907	0.913
AUC	0.991	0.982	0.989
TP rate	0.883	0.905	0.912
FP rate	0.006	0.004	0.005
Kappa statistic	0.876	0.899	0.907
Mean absolute error	0.0118	0.0095	0.0252
RMSE	0.1061	0.0938	0.094
Relative absolute error	0.123	0.100	0.0641

Based on the confusion matrix, various significant classification metrics were calculated, shown in Table 6.2.

Table 6.2 presents the overview of the findings regarding the performance parameters for classical-based classification algorithms, including naive Bayes, logistic regression, and linear regression. The classification parameters show significantly improved results for the linear regression model compared to other classification schemes for ECG biometric authentication.

6.4.3   Performance parameters for graphical model classifiers

The obtained ECG features are then provided to the classification phase in order to evaluate the performance of the AI-based graphical model ML classifiers. Experiments were conducted in this work using classifiers such as Bayesian networks and MLP-NN (ANN) to determine the effectiveness of ECG biometrics.

In Table 6.3, a summary of the findings of the performance parameters for graphical-based classification algorithms, including Bayesian networks and MLP-NN (ANN), was provided. Compared to previous classification systems for ECG biometric authentication, the classification parameters demonstrate significantly improved performance for the MLP-NN model with an overall accuracy of 93.4301%.

6.4.4   Performance parameters for ensemble model classifiers

In order to assess the AI-based ensemble model ML classifier's work, the acquired ECG features are subsequently given to the classification phase. In this work,

Table 6.3   *Performance metrics for graphical model classifiers*

Parameter	Graphical model	
	Bayesian network	MLP-NN
Accuracy (%)	89.781	93.430
Precision (%)	92.92	95.10
Recall (%)	89.87	93.42
F-Score (%)	90.15	93.84
MCC	0.902	0.937
AUC	0.997	0.999
TP rate	0.898	0.934
FP rate	0.005	0.003
Kappa statistic	0.892	0.930
Mean absolute error	0.0096	0.0206
RMSE	0.0935	0.0762
Relative absolute error	0.121	0.0462

Table 6.4   *Performance metrics for ensemble model-I classifiers*

Parameter	Ensemble model-I		
	J48	Decision tree	Random tree
Accuracy (%)	83.941	86.131	81.021
Precision (%)	85.56	87.83	84.15
Recall (%)	83.91	86.14	81.06
F-Score (%)	83.72	86.01	81.32
MCC	0.833	0.858	0.809
AUC	0.923	0.933	0.900
TP rate	0.839	0.861	0.810
FP rate	0.009	0.007	0.010
Kappa statistic	0.8306	0.8537	0.7999
Mean absolute error	0.017	0.0198	0.019
RMSE	0.1238	0.1168	0.1378
Relative absolute error	0.179	0.164	0.184

experiments were done employing classifiers such as SVM, RF, random tree, decision tree, J48, and *K*-NN to determine the efficacy of ECG biometrics.

During the recognition phase, the pattern recognition network built by the training set of data is simulated over the test data, including the ECG signal features structured in the same sequence as the train data. The simulation produces the probability matrix (confusion matrix) for every ECG signal for the full target set. The performance parameters shown in Tables 6.4 and 6.5 were calculated using the confusion matrix generated from the simulation.

Table 6.5   Performance metrics for ensemble model-II
classifiers

Parameter	Ensemble model-II		
	SVM	*K*-NN	Random forest
Accuracy (%)	91.240	92.70	96.62
Precision (%)	92.74	94.16	96.52
Recall (%)	91.25	92.74	95.64
F-Score (%)	91.0	92.91	95.71
MCC	0.910	0.928	0.957
AUC	0.99	0.970	0.995
TP rate	0.912	0.927	0.956
FP rate	0.004	0.004	0.002
Kappa statistic	0.9076	0.9229	0.9538
Mean absolute error	0.0901	0.0103	0.0071
RMSE	0.2085	0.0828	0.0597
Relative absolute error	0.0571	0.0478	0.0384

An overview of the findings regarding the performance parameters for ensemble-based classification algorithms such as SVM, RF, random tree, decision tree, J48, and *K*-NN is presented in Tables 6.3 and 6.4. Compared to the findings of past classification systems for ECG biometric authentication, the classification parameters reveal considerably enhanced performance for the RF model with an overall accuracy of 96.62%.

6.4.5   Overall comparison of AI-based machine learning classifiers for ECG biometrics

This work employs a systematic framework for ECG-based biometric authentication. The methodology consists of ECG data collecting, data pre-processing, PQRST detection, feature extraction, cardiac cycle classification, and ECG signal authentication. The development of an ECG-based biometric authentication system relies heavily on carefully selecting a suitable classifier [56–59]. In this work, several distinct classification strategies, including classical, graphical, and ensemble models, were implemented and evaluated on ECG biometrics. In the classical model, logistic regression and linear regression methods performed well, with 90.51% and 91.24% accuracy, respectively. In terms of graphical methods, MLP-NN outperforms the Bayesian network by 3.65%, with an accuracy of 93.43%. In addition, the ECG biometrics that were analysed in the ensemble model classification were subject to the influence of six distinct classifiers. The findings of the experiments showed that the classifiers of type ensemble model-1, such as J48, decision tree, and random tree, have a significantly low impact on ECG biometrics, whereas the classifiers of type ensemble model-II, such as SVM, *K*-NN, and RF, have reported significantly remarkable performance with an overall highest accuracy of 96.620%. In Table 6.6, we evaluate and contrast the suggested technique to state-of-the-art.

Table 6.6   Comparison with state-of-the-art techniques

S. no.	Author	Classifier	Accuracy (%)
1	Dar *et al.* [21]	Single nearest neighbour classifier	82.30
2	Homer *et al.* [60]	*K*-Nearest neighbour (*K*-NN)	85.20
3	Boumbarov *et al.* [61]	Radial basis function neural network (RBF)	81.60
4	Irvine *et al.* [62]	Minimum distance classifier	91
5	Patro *et al.* [16]	Support vector machine	93.70
6	Choi *et al.* [55]	Support vector machine	95.90
7	Wang *et al.* [63]	Euclidean distance classifier	94.68
8	This study*	MLP-NN	93.43
		Random forest	96.62

*Represents Proposed Methods

6.5   Conclusion

A biometric authentication system that is based on an ECG is becoming more important in the fields of information and security. The ECG signal is universal and persistent within the human body, and the outcome demonstrates that it is also distinct. The fact that a person's heartbeat is a vital indicator of existence and that it cannot be reproduced by any other human offers it the advantage of being a highly secure form of biometric authentication. In this study, we used and compared various classification algorithms to ECG biometrics, including the classical, graphical, and ensemble models. A total of 90 people from the ECG-IDDB were used in the classification process for person authentication. The obtained findings are supportive of ECG as one of the biometric characteristics. Both logistic regression and linear regression approaches did well in the classical model, with 91.24% for logistic regression and 90.51% accuracy for linear regression, respectively. The MLP-NN exceeds the Bayesian network by 3.65%, with an accuracy of 93.43%, making it the superior graphical technique. Additionally, six separate classifiers had an impact on the ECG biometrics that were analysed as part of the ensemble model classification. Experiments revealed that ensemble model-1 classifiers, such as J48, decision tree, and random tree, negatively impact ECG biometrics with an average accuracy of 83.69%. On the other hand, classifiers of the ensemble model-II type, including SVM, *K*-NN, and RF, have exhibited considerably exceptional performance. Overall, the results of the experiments show that the RF classifier had the highest accuracy, at 96.620%.

References

[1]   Jain, Anil K., Arun Ross, and Salil Prabhakar. "An introduction to biometric recognition." *IEEE Transactions on Circuits and Systems for Video Technology* 14, no. 1 (2004): 4–20.

[2]   Priesnitz, Jannis, Rolf Huesmann, Christian Rathgeb, Nicolas Buchmann, and Christoph Busch. "Mobile contactless fingerprint recognition: Implementation, performance and usability aspects." *Sensors* 22, no. 3 (2022): 792.

[3]   Mostofa, Moktari, Salman Mohamadi, Jeremy Dawson, and Nasser M. Nasrabadi. "Deep GAN-based cross-spectral cross-resolution iris recognition." *IEEE Transactions on Biometrics, Behavior, and Identity Science* 3, no. 4 (2021): 443–463.

[4]   Alharbi, Sadeen, Muna Alrazgan, Alanoud Alrashed, *et al.* "Automatic speech recognition: Systematic literature review." *IEEE Access* 9 (2021): 131858–131876.

[5]   Wayman, James L. "The scientific development of biometrics over the last 40 years." In *The History of Information Security*, pp. 263–274. Elsevier Science BV, Amsterdam, 2007.

[6]   Wayman, James L. "Fundamentals of biometric authentication technologies." *International Journal of Image and Graphics* 1, no. 01 (2001): 93–113.

[7]   Pal, Anita, and Yogendra N. Singh. "ECG biometric recognition." In *International Conference on Mathematics and Computing*, pp. 61–73. Springer, Singapore, 2018.

[8]   Agrafioti, Foteini. *ECG in Biometric Recognition: Time Dependency and Application Challenges*. University of Toronto, Toronto, 2011.

[9]   Irvine, John M., Brenda K. Wiederhold, Lauren W. Gavshon, *et al.* "Heart rate variability: A new biometric for human identification." In *Proceedings of the International Conference on Artificial Intelligence (IC-AI'01)*, pp. 1106–1111. 2001.

[10] Zhang, Qingxue, Dian Zhou, and Xuan Zeng. "HeartID: A multi-resolution convolutional neural network for ECG-based biometric human identification in smart health applications." *IEEE Access* 5 (2017): 11805–11816.

[11] Pinto, João R., Jaime S. Cardoso, and André Lourenço. "Evolution, current challenges, and future possibilities in ECG biometrics." *IEEE Access* 6 (2018): 34746–34776.

[12] da Silva Luz, Eduardo J., Gladston J. P. Moreira, Luiz S. Oliveira, William R. Schwartz, and David Menotti. "Learning deep off-the-person heart biometrics representations." *IEEE Transactions on Information Forensics and Security* 13, no. 5 (2017): 1258–1270.

[13] Kim, Hanvit, and Se Y. Chun. "Cancelable ECG biometrics using compressive sensing-generalised likelihood ratio test." *IEEE Access* 7 (2019): 9232–9242.

[14] Islam, Md Saiful, and Naif Alajlan. "Biometric template extraction from a heartbeat signal captured from fingers." *Multimedia Tools and Applications* 76, no. 10 (2017): 12709–12733.

[15] Ingale, Mohit, Renato Cordeiro, Siddartha Thentu, Younghee Park, and Nima Karimian. "ECG biometric authentication: A comparative analysis." *IEEE Access* 8 (2020): 117853–117866.

[16]   Patro, Kiran Kumar, and P. Rajesh Kumar. "Machine learning classification approaches for biometric recognition system using ECG signals." *Journal of Engineering Science and Technology Review* 10, no. 6 (2017): 1–8.

[17]   Patro, Kiran Kumar, Surya Prakasa Rao Reddi, SK. Ebraheem Khalelulla, P. Rajesh Kumar, and K. Shankar. "ECG data optimisation for biometric human recognition using statistical distributed machine learning algorithm." *The Journal of Supercomputing* 76, no. 2 (2020): 858–875.

[18]   Patro, Kiran Kumar, Allam Jaya Prakash, M. Jayamanmadha Rao, and P. Rajesh Kumar. "An efficient optimised feature selection with machine learning approach for ECG biometric recognition." *IETE Journal of Research* 68, no. 4 (2022): 2743–2754.

[19]   Biel, Lena, Ola Pettersson, Lennart Philipson, and Peter Wide. "ECG analysis: A new approach in human identification." *IEEE Transactions on Instrumentation and Measurement* 50, no. 3 (2001): 808–812.

[20]   Choudhary, Tilendra and M. Sabarimalai Manikandan. "A novel unified framework for noise-robust ECG-based biometric authentication." In *2015 Second International Conference on Signal Processing and Integrated Networks (SPIN)*, pp. 186–191. IEEE, Piscataway, NJ, 2015.

[21]   Dar, Muhammad Najam, M. Usman Akram, Anam Usman, and Shoab A. Khan. "ECG biometric identification for general population using multi-resolution analysis of DWT based features." In *2015 Second International Conference on Information Security and Cyber Forensics (InfoSec)*, pp. 5–10. IEEE, Piscataway, NJ, 2015.

[22]   Bashar, Md Khayrul, Yuji Ohta, and Hiroaki Yoshida. "ECG-based biometric authentication using mulscale descriptors: ECG-based biometric authentication." In *2015 International Conference on Intelligent Informatics and Biomedical Sciences (ICIIBMS)*, pp. 1–4. IEEE, Piscataway, NJ, 2015.

[23]   Zhang, Yue, and Youqun Shi. "A new method for ECG biometric recognition using a hierarchical scheme classifier." In *2015 Sixth IEEE International Conference on Software Engineering and Service Science (ICSESS)*, pp. 457–460. IEEE, Piscataway, NJ, 2015.

[24]   Kang, Shin J., Seung Y. Lee, Hyo Il Cho, and Hyunggon Park. "ECG authentication system design based on signal analysis in mobile and wearable devices." *IEEE Signal Processing Letters* 23, no. 6 (2016): 805–808.

[25]   Singh, Yogendra N. "Human recognition using Fisher's discriminant analysis of heartbeat interval features and ECG morphology." *Neurocomputing* 167 (2015): 322–335.

[26]   Gahi, Youssef, Meryem Lamrani, Abdelhak Zoglat, Mouhcine Guennoun, Bill Kapralos, and Khalil El-Khatib. "Biometric identification system based on electrocardiogram data." In *2008 New Technologies, Mobility and Security*, pp. 1–5. IEEE, Piscataway, NJ, 2008.

[27]   Irvine, John M. and Steven A. Israel. "A sequential procedure for individual identity verification using ECG." *EURASIP Journal on Advances in Signal Processing* 2009 (2009): 1–13.

[28]   Venkatesh, N. and Srinivasan Jayaraman. "Human electrocardiogram for biometrics using DTW and FLDA." In *2010 20th International Conference on Pattern Recognition*, pp. 3838–3841. IEEE, Piscataway, NJ, 2010.

[29]   Louis, Wael, Majid Komeili, and Dimitrios Hatzinakos. "Continuous authentication using one-dimensional multi-resolution local binary patterns (1DMRLBP) in ECG biometrics." *IEEE Transactions on Information Forensics and Security* 11, no. 12 (2016): 2818–2832.

[30]   Zahra Fatemian S., and Dimitrios Hatzinakos. "A new ECG feature extractor for biometric recognition." In *2009 16th International Conference on Digital Signal Processing*, pp. 1–6. IEEE, Piscataway, NJ, 2009.

[31]   Odinaka, Ikenna, Po-Hsiang Lai, Alan D. Kaplan, *et al.* "ECG biometrics: A robust short-time frequency analysis." In *2010 IEEE International Workshop on Information Forensics and Security*, pp. 1–6. IEEE, Piscataway, NJ, 2010.

[32]   Li, Ming and Shrikanth Narayanan. "Robust ECG biometrics by fusing temporal and cepstral information." In *2010 20th International Conference on Pattern Recognition*, pp. 1326–1329. IEEE, Piscataway, NJ, 2010.

[33]   Fang, Shih-Chin and Hsiao-Lung Chan. "Human identification by quantifying similarity and dissimilarity in electrocardiogram phase space." *Pattern Recognition* 42, no. 9 (2009): 1824–1831.

[34]   Wan, Yongbo and Jianchu Yao. "A neural network to identify human subjects with electrocardiogram signals." In *Proceedings of the World Congress on Engineering and Computer Science*, pp. 1–4. CiteSeer, 2008.

[35]   Sriram, Janani C., Minho Shin, Tanzeem Choudhury, and David Kotz. "Activity-aware ECG-based patient authentication for remote health monitoring." In *Proceedings of the 2009 International Conference on Multimodal Interfaces*, pp. 297–304. 2009.

[36]   Shen Tsu-Wang, Willis J. Tompkins, and Yu Hen Hu. "Implementation of a one-lead ECG human identification system on a normal population." *Journal of Engineering and Computer Innovations* 2, no. 1 (2011): 12–21.

[37]   Shen, Tsu-Wang, Willis J. Tompkins, and Yu Hen Hu. "One-lead ECG for identity verification." In *Proceedings of the Second Joint 24th Annual Conference and the Annual Fall Meeting of the Biomedical Engineering Society [Engineering in Medicine and Biology]*, vol. 1, pp. 62–63. IEEE, Piscataway, NJ, 2002.

[38]   Safie, Sairul I., John J. Soraghan, and Lykourgos Petropoulakis. "Electrocardiogram (ECG) biometric authentication using pulse active ratio (PAR)." *IEEE Transactions on Information Forensics and Security* 6, no. 4 (2011): 1315–1322.

[39]   Zheng, Gang, Xiaoxia Sun, Shengzhen Ji, Min Dai, and Ying Sun. "ECG based biometric by superposition matrix in unrestricted status." In *Chinese Conference on Biometric Recognition*, pp. 553–561. Springer, Cham, 2018.

[40]   Chu, Yifan, Haibin Shen, and Kejie Huang. "ECG authentication method based on parallel multi-scale one-dimensional residual network with center and margin loss." *IEEE Access* 7 (2019): 51598–51607.

[41] Zhang, Jian, Jun Yu, and Dacheng Tao. "Local deep-feature alignment for unsupervised dimension reduction." *IEEE Transactions on Image Processing* 27, no. 5 (2018): 2420–2432.

[42] Plataniotis, Konstantinos N., Dimitrios Hatzinakos, and Jimmy K. M. Lee. "ECG biometric recognition without fiducial detection." In *2006 Biometrics Symposium: Special Session on Research at the Biometric Consortium Conference*, pp. 1–6. IEEE, Piscataway, NJ, 2006.

[43] Agrafioti, Foteini and Dimitrios Hatzinakos. "ECG based recognition using second order statistics." In *Sixth Annual Communication Networks and Services Research Conference (CNSR 2008)*, pp. 82–87. IEEE, Piscataway, NJ, 2008.

[44] Hejazi, Maryamsadat, Syed A. R. Al-Haddad, Yashwant P. Singh, Shaiful J. Hashim, and Ahmad F. A. Aziz. "ECG biometric authentication based on non-fiducial approach using kernel methods." *Digital Signal Processing* 52 (2016): 72–86.

[45] LeCun, Yann, Yoshua Bengio, and Geoffrey Hinton. "Deep learning." *Nature* 521, no. 7553 (2015): 436–444.

[46] Labati, Ruggero D., Enrique Muñoz, Vincenzo Piuri, Roberto Sassi, and Fabio Scotti. "Deep-ECG: Convolutional neural networks for ECG biometric recognition." *Pattern Recognition Letters* 126 (2019): 78–85.

[47] Goldberger Ary. L., Luis AN Amaral, Leon Glass, *et al.* PhysioBank, PhysioToolkit, and PhysioNet: Components of a new research resource for complex physiologic signals. *Circulation* 101, no. 23 (2000): e215–e220 [Circulation Electronic Pages; http://circ.ahajournals.org/cgi/content/full/101/23/e215].

[48] Patro, Kiran Kumar, and P. Rajesh Kumar. "De-noising of ECG raw signal by cascaded window based digital filters configuration." In *2015 IEEE Power, Communication and Information Technology Conference (PCITC)*, pp. 120–124. IEEE, Piscataway, NJ, 2015.

[49] Patro, Kiran Kumar, and P. Rajesh Kumar. "A novel frequency-time based approach for the detection of characteristic waves in electrocardiogram signal." In *Microelectronics, Electromagnetics and Telecommunications*, pp. 57–67. Springer, New Delhi, 2016.

[50] Pan, Jiapu and Willis J. Tompkins. "A real-time QRS detection algorithm." *IEEE Transactions on Biomedical Engineering* 3 (1985): 230–236.

[51] Patro, Kiran Kumar, and P. Rajesh Kumar . "Effective feature extraction of ECG for biometric application." *Procedia Computer Science* 115 (2017): 296–306.

[52] Lugovaya, Tatiana S. "Biometric human identification based on electro-cardiogram." *Master's thesis*, Faculty of Computing Technologies and Informatics, Electrotechnical University 'LETI', Saint-Petersburg, Russian Federation (2005).

[53] Jović, Alan, Karla Brkić, and Nikola Bogunović. "A review of feature selection methods with applications." In *2015 38th International Convention*

on Information and Communication Technology, Electronics and Microelectronics (MIPRO), pp. 1200–1205. IEEE, Piscataway, NJ, 2015.

[54] Pedregosa, Fabian, Gaël Varoquaux, Alexandre Gramfort, *et al.* "Scikit-learn: Machine learning in Python." *Journal of Machine Learning Research* 12 (2011): 2825–2830.

[55] Choi, Hyun-Soo, Byunghan Lee, and Sungroh Yoon. "Biometric authentication using noisy electrocardiograms acquired by mobile sensors." *IEEE Access* 4 (2016): 1266–1273.

[56] Hammad Mohamed, Abdullah M. Iliyasu, Ibrahim A. Elgendy, and Ahmed A. Abd El-Latif "End-to-end data authentication deep learning model for securing IoT configurations." *Human-Centric Computing and Information Sciences* 12, no. 4 (2022).

[57] Allam, Jaya Prakash, Kiran Kumar Patro, Saunak Samantray, Paweł Pławiak, and Mohamed Hammad. "A deep learning technique for biometric authentication using ECG beat template matching." *Information* 14, no. 2 (2023): 65.

[58] Sakr, Ahmed S., Paweł Pławiak, Ryszard Tadeusiewicz, and Mohamed Hammad. "Cancelable ECG biometric based on combination of deep transfer learning with DNA and amino acid approaches for human authentication." *Information Sciences*, 585 (2022): 127–143.

[59] Allam, Jaya Prakash, Kiran Kumar Patro, Mohamed Hammad, Ryszard Tadeusiewicz., and Paweł Pławiak. "BAED: A secured biometric authentication system using ECG signal based on deep learning techniques." *Biocybernetics and Biomedical Engineering*, 42, no. 4 (2022): 1081–1093.

[60] Homer, Mark, John M. Irvine, and Suzanne Wendelken. "A model-based approach to human identification using ECG." In *Optics and Photonics in Global Homeland Security V and Biometric Technology for Human Identification VI*, vol. 7306, pp. 416–425. SPIE, Bellingham, WA, 2009.

[61] Boumbarov, Ognian, Yuliyan Velchev, and Strahil Sokolov. "ECG personal identification in subspaces using radial basis neural networks." In *2009 IEEE International Workshop on Intelligent Data Acquisition and Advanced Computing Systems: Technology and Applications*, pp. 446–451. IEEE, Piscataway, NJ, 2009.

[62] Irvine, John M., Steven A. Israel, W. Todd Scruggs, and William J. Worek. "eigenPulse: Robust human identification from cardiovascular function." *Pattern Recognition* 41, no. 11 (2008): 3427–3435.

[63] Wang, Kuikui, Gongping Yang, Yuwen Huang, and Yilong Yin. "Multiscale differential feature for ECG biometrics with collective matrix factorisation." *Pattern Recognition* 102 (2020): 107211.

Chapter 7

A comparative analysis of email phishing detection methods: a deep learning perspective

Cong Khoa Truong[1], Phuc Hao Do[2,3] and Tran Duc Le[1,4]

The study comprehensively evaluates deep learning models for detecting email phishing attacks. The study applies deep learning models, including convolutional neural networks, recurrent neural networks (RNNs), long short-term memory (LSTM), and bidirectional long short-term memory, to a dataset of phishing and legitimate emails. It evaluates their performance based on several metrics, including accuracy and precision, recall, and $F1$-score. The LSTM model achieved the highest accuracy of 99.41%, outperforming all other models, while the RNN model had the worst accuracy among all the models evaluated. This chapter provides valuable insights into the potential of deep learning models for detecting email phishing attacks. It highlights the need for further research to develop more effective and reliable approaches. The study also underscores the importance of developing robust and accurate phishing detection systems, given the significant impact that emails phishing attacks can have on individuals and organizations. The findings of this study have practical implications for the development of email phishing detection systems and provide a foundation for future research in this area.

7.1 Introduction

Email phishing is a malicious activity where attackers masquerade as trustworthy entities to deceive recipients into revealing sensitive information or taking actions that compromise their security. Phishing attacks have become increasingly sophisticated, making it more challenging for traditional detection methods to identify and prevent them effectively. The substantial rise in phishing incidents and

[1]Department of Computer Networking and Communication, University of Science and Technology— The University of Da Nang, Viet Nam
[2]Department of Software Engineering and Computing, The Bonch-Bruevich Saint Petersburg State University of Telecommunications, Russian Federation
[3]Faculty of Information Technology, Da Nang Architecture University, Viet Nam
[4]Department of Marketing and Information Systems, Université du Québec à Trois-Rivières, Canada

their severe consequences, including financial losses, identity theft, and reputational damage, has necessitated the development of advanced detection methods.

In recent years, machine learning techniques, particularly deep learning, have shown promising results in various applications, including image recognition, natural language processing, and anomaly detection. Deep learning is a subset of machine learning that leverages neural networks to learn from large datasets and discover complex patterns. The use of deep learning models in phishing detection has also gained considerable attention in recent years due to its ability to extract relevant features automatically from email content and metadata.

Moreover, the motivation behind this research stems from the need to address the limitations of traditional phishing detection methods, such as rule-based filters and blacklist databases. These methods often struggle to adapt to the evolving tactics employed by attackers. They may produce high false positive (FP) and false negative (FN) rates. On the other hand, deep learning techniques offer the potential to learn complex patterns and features from large datasets automatically. It potentially enhances their ability to identify phishing emails more accurately and efficiently.

Therefore, this study contributes to the growing body of knowledge in the field of email phishing detection and deep learning by systematically comparing prominent techniques. The insights gained from this research will help researchers and practitioners develop more effective and adaptable phishing detection systems, ultimately strengthening cybersecurity defenses against this pervasive threat.

The primary objective of this study is to provide a comprehensive comparative analysis of four deep learning techniques—convolutional neural networks (CNNs), recurrent neural networks (RNNs), long short-term memory (LSTM), and bidirectional long short-term memory (Bi-LSTM)—in the context of email phishing detection. To achieve this goal, the research will focus on the following specific objectives:

- Implement and train each model using a large dataset of phishing and non-phishing emails to ensure a robust comparison of the models' capabilities to generalize across various types of attacks.
- Evaluate the performance of the models using multiple metrics, such as accuracy, precision, recall, and $F1$-score, to provide a comprehensive understanding of their effectiveness in detecting email phishing.
- Discuss the most suitable deep learning technique depending on a phishing detection scenario's requirements and constraints.

The main contributions of this study include a thorough comparison of the four deep learning techniques in the domain of email phishing detection, highlighting their respective strengths and weaknesses; a detailed analysis of the experimental results, enabling researchers and practitioners to make informed decisions on the most suitable technique for their specific use cases; and identification of areas for future research, aimed at enhancing the effectiveness of deep learning methods in detecting email phishing attacks.

The rest of this study is organized: Section 7.2 reviews traditional phishing detection methods and deep learning approaches. Section 7.4 describes the dataset description, preprocessing, model architectures, and evaluation setup. Section 7.5

compares the performance of the models based on various metrics. Finally, Sections 7.6 and 7.7 summarize the findings, implications for practitioners and researchers, and suggestions for future work.

7.2 Related work

7.2.1 Traditional phishing detection methods

Various traditional phishing detection methods have been developed to counter email phishing attacks. These methods can be broadly categorized into the following:

Rule-based filters [1,2]: Rule-based filters are one of the most commonly used methods for detecting phishing emails. These filters operate based on predefined rules or heuristics that scan emails for specific characteristics such as keywords, suspicious links, or inconsistencies in email headers. Rule-based filters effectively detect known phishing patterns and can be particularly useful in identifying simple, low-level attacks that rely on common tactics like misspelled URLs or other telltale signs.

However, despite their effectiveness, rule-based filters have a significant limitation: they struggle to adapt to new or evolving phishing tactics. For instance, if a phishing attack relies on a previously unknown keyword or a sophisticated social engineering technique, the rule-based filter may not be able to detect it. This is because these filters rely on predefined rules, which can become outdated as phishing tactics evolve and attackers become more sophisticated. As a result, rule-based filters may not provide sufficient protection against advanced phishing attacks, which can evade detection.

Another significant limitation of rule-based filters is their high maintenance cost. The rules must be regularly updated and maintained to ensure that they are up-to-date and effective in detecting new phishing attacks. This requires considerable effort and expertise, and the need for manual rule updates can be labor-intensive and time-consuming. Moreover, it is challenging to keep up with the ever-evolving tactics of phishers, making it difficult for rule-based filters to remain effective.

Despite these limitations, rule-based filters can still be a valuable component of an overall email security strategy, mainly when used with other methods such as machine learning and behavioral analysis. By combining multiple approaches, organizations can achieve a more comprehensive and robust defense against phishing attacks, minimizing the risk of falling victim to these scams.

Blacklist databases [3,4]: Blacklist databases are commonly used to identify and flag potential email phishing attempts. These databases contain lists of known malicious URLs, IP addresses, or domain names identified as sources of phishing attacks. An email containing any of these elements is flagged as a possible phishing attempt. Further analysis is performed to determine if the email is a phishing attack.

One of the main advantages of blacklist databases is their ability to stay current with emerging threats. They are typically updated regularly, ensuring that the database contains the latest information on known malicious sources. It makes blacklist databases essential for detecting and preventing known phishing attacks.

However, one of the significant limitations of blacklist databases is their reactive nature. These databases can only detect phishing attacks already identified and add to the database. As a result, they may not provide adequate protection against novel or rapidly evolving phishing campaigns that have not yet been identified and added to the database. This is a concern as attackers continually develop new tactics and techniques to evade detection.

Another limitation of blacklist databases is their potential for FPs. Sometimes legitimate websites may be inadvertently added to the blacklist, flagging legitimate emails as potential phishing attacks. This can lead to unnecessary inconvenience and loss of productivity for users who have to spend time verifying the legitimacy of the flagged emails.

Whitelist databases [5,6]: Whitelist databases are an alternative approach to detecting phishing attacks. Unlike blacklist databases, which maintain lists of known malicious entities, whitelist databases contain lists of trusted entities, such as email addresses, domain names, or IP addresses. Any email originating from an entity, not on the whitelist, is subjected to further scrutiny or flagged as suspicious. By only allowing emails from trusted entities, organizations can reduce the risk of falling victim to phishing scams.

However, the whitelist databases can also lead to a higher rate of FPs. Legitimate emails from unknown sources may be flagged as potential phishing attempts, subjected to additional scrutiny, or even blocked. This can lead to inconvenience and lost productivity for users who have to spend time verifying the legitimacy of the flagged emails.

Moreover, maintaining an up-to-date whitelist database can be challenging. As organizations continue interacting with new entities, the list of trusted sources may need to be continually updated. This requires careful management and monitoring to ensure the list remains accurate and up-to-date.

Machine learning techniques [7,8]: Machine learning techniques are increasingly used to detect email phishing attacks. Both supervised and unsupervised machine learning algorithms have been employed to extract features from the email content and metadata and identify patterns indicative of phishing attacks. Standard techniques include Decision Trees, Support Vector Machines, Naive Bayes Classifiers, and Clustering Algorithms.

Supervised machine learning algorithms learn to identify phishing patterns from labeled datasets and generalize them to new instances. This means that the algorithms can automatically detect recent phishing attacks with high accuracy once trained. However, the performance of these algorithms may be affected by the quality and representativeness of the training data. If the training data is biased or unrepresentative, the algorithm may not be effective in detecting real-world phishing attacks.

On the other hand, unsupervised machine learning algorithms do not rely on labeled datasets but instead identify patterns and anomalies in the data. This makes them useful for detecting novel or previously unknown phishing attacks that do not fit known patterns. However, they may not be as effective in detecting highly sophisticated or targeted phishing attacks that exhibit subtle differences from known patterns.

Machine learning–based approaches have shown promising results in detecting phishing attacks. Some studies report detection rates of up to 99% [9]. However, these techniques are not without limitations. Highly sophisticated phishing attacks can evade detection by machine learning algorithms, especially those that use social engineering techniques to manipulate users into taking specific actions.

Another limitation of machine learning–based approaches is the need for continuous training and updating of the algorithms to remain effective. As phishing attacks evolve, the algorithms must be retrained with updated data to accurately detect new patterns and anomalies.

Despite their widespread use, traditional phishing detection methods have limitations that can result in high FP and FN rates and the inability to adapt to evolving attack patterns. These shortcomings have prompted researchers to explore alternative approaches, such as deep learning techniques.

Deep learning techniques are a subset of machine learning that uses neural networks with multiple layers to identify patterns and features in data. They are particularly effective in processing large and complex datasets, such as those in email systems. They can learn to identify patterns that may be missed by traditional detection methods [10].

One advantage of deep learning techniques is their ability to adapt to evolving attack patterns. Unlike traditional methods, which rely on predefined rules or heuristics, deep learning algorithms can learn to identify new patterns and anomalies [11] in data through continuous training and improvement.

Another advantage is their potential to reduce FPs and FNs. The use of deep learning algorithms allows for processing substantial amounts of data and detecting intricate patterns that may evade other methods. This capacity mitigates the risk of erroneously categorizing legitimate emails as phishing attempts or overlooking actual phishing attacks.

In conclusion, traditional phishing detection methods have limitations that can result in high FP and FN rates and the inability to adapt to evolving attack patterns. Deep learning techniques [12,13] promise to overcome these limitations and provide more accurate and adaptive phishing detection capabilities. While these techniques may present some challenges, they offer a potentially powerful tool for organizations seeking to protect against the ever-evolving threat of phishing attacks.

7.2.2 Deep learning approaches for phishing detection

Deep learning methodologies have garnered considerable interest in recent years because they can autonomously acquire and derive intricate patterns and features from voluminous datasets without requiring explicit feature engineering. In the context of email phishing detection, several deep learning architectures have been applied and shown promising results [14]. In this study, we consider the following deep learning models, such as CNNs, RNNs, LSTM, and Bi-LSTM.

7.2.2.1 Convolutional neural networks

CNNs [15]: CNNs were initially developed for image recognition tasks (Figure 7.1). However, researchers have successfully adapted them to process

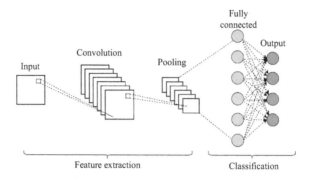

Figure 7.1   The basic structure of CNN

textual data in phishing detection. CNNs use convolutional layers to automatically learn features and patterns from the email content by applying multiple filters to different regions of the input text. These filters can capture local patterns, such as word groupings or specific textual structures, indicating phishing attempts.

The formula for CNN classification varies depending on the specific architecture and design of the CNN model. However, a general procedure for CNN classification can be broken down into the following steps:

- Convolutional layers: The data input is passed through one or more convolutional layers. Each convolutional layer applies filters to the data input, creating feature maps that capture different aspects of the data.
- Activation function: After each convolutional layer, an activation function is applied to introduce nonlinearity to the output feature maps. The most commonly used activation function is ReLU (rectified linear unit).
- Pooling layers: The feature maps are passed through one or more pooling layers after the activation function. Pooling layers downsample the feature maps by taking the maximum or average value within a specific window size. This reduces the size of the feature maps and makes the model more computationally efficient.
- Flatten layer: The feature maps are flattened into a one-dimensional vector after the final pooling layer.
- Fully connected layers: The flattened feature vector is passed through one or more fully connected layers. Each fully connected layer applies a set of weights to the input vector and outputs a new vector of a specified size.
- Softmax: The final fully connected layer uses the Softmax function to convert the output vector into a probability distribution over the different classes in the classification task. The class with the highest probability is then selected as the predicted class.

The above steps can be represented as a mathematical formula for a basic CNN classification model as follows:

$$y = softmax\left(W_2 \times ReLU(W_1 \times pool(conv(x)) + b_1) + b_2\right) \tag{7.1}$$

In (7.1), the input data x is subjected to convolutional and pooling layers represented by *conv* and *pool*, respectively. The output of these layers is then passed through the first fully connected layer, represented by the weights W_1 and biases b_1. The *ReLU* activation function is applied to the output of the first fully connected layer. The resulting output is then passed through the final fully connected layer, represented by the weights W_2 and biases b_2. The Softmax function is applied to the output of the final fully connected layer, which produces the probability distribution over the different classes.

One advantage of using CNNs in phishing detection is their ability to automatically learn features and patterns without requiring manual feature engineering or rule-based filters. This can save considerable time and effort in model development and maintenance and improve the model's ability to adapt to evolving phishing attacks.

7.2.2.2   Recurrent neural networks

RNNs [16,17]: RNNs are a specialized type of neural network architecture designed to process sequential data, rendering them appropriate for analyzing the temporal structure of textual data within emails. By preserving an internal state, RNNs can capture contextual information and dependencies within the email content, which is essential since the connotation of words or phrases in an email may hinge on their context within the message.

A basic RNN architecture comprises three layers: input, recurrent hidden, and output, as illustrated in Figure 7.2(a). The input layer consists of N input units that receive a sequence of vectors over time t, denoted as $\{ \ldots, x_{t-1}, x_t, x_{t+1}, \ldots \}$, where $x_t = (x_1, x_2, \ldots, x_N)$. In a fully connected RNN, the input units are connected to the hidden units in the hidden layer via a weight matrix W_{IH}. The hidden layer comprises M hidden units $h_t = (h_1, h_2, \ldots, h_M)$ connected through time by recurrent

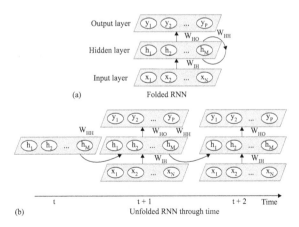

Figure 7.2   A simple recurrent (a) neural network (RNN) and (b) its unfolded structure through time t. Each arrow shows a full connection of units between the layers. To keep the figure simple, biases are not shown.

connections, as shown in Figure 7.2(b). Initializing the hidden units with small nonzero values can enhance the overall performance and stability of the network. The hidden layer defines the state space or *memory* of the system as

$$h_t = f_H(o_t) \tag{7.2}$$

where o_t is defined by the following equation:

$$o_t = W_{IH}x_t + W_{HH}h_{t-1} + b_h, \tag{7.3}$$

where $f_H(\cdot)$ denotes the activation function of the hidden layer, and b_h is the bias vector of the hidden units. The hidden units are connected to the output layer via weighted connections W_{HO}. The output layer comprises P units $y_t=(y_1, y_2, \ldots, y_P)$ that are computed as

$$y_t = f_O(W_{HO}h_t + b_o) \tag{7.4}$$

where $f_O(\cdot)$ represents the activation function of the output layer, and b_o is the bias vector of the output layer. Since the input-target pairs are sequential over time, the above equations are iterated over time $t= (1, \ldots, T)$. Equations (7.2) and (7.4) highlight that an RNN consists of nonlinear state equations that can be iterated over time. The hidden states predict the output layer based on the input vector in each time step.

The hidden state of an RNN comprises a set of values that summarize all the necessary unique information about the past states of the network over many time steps, independent of any external influences. This integrated information can define the future behavior of the network and enable accurate predictions at the output layer. While a simple nonlinear activation function is used in every unit of an RNN, a basic structure can capture complex dynamics if trained effectively over time steps.

Another advantage is their ability to capture long-range dependencies in sequences, allowing them to consider the entire email content when making a phishing detection decision. This can improve the accuracy of phishing detection, especially in the case of complex or sophisticated phishing attacks.

However, conventional RNNs may suffer from the vanishing gradient problem, which hinders their ability to learn long-range dependencies in sequences. This can sometimes limit their effectiveness, especially when dealing with long, complex email content.

7.2.2.3   Long short-term memory

LSTM [18]: LSTM is a specialized type of RNN that addresses the vanishing gradient problem by introducing memory cells and gating mechanisms. These features allow LSTMs to effectively learn and retain long-range dependencies in sequences, improving their performance in various text-based tasks, including phishing detection.

RNNs with LSTM have emerged as a robust and scalable approach for various learning tasks that involve sequential data. LSTMs effectively capture long-term

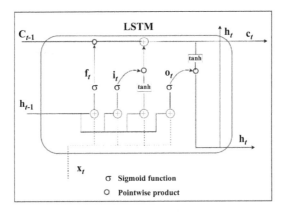

Figure 7.3   The structure of a long short-term memory (LSTM) algorithm

temporal dependencies since they are generic and can be applied broadly. The LSTM architecture is similar to that of an RNN. However, it includes gates that regulate the flow of information between cells. The input and forget gate structures can modify information traveling along the cell state. At the same time, the final output is a filtered version of the cell state based on the input context. Despite the success of LSTMs, the design has been criticized for being ad hoc and containing several components whose purpose is unclear. Therefore, whether LSTMs are the best design remains uncertain, and superior alternatives may exist. The structure of an LSTM algorithm is illustrated in Figure 7.3.

The forward training process of an LSTM can be formulated with the following equations:

$$f_t = \sigma(W_f \cdot [h_{t-1}, x_t] + b_f) \tag{7.5}$$

$$i_t = \sigma(W_f \cdot [h_{t-1}, x_t] + b_i) \tag{7.6}$$

$$C_t = f_t \times C_{t-1} + i_t \times \tanh(W_c \cdot [h_{t-1}, x_t] + b_c) \tag{7.7}$$

$$o_t = \sigma(W_0 \cdot [h_{t-1}, x_t] + b_0) \tag{7.8}$$

$$h_t = o_t \times \tanh(C_t) \tag{7.9}$$

In the above equations, i_t, o_t, and f_t denote the activation of the input, output, and forget gates, respectively. C_t and h_t denote the activation vector for each cell and memory block, respectively, while W and b represent the weight matrix and bias vector, respectively. Furthermore, $\sigma(.)$ denotes the sigmoid function.

One of the main advantages of LSTMs is their ability to capture complex patterns in email content and metadata. By maintaining an internal memory state and using gating mechanisms to control the flow of information, LSTMs can identify subtle cues and dependencies that may signify a phishing attack. This allows them to differentiate between legitimate and phishing emails more accurately than traditional RNNs.

Another advantage is their ability to learn and adapt to new patterns and anomalies in the email content. By continuously training and updating the model with new data, LSTMs can adapt to evolving phishing attack tactics and detect new threats effectively.

LSTMs have been shown to be highly effective in various text-based tasks, including sentiment analysis, text classification, and language translation. In phishing detection, LSTMs have shown promise in detecting highly sophisticated attacks that may evade traditional detection methods.

7.2.2.4   Bidirectional long short-term memory

Bi-LSTM is an elaboration of the LSTM architecture that undertakes the processing of input sequences in both forward and backward directions. This dual direction-ality empowers the model to capture dependencies and context from both past and future elements of the sequence. This bidirectional processing enables Bi-LSTMs to have a more comprehensive understanding of the email content. It can be ben-eficial in detecting phishing attempts that employ subtle obfuscation techniques or exhibit unusual textual patterns.

By processing the input sequence in both directions, Bi-LSTMs can identify patterns and dependencies that unidirectional LSTMs may miss. This allows them to detect complex and sophisticated phishing attacks that may involve context-dependent manipulations or social engineering techniques.

One advantage of Bi-LSTMs is their ability to learn and adapt to new patterns and anomalies in the email content. By continuously training and updating the model with new data, Bi-LSTMs can effectively adapt to evolving phishing attack tactics and detect new threats.

Additionally, Bi-LSTMs can be used with other detection methods, such as rule-based filters or blacklist databases, to provide a more comprehensive and robust defense against phishing attacks.

Applying deep learning approaches to phishing detection has shown significant improvements compared to traditional methods. However, several factors, such as the choice of architecture, dataset quality and size, and model hyperparameters, can influence the performance of these techniques. Therefore, a systematic comparison of deep learning techniques for phishing detection is necessary to better understand their strengths and weaknesses.

The bidirectional recurrent neural network (BRNN) model has been proposed to remove various constraints from conventional RNNs. One version of this model is the Bi-LSTM, which can improve the performance of LSTM models in classi-fication tasks. In the BLSTM architecture, two different LSTM networks are trained for sequential inputs. Figure 7.4 illustrates the basic structure of a BLSTM running on sequential inputs. The neurons in the forward state of the BLSTM function as unidirectional LSTM structures. Since the neurons in both networks are not interconnected, network training can be provided as a normal unidirectional LSTM.

The training procedure for BLSTMs is typically as follows. In the forward pass, all input data for a time slice ($1 \leq t \leq T$) is processed through the BRNNs, and

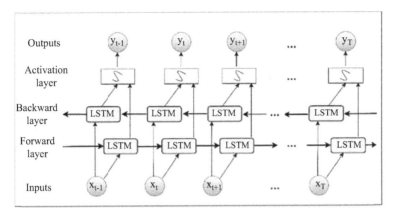

Figure 7.4   The basic structure of the Bi-LSTM network. The LSTM nets at the bottom indicate the forward feature. The above nets are used for backward.

all predicted outputs are determined. Forward passes are carried out from time $t=1$ to $t=T$ and backward from $t=T$ to $t=1$. A forward pass is also conducted for the output neurons. In the backward pass, the error function derivative is calculated for the time slice ($1 \leq t \leq T$) used in the forward pass. A backward pass is carried out for the output neurons, and another backward pass is carried out for the forward states from $t=T$ to $t=1$ and the backward states from $t=1$ to $t=T$. Finally, all weights are updated. Depending on the problem area, BLSTM structures can produce better results than other network structures. For instance, it has been demonstrated that Bi-LSTMs are particularly successful in natural language processing tasks where content is critical.

Such a comparison can help researchers and practitioners select and implement the most suitable approach for a given scenario. It can also guide the development of new and improved deep learning architectures for phishing detection.

A systematic comparison can be performed by evaluating deep learning techniques on a standard dataset, using common performance metrics such as precision, recall, $F1$-score, and accuracy. Besides, the choice of architecture, dataset quality and size, and model hyperparameters can significantly influence the performance of deep learning techniques. As the threat landscape of phishing attacks continues to evolve, ongoing research is necessary to develop and improve deep learning–based approaches for phishing detection.

7.3   Data collection and preprocessing

As illustrated in Figure 7.5, the workflow encompasses both data collection and data normalization [19,20] processes. The phishing email data was procured from the *CLAIR collection of fraudulent emails* [21]. This dataset comprises over 2,500 "Nigerian" phishing messages from 1998 to 2007. The information is stored in a text file containing emails and basic headers. It is worth noting that the emails in this dataset are assigned a label of 1.

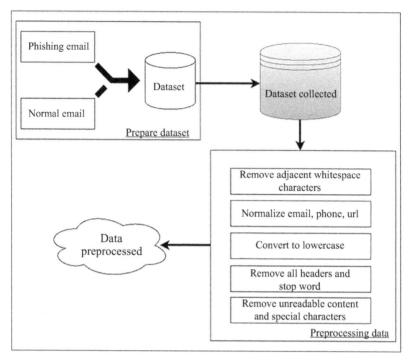

Figure 7.5   Data collection and preprocessing

Figure 7.6 presents the content of an email phishing sample from the dataset.

The non-phishing email data, otherwise referred to as normal email data, was sourced from the Enron email dataset [22]. This dataset encompasses approximately 500,000 emails generated by nearly 150 users, predominantly consisting of Enron senior management. The Federal Energy Regulatory Commission (FERC) obtained this data while investigating Enron's collapse. The information is stored in a CSV file, comprising two columns that include the email file name and the message containing the email content. It is important to note that these emails are labeled as 0. Figure 7.7 presents a part of the .csv file containing the emails from the *Enron* dataset.

Subsequently, the two datasets are combined by randomly selecting 8,000 emails from the 500,000 Enron emails and integrating them with the entire phishing email data. The final dataset comprises 11,766 emails divided into training, testing, and validation subsets at ratios of 60%, 20%, and 20%, respectively.

The present study employs a structured data preprocessing approach that comprises several sequential steps. Initially, headers and illegible data are removed. The data is then converted to lowercase and processed to eliminate adjacent whitespace characters. Subsequently, the normalization of variable values, including addresses, phone numbers, and URLs, is performed. Further, HTML tags are extracted and removed. Special characters and stop words are subsequently eliminated. Finally, the data is returned to its original form of words. Figures 7.8 and 7.9 present the raw data and the processed data.

From r Wed Oct 30 21:41:56 2002
Return-Path: <james_ngola2002@maktoob.com>
X-Sieve: cmu-sieve 2.0
Return-Path: <james_ngola2002@maktoob.com>
Message-Id: <200210310241.g9V2fhm002828IQ4s.CU>
From: "MR. JAMES NGOLA." <james_ngola2002@maktoob.com>
Reply-To: james_ngola2002@maktoob.com
To: webmaster@aclweb.org
Date: Thu, 31 Oct 2002 02:38:20 +0000
Subject: URGENT BUSINESS ASSISTANCE AND PARTNERSHIP
X-Mailer: Microsoft Outlook Express 5.00.2919.6900 DM
MIME-Version: 1.0
Content-Type: text/plain; charset="us-ascii"
Content-Transfer-Encoding: 8bit
X-MIME-Autoconverted: from quoted-printable to 8bit by sideshome1.si.um id g9V2fG024311
Status: O

FROM:MR. JAMES NGOLA.
CONFIDENTIAL TEL: 233-27-587908.
E-MAIL: (james_ngola2002@maktoob.com).

URGENT BUSINESS ASSISTANCE AND PARTNERSHIP.

DEAR FRIEND,

I AM (DR.) JAMES NGOLA, THE PERSONAL ASSISTANCE TO THE LATE CONGOLESE (PRESIDENT LAURENT KABILA) WHO WAS ASSASSINATED BY HIS BODY GUARD ON 16TH JAN. 2001.

THE INCIDENT OCCURRED IN OUR PRESENCE WHILE WE WERE HOLDING MEETING WITH HIS EXCELLENCY OVER THE FINANCIAL RETURNS FROM THE DIAMOND SALES IN THE AREAS CONTROLLED BY (D.R.C.) DEMOCRATIC REPUBLIC OF CONGO FORCES AND THEIR FOREIGN ALLIES ANGOLA AND ZIMBABWE, HAVING RECEIVED THE PREVIOUS DAY (USD$100M) ONE HUNDRED MILLION UNITED STATES DOLLARS, CASH IN THREE DIPLOMATIC BOXES ROUTED THROUGH ZIMBABWE.

MY PURPOSE OF WRITING YOU THIS LETTER IS TO SOLICIT FOR YOUR ASSISTANCE AS TO BE A COVER TO THE FUND AND ALSO COLLABORATION IN MOVING THE SAID FUND INTO YOUR BANK ACCOUNT THE SUM OF (USD$25M) TWENTY FIVE MILLION UNITED STATES DOLLARS ONLY, WHICH I DEPOSITED WITH A SECURITY COMPANY IN GHANA, IN A DIPLOMATIC BOX AS GOLDS WORTH (USD$25M) TWENTY FIVE MILLION UNITED STATES DOLLARS ONLY FOR SAFE KEEPING IN A SECURITY VAULT FOR ANY FURTHER INVESTMENT PERHAPS IN YOUR COUNTRY.

YOU WERE INTRODUCED TO ME BY A RELIABLE FRIEND OF MINE WHO IS A TRAVELLER,AND ALSO A MEMBER OF CHAMBER OF COMMERCE AS A RELIABLE AND TRUSTWORTHY PERSON WHOM I CAN RELY ON AS FOREIGN PARTNER, EVEN THOUGH THE NATURE OF THE TRANSACTION WAS NOT REVEALED TO HIM FOR SECURITY REASONS.

THE (USD$25M) WAS PART OF A PROCEEDS FROM DIAMOND TRADE MEANT FOR THE LATE PRESIDENT LAURENT KABILA WHICH WAS DELIVERED THROUGH ZIMBABWE IN DIPLOMATIC BOXES. THE BOXES WERE KEPT UNDER MY CUSTODY BEFORE THE SAD EVENT THAT TOOK THE LIFE OF (MR. PRESIDENT).THE CONFUSION THAT ENSUED AFTER THE ASSASSINATION AND THE SPORADIC SHOOTING AMONG THE FACTIONS, I HAVE TO RUN AWAY FROM THE COUNTRY FOR MY DEAR LIFE AS I AM NOT A SOLDIER BUT A CIVIL SERVANT I CROSSED RIVER CONGO TO OTHER SIDE OF CONGO LIBREVILLE FROM THERE I MOVED TO THE THIRD COUNTRY GHANA WHERE I AM PRESENTLY TAKING REFUGE.

AS A MATTER OF FACT, WHAT I URGENTLY NEEDED FROM YOU IS YOUR ASSISTANCE IN MOVING THIS MONEY INTO YOUR ACCOUNT IN YOUR COUNTRY FOR INVESTMENT WITHOUT RAISING EYEBROW. FOR YOUR ASSISTANCE I WILL GIVE YOU 20% OF THE TOTAL SUM AS YOUR OWN SHARE WHEN THE MONEY GETS TO YOUR ACCOUNT, WHILE 75% WILL BE FOR ME, OF WHICH WITH YOUR KIND ADVICE I HOPE TO INVEST IN PROFITABLE VENTURE IN YOUR COUNTRY IN OTHER TO SETTLE DOWN FOR MEANINGFUL LIFE, AS I AM TIRED OF LIVING IN A WAR ENVIRONMENT.

THE REMAINING 5% WILL BE USED TO OFFSET ANY COST INCURRED IN THE CAUSE OF MOVING THE MONEY TO YOUR ACCOUNT. IF THE PROPOSAL IS ACCEPTABLE TO YOU PLEASE CONTACT ME IMMEDIATELY THROUGH THE ABOVE TELEPHONE AND E-MAIL, TO ENABLE ME ARRANGE FACE TO FACE MEETING WITH YOU IN GHANA FOR THE CLEARANCE OF THE FUNDS BEFORE TRANSFERRING IT TO YOUR BANK ACCOUNT AS SEEING IS BELIEVING.

FINALLY, IT IS IMPORTANT ALSO THAT I LET YOU UNDERSTAND THAT THERE IS NO RISK INVOLVED WHATSOEVER AS THE MONEY HAD NO RECORD IN KINSHASA FOR IT WAS MEANT FOR THE PERSONAL USE OF (MR. PRESIDENT) BEFORE THE NEFARIOUS INCIDENT OCCURRED, AND ALSO I HAVE ALL THE NECESSARY DOCUMENTS AS REGARDS TO THE FUNDS INCLUDING THE (CERTIFICATE OF DEPOSIT), AS I AM THE DEPOSITOR OF THE CONSIGNMENT.

LOOKING FORWARD TO YOUR URGENT RESPONSE.

YOUR SINCERELY,

Figure 7.6 Email phishing sample

	message
45701	Message-ID: <15791592.1075857929040.JavaMail.evans@thyme>\nDate: Sat, 21 Apr 2001 16:38:00 -0700 (PDT)\nFrom: kvanpelt@flash.net\nTo: vi_dare@yahoo.com, vpsurry@aol.com, dynomitetnt8433@aol.com, \nltstp19992000@yahoo.com, sblanehart@earthlink.net, \nltilly_osu@provalue.net, thefoxs@flash.net, neelyshaw@aol.com, tulsadad@att.net, kingye@aol.com, \nltphysics123@yahoo.com, meldenkey@yahoo.com, lsabbar@aol.com, \nltlcampbel@aol.com, mboyce4961@aol.com, jjdanker@hotmail...
58663	Message-ID: <11954150.1075842930862.JavaMail.evans@thyme>\nDate: Wed, 22 Sep 1999 16:11:00 -0700 (PDT)\nFrom: businessbrowser_support@onesource.com\nTo: dasovich@haas.berkeley.edu\nSubject: Your OneSource Account.\nMime-Version: 1.0\nContent-Type: text/plain; charset=us-ascii\nContent-Transfer-Encoding: 7bit\nX-From: BusinessBrowser_Support@onesource.com\nX-To: dasovich@haas.berkeley.edu\nX-cc: \nX-bcc: \nX-Folder: \Jeff_Dasovich_Dec2000\Notes Folders\All documents\nX-Origin: DASOVICH-J\nX-F...
352344	Message-ID: <6332707.1075842653311.JavaMail.evans@thyme>\nDate: Tue, 3 Oct 2000 01:21:00 -0700 (PDT)\nFrom: kckrisa@apex2000.net\nTo: dan.j.bump@enron.com, gerald.nemec@enron.com, joan.quick@enron.com, \nltmwhitt@enron.com, scott.josey@enron.com\nSubject: Status of Field Pressures and Wildhorse\nXcc: amartin@enron.com\nMime-Version: 1.0\nContent-Type: text/plain; charset=us-ascii\nContent-Transfer-Encoding: 7bit\nBcc: amartin@enron.com\nX-From: "Ken" <kckrisa@apex2000.net>\nX-To: "Dan Bump \/...
107180	Message-ID: <30446668.1075854286990.JavaMail.evans@thyme>\nDate: Thu, 8 Feb 2001 02:53:00 -0800 (PST)\nFrom: gary.hanks@enron.com\nTo: cstone1@txu.com, ggreen2@txu.com, daren.j.farmer@enron.com, \nltgary.a.hanks@enron.com, carlos.j.rodriguez@enron.com, unteari.tisdale@enron.com, davila1@txu.com, liz.bellamy@enron.com, kponton@duke-energy.com\nSubject: 2/07/01 GAS FLOW\nMime-Version: 1.0\nContent-Type: text/plain; charset=us-ascii\nContent-Transfer-Encoding: 7bit\nX-Fro...
295433	Message-ID: <16420089.1075841083987.JavaMail.evans@thyme>\nDate: Wed, 23 Jan 2002 11:01:33 -0800 (PST)\nFrom: m_love@enron.com\nTo: chance.rabon@enron.com\nSubject: FW: Deals to be moved to Bankruptcy Books (From Russell's Exposure\n Report)\nMime-Version: 1.0\nContent-Type: text/plain; charset=us-ascii\nContent-Transfer-Encoding: 7bit\nX-From: Love, Phillip M. </O=ENRON/OU=NA/CN=RECIPIENTS/CN=PLOVE>\nX-To: Rabon, Chance </O=ENRON/OU=NA/CN=RECIPIENTS/CN=Crabon>\nX-cc: \nX-bcc: \nX-Folder: \...

Figure 7.7 Sample of Eron dataset

Wed Oct 30 21:41:56 2002\nReturn-Path: <james_ngola2002@maktoob.com>\nX-Sieve: cmu-sieve 2.0\nReturn-Path: <james_ngola2002@maktoob.com>\nReply-To: james_ngola2002@maktoob.com>\nMessage-Id: <20021031041.g9V2hNm6028281@cs.CU>\nFrom: "MR. JAMES NGOLA." <james_ngola2002@maktoob.com>\nReply-To: james_ngola2002@maktoob.com>\nTo: webmaster@aclweb.org\nDate: Thu, 31 Oct 2002 02:38:20 +0000\nSubject: URGENT BUSINESS ASSISTANCE AND PARTNERSHIP\nX-Mailer: Microsoft Outlook Express 5.00.2919.6900 DM\nMIME-Version: 1.0\nContent-Type: text/p...

Thu Oct 31 08:11:39 2002\nReturn-Path: <bensul2004nng@spinfinder.com>\nX-Sieve: cmu-sieve 2.0\nReturn-Path: <bensul2004nng@spinfinder.com>\nMessage-Id: <200210311310.g9VDANt24674@bloodwork.mr.itd.UM>\nFrom: "Mr. Ben Suleman" <bensul2004nng@spinfinder.com>\nDate: Thu, 31 Oct 2002 05:10:00\nTo: R@M\nSubject: URGENT ASSISTANCE /RELATIONSHIP (P)\nMIME-Version: 1.0\nContent-Type: text/plain;charset="iso-8859-1"\nContent-Transfer-Encoding: 7bit\nStatus: O\nDear Friend,\n\nI am Mr. Ben Suleman ...

Thu Oct 31 17:27:16 2002\nReturn-Path: <obong_715@epatra.com>\nX-Sieve: cmu-sieve 2.0\nReturn-Path: <obong_715@epatra.com>\nReply-To: obong_715@epatra.com>\nMessage-Id: <20021031227.g9VMQvDj017949@bluewhale.cs.CU>\nFrom: "PRINCE OBONG ELEME" <obong_715@epatra.com>\nTo: webmaster@aclweb.org\nDate: Thu, 31 Oct 2002 22:17:55 +0100\nSubject: GOOD DAY TO YOU\nX-Mailer: Microsoft Outlook Express 5.00.2919.6900\nDM\nMIME-Version: 1.0\nContent-Type: text/plain; charset="us-ascii"\nContent-Transfer-E...

Thu Oct 31 17:53:56 2002\nReturn-Path: <obong_715@epatra.com>\nX-Sieve: cmu-sieve 2.0\nReturn-Path: <obong_715@epatra.com>\nReply-To: obong_715@epatra.com>\nMessage-Id: <20021031253.g9VMreDj018024@bluewhale.cs.CU>\nFrom: "PRINCE OBONG ELEME" <obong_715@epatra.com>\nTo: webmaster@aclweb.org\nSubject: GOOD DAY TO YOU\nMIME-Version: 1.0\nContent-Type: text/plain;charset="iso-8859-1"\nContent-Transfer-Encoding: 7bit\nStatus: RO\n\nFROM HIS ROYAL MAJESTY (HRM) CROWN RULER OF ELEME KINGDOM \nCH...

Fri Nov 1 04:48:39 2002\nReturn-Path: <m_abacha03@www.com>\nX-Sieve: cmu-sieve 2.0\nReturn-Path: <m_abacha03@www.com>\nReply-To: m_abacha03@www.com>\nTo: R@M\nDate: Fri, 1 Nov 2002 01:45:04 +0100\nSubject: I Need Your Assistance.\nMessage-Id: <20021101094B.gA19mLu22932@perfectworld.mr.itd.UM>\nFrom: "Maryam Abacha" <m_abacha03@www.com>\nX-Mailer: Microsoft Outlook Express 5.00.2919.6900 DM\nMIME-Version: 1.0\nContent-Type: text/plain; charset="us-ascii"\nContent-Transfer-Encoding: 8bit\nX...

Figure 7.8 Raw data

guess wont know doesnt fault teaching correctly supplemental conversation yesterday would come back help project job needed talent involves working guy forget p taught well thing still done incorrectly ken forwarded kenneth seamanhouect 020120000 0911 robert e lloyd 020120000 0858 kenneth seamanhouectect cc subject schedule simple want know personally appreciate time spent ken taught well confidence carry torch thanks available kenneth seaman 020120000 0751 robert e lloydhouectect cc subject sc...

forwarded eve puckettcorpenron 11162000 0953 brenna neve 11162000 0916 mark thornehouectect eve puckettcorpenronenron michael neveshouectect EMAILADDRESS EMAILADDRESS EMAILADDRESS EMAILADDRESS EMAILADDRESS EMAILADDRESS EMAILADDRESS cc subject great day deborah miller 11162000 074123 cc subject great day get private free email msn hotmail URL share information create public profile URL URL

yuk sorry cancel deal making like want close trader scheduled 430 call wrap dont know better thing getting back track thanksgiving sorry

sharen deal changed caiso real time fyi sharen cason 04252001 0759 kate symespdxectect cc subject energy type several deal npsp delivery point firm energy thanks 590527 590523 589943 589942 589941 589919 589909 sent fillinger regarding roseville plant gas supply

Figure 7.9 Processed data

The ultimate data to train and validate the models consists of strings containing normalized words separated by spaces.

7.4   Methodology

As demonstrated in Figure 7.10, the core progression of this investigation involves several steps. Following data preparation, we execute word embedding [23,24] and employ deep learning models, such as CNN, RNN, LSTM, and Bi-LSTM, to classify data.

7.4.1   Word embedding

After data preparation and preprocessing, the original data is transformed into vectors. One vector conversion method involves constructing a library of words from the training dataset, assigning each word an index based on its frequency. Subsequently, the entire text is converted into a vector by substituting each word with its corresponding index in the library. Once the vector is derived from the text, an embedding class transforms each word into a numerical vector. The embedding class operates as a reference table that establishes an association between the indices of each term and a corresponding vector.

The parameters within the embedding class are initialized randomly. Throughout the training process, these parameters are updated via backpropagation. Once trained, the embedding class can encode words with similar meanings.

As depicted in Figure 7.11, the embedding class has a dimension of four. The maximum number of words in the dictionary for the embedding class is 40,000, with the dimension of the embedding vector being 100. The maximum number of

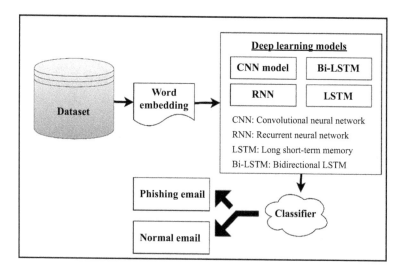

Figure 7.10   The main research flow

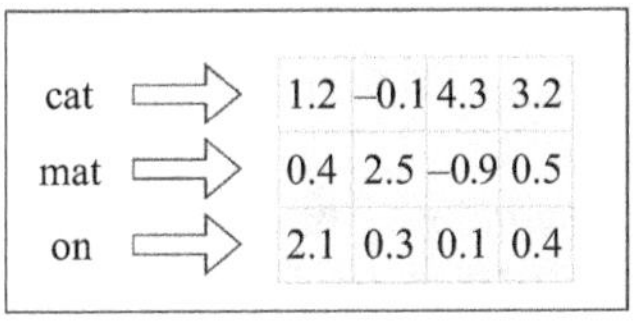

cat ⟹	1.2	–0.1	4.3	3.2
mat ⟹	0.4	2.5	–0.9	0.5
on ⟹	2.1	0.3	0.1	0.4

Figure 7.11   Description of embedding layer with four dimensions

tokens allowed in a document is 500; if the number is smaller, trailing zeros are added to meet the requirement. Subsequently, experiments are conducted using popular deep learning models such as CNN, RNN, LSTM, and Bi-LSTM.

7.4.2   Evaluation criteria

Binary classification tackles classification problems with only two labels. Generally, binary problems involve yes/no questions or 0–1 settings, such as determining whether an email is a scam. With two labels, distinctions can be made between positive and negative samples. For instance, an email can be classified as fraudulent (positive) or non-fraudulent (negative). The outcomes can be categorized as follows:

- True positive (TP): The prediction and the actual result are positive (the model correctly classifies positive samples).
- False positive (FP): The actual result is positive, but the prediction is negative (the model incorrectly classifies a positive sample as negative).
- True negative (TN): The prediction and the actual result are negative (the model correctly classifies negative samples).
- False negative (FN): The actual result is negative, but the prediction is positive (the model incorrectly classifies a negative sample as positive).

7.4.2.1   Accuracy

The most straightforward and widely used evaluation metric is accuracy. It calculates the ratio of correctly predicted samples to the total number of samples in the dataset. The formula for computing accuracy is as follows:

$$\text{Accuracy} = \frac{\text{TP} + \text{TN}}{\text{TP} + \text{TN} + \text{FP} + \text{FN}} \tag{7.10}$$

Assuming an accuracy of 90% implies that out of 100 samples, 90 are classified correctly. However, this evaluation metric can be misleading for an imbalanced test dataset (i.e., when the number of positive samples significantly exceeds the number of negative samples).

7.4.2.2   Precision and recall

Precision is the ratio of TP samples among those classified as positive (TP+FP). With a precision of 0.9, the model correctly predicts 90 out of 100 samples it classifies as positive.

Recall is defined as the ratio of TP samples among the points that are actually positive (TP+FN). With a recall of 0.9, it means that the model correctly predicts 90 samples out of 100 that are truly positive. High precision indicates high accuracy for correctly classified samples, while high recall signifies a low number of missed TP samples. An effective classification model exhibits high precision and recall, ideally as close to one.

In the context of phishing email detection, choosing a model with the highest recall is preferable, as a higher value minimizes the likelihood of the model overlooking phishing emails:

$$\text{Precision} = \frac{\text{TP}}{\text{TP} + \text{FP}} \tag{7.11}$$

$$\text{Recall} = \frac{\text{TP}}{\text{TP} + \text{FN}} \tag{7.12}$$

7.4.2.3 *F1-Score*

The *F*1-score is the harmonic mean of precision and recall, assigning equal importance to FNs and FPs. The *F*1-score value is calculated using the following formula:

$$\text{F1} - \text{score} = \frac{2 \times \text{Precision} \times \text{Recall}}{\text{Precision} + \text{Recall}} \tag{7.13}$$

A higher *F*1-score indicates higher precision and recall, resulting in a better classification model.

7.5 Results and analysis

In this research, experiments are conducted using CNN, RNN, LSTM, and Bi-LSTM models. For the CNN model, the following sequence is implemented: a 1D convolution layer with 128 filters, kernel size of 5, ReLU activation function, and a MaxPooling layer with a kernel size of 5. This sequence is iterated twice or more. Subsequently, a flatten layer and two fully connected layers are employed to obtain the final result, utilizing ReLU and Softmax activation functions.

Regarding the RNN model, the implementation consists of the following layers: a simpleRNN layer and a final fully connected layer employing the Softmax activation function. For the LSTM models, the implementation includes an LSTM layer with an output size of 16, followed by a flattened layer and a fully connected layer using the Softmax activation function. Lastly, the Bi-LSTM model is designed as follows: a BiLSTM layer with an output size of 32, a 1D convolution layer with a kernel size of 3, and a GlobalMaxPool1D layer. A flatten layer and a fully connected layer are then used to obtain the final result, employing ReLU and Softmax activation functions.

7.5.1 With CNN model

Figure 7.12 shows the accuracy and loss values when working with the CNN model. The CNN model appears to have performed very well in detecting phishing emails. The accuracy of 98.91% indicates that the model can correctly classify the vast majority of emails in the dataset.

The convergence of the accuracy pattern after epoch 20 suggests that the model has been sufficiently trained, and further training may not yield significant improvements.

The confusion matrix in Figure 7.13 also indicates a relatively good perfor-mance on the test set, with most emails correctly classified as either phishing or non-phishing. The high precision, recall, and $F1$-score values of 0.9986, 0.9795, and 0.9890, respectively, further confirm the effectiveness of the CNN model in detecting phishing emails.

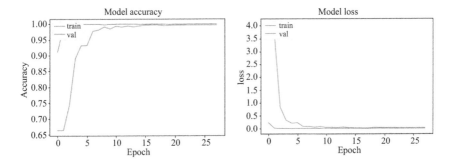

Figure 7.12   Accuracy and loss values of the CNN model

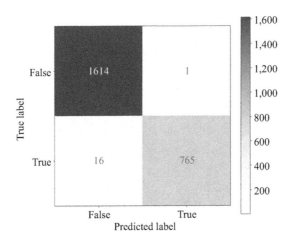

Figure 7.13   Confusion matrix of the CNN model

However, it is essential to note that the quality and representativeness of the dataset used to train the model can significantly impact its performance in real-world scenarios. Therefore, it is necessary to validate the model's performance on other datasets and evaluate its performance on new and evolving phishing attacks.

7.5.2   With RNN model

Figure 7.14 shows the accuracy and loss values when working with the RNN model. Comparing the results of the RNN model with the CNN model, it appears that the RNN model has a slightly lower accuracy of 98.16% compared to the CNN model's accuracy of 98.91%. However, the difference in accuracy is not very significant, and both models have performed very well in detecting phishing emails.

The confusion matrix for the RNN model, presented in Figure 7.15, shows a relatively good performance on the test set. The precision, recall, and *F*1-score of

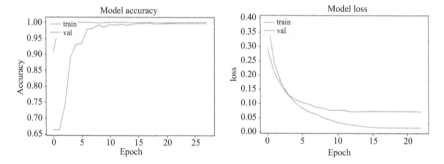

Figure 7.14   Accuracy and loss values of the RNN model

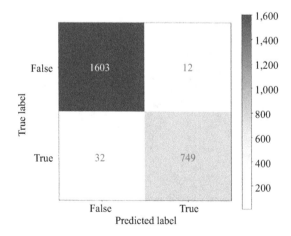

Figure 7.15   Confusion matrix of the RNN model

0.9842, 0.9590, and 0.9714, respectively, indicate that the model has a high ability to correctly identify phishing emails, with low FPs and FNs.

Compared to the CNN model, the RNN model has a lower recall, indicating a higher rate of FNs. However, the difference in the recall is relatively small, and the overall performance of the RNN model is still very good.

7.5.3 With LSTM model

Figure 7.16 shows the accuracy and loss values when working with the LSTM model. The LSTM model appears to have performed very well in detecting phishing emails, with an accuracy of 99.41%. The convergence of the accuracy pattern after about ten epochs indicates that the model has been sufficiently trained, and further training may not yield significant improvements.

The confusion matrix in Figure 7.17 shows that the LSTM model has achieved perfect precision and a high recall of 0.9820. This indicates that the model can correctly identify phishing emails while maintaining low FPs.

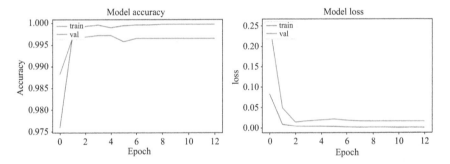

Figure 7.16   Accuracy and loss values of the LSTM model

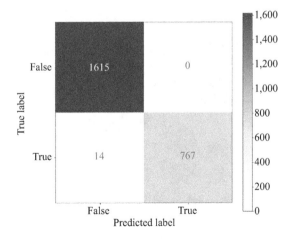

Figure 7.17   Confusion matrix of the LSTM model

The $F1$-score of 0.9909 further confirms the effectiveness of the LSTM model in detecting phishing emails. Compared to the CNN and RNN models, the LSTM model has the highest accuracy and precision and a slightly higher recall than the RNN model.

7.5.4   With Bi-LSTM model

Figure 7.18 shows the accuracy and loss values when implemented with the Bi-LSTM model. According to the results, the Bi-LSTM model has performed exceptionally well in detecting phishing emails, with an accuracy of 99.37%. The model's convergence was observed after about six epochs of training, indicating that it was sufficiently trained and did not require further iterations.

The confusion matrix in Figure 7.19 demonstrates that the Bi-LSTM model has achieved perfect precision and a high recall of 0.9807. This indicates that the model can accurately identify phishing emails while minimizing FPs.

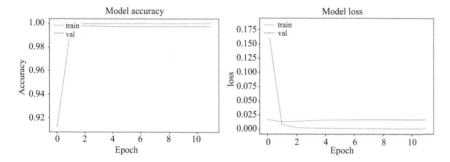

Figure 7.18   Accuracy value based on the Bi-LSTM model

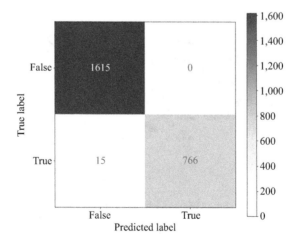

Figure 7.19   Confusion matrix based on the Bi-LSTM model

Table 7.1   Comparison table of measures between algorithms

Metrics	CNN	RNN	LSTM	Bi-LSTM
Precision	0.9986	0.9842	1.00	1.00
Recall	0.9795	0.9590	**0.9820**	0.9807
$F1$-score	0.9890	0.9714	**0.9909**	**0.9903**
Accuracy (%)	98.91	98.16	**99.41**	99.37

The bolded values indicate which metric will have the highest value for the respective algorithm.

The $F1$-score of 0.9903 further confirms the effectiveness of the Bi-LSTM model in detecting phishing emails. Compared to the CNN, RNN, and LSTM models, the Bi-LSTM model has achieved the second-highest accuracy, with slightly lower recall than the LSTM model.

Table 7.1 compares performances between CNN, RNN, LSTM, and Bi-LSTM in detecting phishing emails.

7.6   Discussion

Table 7.1 presents the performance metrics of four different models: CNN, RNN, LSTM, and Bi-LSTM, in detecting phishing emails.

The precision scores for all models are relatively high, ranging from 0.9842 to 1.00, indicating that the models have a low rate of FPs. The LSTM and Bi-LSTM models achieved perfect precision, the highest precision score possible.

The recall scores for all models range from 0.9590 to 0.9820, indicating that the models can correctly identify phishing emails but may have a higher rate of FNs. The LSTM model achieved the highest recall score of 0.9820, followed closely by the Bi-LSTM model, with a recall score of 0.9807.

The $F1$-scores for all models are relatively high, ranging from 0.9714 to 0.9909, indicating that the models perform well in detecting phishing emails. The LSTM model achieved the highest $F1$-score of 0.9909, followed by the Bi-LSTM model with an $F1$-score of 0.9903.

The accuracy scores for all models are high, ranging from 98.16% to 99.41%, indicating that the models can correctly classify phishing emails. The LSTM and Bi-LSTM models achieved the highest accuracy scores of 99.41% and 99.37%, respectively.

In conclusion, based on the performance metrics presented in the table, all models have demonstrated a high ability to detect phishing emails, with the LSTM and Bi-LSTM models performing slightly better than the CNN and RNN models' accuracy, recall, and $F1$-score. However, the choice of the most suitable model will depend on the specific requirements of a given scenario. Further validation of other datasets is necessary to confirm the models' effectiveness in real-world scenarios.

The study provides valuable insights into applying deep learning models for email phishing detection and highlights the need for further research. It also underscores the importance of developing effective and reliable methods for detecting email phishing attacks, given their significant impact on individuals and organizations. The study is an essential contribution to cybersecurity. It provides valuable insights into applying deep learning models for detecting email phishing attacks. It highlights the strengths and weaknesses of various models. It underscores the need for further research to develop more effective and reliable approaches for detecting these types of attacks.

7.7 Conclusion

In conclusion, the study provides important insights into applying deep learning models for detecting email phishing attacks. The evaluation of various models, including CNN, RNN, LSTM, Bi-LSTM, and LSTM, showed that LSTM achieved the highest accuracy of 99.41%. The study also revealed that the RNN model had the worst accuracy among all the models evaluated. These findings highlight the potential of deep learning models in improving the detection of email phishing attacks and the need for further research to develop more effective and efficient models.

In terms of future work, there is a need to develop more robust and reliable deep learning models for detecting email phishing attacks. The use of more advanced deep learning architectures, such as CNNs and transformer models, could be explored. Additionally, the study could be extended to include a larger dataset to evaluate the performance of the models in a more realistic setting. Furthermore, the effectiveness of the models could be assessed on different types of phishing attacks, including spear-phishing and whaling attacks, which are becoming increasingly common. Finally, integrating deep learning models with other traditional techniques, such as rule-based systems and machine learning algorithms, could be explored to improve the overall detection accuracy.

References

[1] SatheeshKumar, M., K. G. Srinivasagan, and G. UnniKrishnan. "A lightweight and proactive rule-based incremental construction approach to detect phishing scam." *Information Technology and Management* 23(4) (2022): 271–298.

[2] Xia, Tian. "A constant time complexity spam detection algorithm for boosting throughput on rule-based filtering systems." *IEEE Access* 8 (2020): 82653–82661.

[3] Bell, Simon and Peter Komisarczuk. "An analysis of phishing blacklists: Google safe browsing, openphish, and phishtank." In: *Proceedings of the Australasian Computer Science Week Multiconference*. 2020.

[4] Razaque, Abdul, Mohamed Ben Haj Frej, Dauren Sabyrov, Aidana Shaikhyn, Fathi Amsaad, and Ahmed Oun, "Detection of phishing websites using machine learning." In: *2020 IEEE Cloud Summit*, Piscataway, NJ: IEEE, 2020. pp. 103–107.

[5] Krupalin, Vijjeswarapu Abishek Heyer, G. V. Sriramakrishnan, and T. Daniya. "A survey and taxonomy of anti-phishing techniques for detecting fake websites." In: *2022 Fourth International Conference on Inventive Research in Computing Applications (ICIRCA)*. Piscataway, NJ: IEEE, 2022. pp. 601–604.

[6] Azeez, Nureni Ayofe, Sanjay Misra, Ihotu Agbo Margaret, Luis Fernandez-Sanz, and Shafi'i Muhammad Abdulhamid. "Adopting automated whitelist approach for detecting phishing attacks." *Computers & Security* 108 (2021): 102328.

[7] Fatima, Rubab, Muhammad Sadiq, Saleem Ullah, Gulnaz Ahmed, and Saqib Mahmood. "An optimized approach for detection and classification of spam email's using ensemble methods." (2023).

[8] Karim, Abdul, Mobeen, Shahroz, Khabib Mustofa, Samir Brahim Belhaouari, and S. Ramana Kumar Joga. "Phishing detection system through hybrid machine learning based on URL." *IEEE Access* 11 (2023): 36805–36822.

[9] Alhogail, Areej and Afrah Alsabih. "Applying machine learning and natural language processing to detect phishing email." *Computers & Security* 110 (2021): 102414.

[10] Bagui, Sikha, Debarghya Nandi, Subhash Bagui, and Robert Jamie White. "Classifying phishing email using machine learning and deep learning." In: *2019 International Conference on Cyber Security and Protection of Digital Services (Cyber Security)*. Piscataway, NJ: IEEE, 2019, pp. 1–2.

[11] Do, Phuc Hao, Tran Duc Le, Vladimir Vishnevsky, Aleksandr Berezkin, and Ruslan Kirichek. "A horizontal federated-learning model for detecting abnormal traffic generated by malware in IoT networks." In: *2023 25th International Conference on Advanced Communication Technology (ICACT), Pyeongchang, Republic of Korea*. Piscataway, NJ: IEEE, 2023, pp. 28–36, doi:10.23919/ICACT56868.2023.10079624.

[12] Reguig, Sara Azzouz. Intelligent detection: a classification-based approach to email (text) filtering. MS thesis. Altınbaş Üniversitesi/Lisansüstü Eğitim Enstitüsü, 2022.

[13] Tareen, Saima, Sibghat Ullah Bazai, Shafi Ullah, Rehmat Ullah, Shah Marjan, and Muhmmad, Imran Ghafoor. "Phishing and intrusion attacks: an overview of classification mechanisms." In: *2022 Third International Informatics and Software Engineering Conference (IISEC)*. Piscataway, NJ: IEEE, 2022. pp. 1–5.

[14] Hiransha, M., Nidhin A. Unnithan, R. Vinayakumar, K. Soman, and A. D. R. Verma. "Deep learning based phishing email detection." In: *Proceedings of the First AntiPhishing Shared Pilot Fourth ACM International Workshop on Security Privacy Analysis (IWSPA)*, Tempe, AZ, USA. 2018. pp. 1–5.

[15] Yin, Wenpeng, Katharina Kann, Mo Yu, and Hinrich Schütze. "Comparative study of CNN and RNN for natural language processing." arXiv preprint arXiv:1702.01923 (2017).

[16]   Xiao, Jianqiong and Zhiyong Zhou. "Research progress of RNN language model." In: *2020 IEEE International Conference on Artificial Intelligence and Computer Applications (ICAICA)*. Piscataway, NJ: IEEE, 2020. pp. 1285–1288.

[17]   Van, Nguyen Nang Hung, Pham Minh Tuan, Do Phuc Hao, Pham Cong Thang, and Tachibana Kanta. "Human action recognition method based on conformal geometric algebra and recurrent neural network." *Information and Control Systems*, 5(108) (2020): 2–11.

[18]   Ullah, Waseem, Amin Ullah, Ijaz Ul Haq, Khan Muhammad, Muhammad Sajjad, and Sung Wook Baik. "CNN features with bi-directional LSTM for real-time anomaly detection in surveillance networks." *Multimedia Tools and Applications* 80 (2021): 16979–16995.

[19]   Pham, Minh Tuan, Phuc Hao Do, and Kanta Tachibana. "Feature extraction for classification method using principal component based on conformal geometric algebra." In: *2016 International Joint Conference on Neural Networks (IJCNN)*, Vancouver, BC, Canada, 2016, pp. 4112–4117, doi:10.1109/IJCNN.2016.7727735.

[20]   Do, Phuc Hao, Truong Duy Dinh, Duc Tran Le, Lyudmila Myrova, and Ruslan Kirichek. "An efficient feature extraction method for attack classification in IoT networks." In: *Thirteenth International Congress on Ultra Modern Telecommunications and Control Systems and Workshops (ICUMT)*, Brno, Czech Republic, 2021, pp. 194–199, doi:10.1109/ICUMT54235.2021.9631726.

[21]   Radev, Dragomir. "CLAIR collection of fraud email, ACL data and code repository." ADCR2008T001 (2008).

[22]   Kaelbling, L. "Enron email dataset," CALO Project. http://www.cs.cmu.edu/~enron/, 2011.

[23]   Li, Yang and Tao Yang. "Word embedding for understanding natural language: a survey." *Studies in Big Data*, vol. 26. Springer, Cham, doi.org/10.1007/978-3-319-53817-4_4.

[24]   Grand, Gabriel, Idan Asher Blank, Francisco Pereira, and Evelina Fedorenko "Semantic projection recovers rich human knowledge of multiple object features from word embeddings." *Nature Human Behaviour* 6(7) (2022): 975–987.

Chapter 8

Securing hardware coprocessors against piracy using biometrics for secured IoT systems

Aditya Anshul[1], Rahul Chaurasia[1] and Anirban Sengupta[1,2]

Two crucial aspects need serious consideration concerning the underlying hardware used on the Internet of Things (IoT) systems: security and design optimization. Pirated or counterfeited hardware integrated into IoT systems may lead to different security threats such as confidential data leakage, malfunctioning of the device, and performance degradation. Therefore, the security of underlying hardware in IoT systems must be ensured for safe and reliable usage to end-users. This chapter discusses biometric-based methodologies to secure IoT hardware coprocessors against piracy and isolate counterfeited designs. Biometric-based approaches, such as fingerprint, facial, and palmprint biometrics, are discussed regarding their design flow, security strength, design cost overhead, tamper tolerance ability, and probability of coincidence (Pc). The biometric security in corresponding IoT hardware coprocessors is incorporated during the high-level synthesis phase (during the higher abstraction level of design) of the design process to ensure minimal design overhead and easy isolation of counterfeited designs. Moreover, for an adversary, the exact regeneration of digital templates to evade counterfeit detection is not possible due to incorporating unique biometric features during signature generation, unlike non-biometric-based approaches. The palmprint biometric hardware security approach renders higher tamper tolerance than the facial and fingerprint approaches (due to the larger encoding bits and signature strength), whereas the fingerprint biometric approach offers a smaller Pc than the facial and palmprint hardware security approaches.

8.1 Introduction

In the present era of advancement in modern technology, we observe the usefulness of the Internet of Things (IoT), from smartphones and smart homes to smart cities and several electronic gadgets. IoT exhibits the interconnectivity of the physical objects or devices termed things for performing several tasks such as

[1]Department of Computer Science and Engineering, Indian Institute of Technology Indore, India
[2]Computing and Microelectronics Unit, Indian Statistical Institute Kolkata, India

communication and transferring operational data among devices and systems over the Internet [1,2]. A thing can be a person, an object, or a device that can be configured with an Internet protocol address. However, the IoT framework may be prone to several security threats and vulnerabilities due to its underlying hardware as well as the network stack, which could lead to a loss of important information and degradation in performance. Therefore, the integrity and security of the IoT hardware devices must also be assured. Hence, security is the major concern for hardware researchers, IoT developers, and system architects, irrespective of the platforms.

Mainly there are three fronts on which security of the IoT devices must be assured: networking, software, and hardware. This chapter mainly focuses on securing the underlying hardware in IoT systems. The underlying IoT hardware or device may be composed of dedicated processors, coprocessors, and several digital signal coprocessors (DSP) hardware coprocessors for efficient usage and high performance [3,4]. Further, the IoT system developer must ensure the authenticity (genuineness) of IoT hardware being used in IoT system integration. Some well-known hardware or DSP hardware coprocessors are finite impulse response filter, infinite impulse response filter, discrete cosine transformation, fast Fourier transform, and JPEG-CODEC coprocessors. These hardware coprocessors are used in several IoT systems in the context of images, audio, and video-processing applications.

In the modern supply chain, these hardware coprocessors are imported from third-party (intellectual property) IP vendors to address time to market and design costs, which may not be trustworthy. However, these hardware coprocessors can be compromised at different levels of the design process-IP vendor level (third-party IP vendors), system-on-chip (SoC) integration level, where these IPs are integrated at fabless design houses and fabrication level. Therefore, by affecting the functionality or operations of these hardware coprocessors by malicious sources (at any stage of the design process), the functionality and security of the underlying hardware used in the IoT framework can be compromised. Moreover, the usage of counterfeited hardware coprocessor design may lead to backdoor Trojan insertion, resulting in leakage of confidential user information, excessive heat dissipation, and the malfunction of IoT devices. Therefore, anti-piracy and counterfeit hardware detection solutions are essential to ensure that IoT devices and systems are safe and reliable.

The crucial issues related to the hardware used in IoT devices are (a) the security of IoT hardware, (b) reliability, and (c) hardware design cost. To ensure the security (detective control against pirated hardware) of coprocessors used in IoT hardware, several methodologies, such as watermarking approaches, steganography-based approaches, and biometric-based approaches, have been presented by researchers. More specifically, the biometric-based approaches adopted are fingerprint-based, facial biometric-based, and palmprint biometric-based. The biometric-based approaches are more robust than the non-biometric-based approaches as they are non-replicable because of incorporating unique biometric features during secret signature generation. Biometric approaches are capable of detecting the IP piracy and counterfeiting of hardware coprocessors employed in IoT systems. We first extract the digital signature based on unique biometric features in biometric-based approaches. Then, the implantation of the digital signature into the hardware design is performed by exploiting the high-level synthesis (HLS) process [5,6].

8.2 IoT hardware security, threat model, and its significance

In the rapidly evolving landscape of technology, IoT hardware has become indispensable in various sectors, including information technology (IT) and global supply chain and management. These IoT devices play a pivotal role in the collection and transmission of essential and sensitive information on a global scale. However, the production process of IoT hardware involves the integration of diverse DSP IP cores sourced from multiple offshore entities, driven by the need to meet demanding time-to-market requirements. While this approach enables rapid innovation and deployment, it also exposes IoT hardware to a multitude of hardware threats.

Securing IoT/IP cores from piracy, counterfeiting, cloning, and fraudulent claim of ownership is crucial to maintain the integrity and reliability of IoT hardware. Counterfeit IoT devices, which have bypassed rigorous hardware testing and reliability analysis, can introduce various problems for end consumers. Such devices may exhibit substandard performance, vulnerability to attacks, and compromised security. Beyond individual impact, the proliferation of counterfeited or pirated IoT hardware at a global level can have far-reaching consequences, potentially leading to the leakage of important information and undermining relationships among different countries.

Moreover, the IP cores used in the production of IoT hardware are susceptible to fraudulent claims by SoC integrators during in-house system integration. Through counterfeiting practices, unscrupulous actors may falsely assert ownership over the IP cores, jeopardizing the reputation and IP rights of both the IoT/IP designer and the SoC integrator. As a result, the detection and isolation of counterfeit IoT hardware are critical at both the IoT/IP designer level and the SoC integration level to protect the esteem, trust, and integrity of all involved parties.

To address these challenges and mitigate the risks associated with hardware threats, various biometric-based security methodologies discussed later can provide security to the IoT hardware against these challenges. Biometric-based security leverages unique physical or behavioral characteristics of individuals to establish their identity and authenticate their access to IoT hardware. These methodologies encompass a range of techniques, including fingerprint recognition, iris scanning, voice recognition, and facial recognition. By incorporating these techniques at different stages of the IoT hardware lifecycle, from manufacturing to deployment and usage, manufacturers can fortify the security of their devices and ensure their authenticity and integrity.

The integration of biometric-based security methodologies into IoT hardware enhances the overall security posture and resilience of these devices. It provides a robust system for verifying the authenticity of IoT/IP cores and detecting any attempts at counterfeiting or fraudulent claims of ownership. By implementing biometric authentication mechanisms, manufacturers can establish a strong defense against hardware threats, reinforcing the trustworthiness and reliability of IoT hardware deployments.

8.3   Fingerprint biometric-based hardware security

Securing DSP hardware used in the production of IoT hardware against piracy, counterfeiting, and cloning using biometrics involves embedding/implanting an additional unique signature obtained through a different biometric approach into the register allocation phase of the HLS framework. In the counterfeit detection process, the extra information (unique signature) added to the design can be used to authenticate the IP originality and ownership.

8.3.1   Overview of the fingerprint biometric-based approach

The fingerprint biometric-based hardware security methodology offers an effective means to enhance the security of IoT hardware. In this approach [7], the unique signature used for embedding into the original design to provide security is derived from an image of a fingerprint captured using an optical scanner. The captured fingerprint image is processed to extract various features, particularly the minutiae points that represent unique characteristics of the fingerprint.

The generated minutiae points serve as the basis for creating a unique signature that will be associated with the IoT hardware. To establish the link between the fingerprint-based signature and the corresponding hardware security constraints, a predefined mapping rule is applied. This mapping ensures that the generated fingerprint-based signature aligns with the specific security requirements and constraints of the IoT hardware design.

To incorporate the fingerprint-based signature into the IP core design, the register allocation phase of the HLS framework is utilized. HLS involves the transformation of the IP core's algorithmic representation (typically written in high-level languages such as C/C++) into a scheduled hardware allocation design. This transformation takes into account the module library, which provides essential information about the area and latency of different functional units required for the target IP core, as well as any resource constraints specified by the user or obtained through optimization algorithms.

By embedding the fingerprint-based signature into the IP core design using the HLS framework, the resulting IoT hardware becomes resilient against various hardware security threats, including counterfeiting, cloning, piracy, and fraudulent claims of ownership. The integration of the fingerprint biometric-based approach enhances the security of the IoT hardware, ensuring that only authorized and legitimate devices can be used and reducing the risk of unauthorized access or tampering.

In Figure 8.1, an overview of the fingerprint biometric-based approach is presented, showcasing the key steps involved in capturing the fingerprint image, generating the fingerprint-based signature, mapping it to the hardware security constraints, and embedding it into the IP core design.

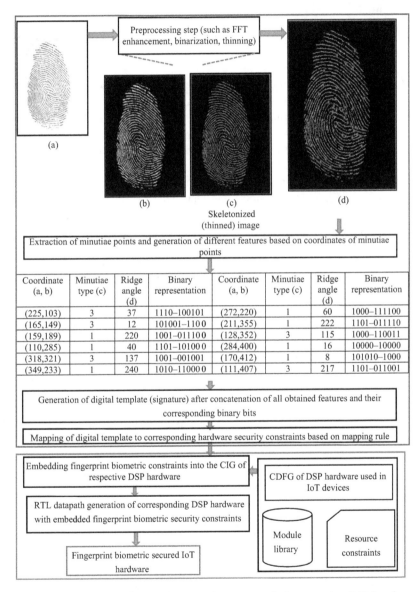

Figure 8.1   Fingerprint biometric security approach for securing IoT hardware: (a) actual fingerprint image, (b) binarized image, (c) skeletonized (thinned) image, and (d) minutiae points generation and extract

Overall, the fingerprint biometric-based hardware security methodology provides a robust and reliable solution for protecting IoT hardware against various hardware threats. By leveraging the unique characteristics of fingerprints and incorporating them into the design process, manufacturers can enhance the security and integrity of their IoT devices, bolstering the overall trustworthiness and reliability of the IoT ecosystem.

8.3.2 Details of the fingerprint biometric-based methodology

1. First, an optical scanner captures the DSP hardware vendor's fingerprint image. Fingerprint images contain distinct patterns known as ridges and valleys. The points in the fingerprint where ridge lines bifurcate (fork) into branch ridges are known as minutiae. These minutiae points are used as unique fingerprint biometric features implanted in the IoT hardware design in the fingerprint-based biometric approach.
2. Preprocessing of the captured fingerprint image followed after the first step for removing the unnecessary noise and increasing the quality of the fingerprint image. The important steps involved in the preprocessing are FFT enhancement, binarization, and thinning [7]. Furthermore, minutiae points are extracted from the improved thinned fingerprint image.
3. Then, a digital template (signature) is generated using the coordinates of the minutiae points (features). A single minutia point feature has four parameters: (a) x-axis coordinates, (b) y-axis coordinates, (c) minutiae type (e.g., if $c = 1$, then it indicates that the minutiae point is ridge ending, and if $c = 3$, then it indicates a ridge bifurcation, and so on), (d) ridge angle (clockwise angle from the horizontal axis). All the decimal values are converted into their corresponding binary equivalents, and then all the feature parameters $((a)+(b)+(c)+(d))$ are concatenated together to generate the final digital template (fingerprint-based signature).
4. The generated fingerprint-based signature is then converted/mapped into their corresponding hardware security constraints on the basis of a predefined mapping rule (e.g., embedding an extra edge between (even, even) node pair into the colored interval graph (CIG) in the case of "0" signature bit (during register allocation phase of the HLS), and embedding an extra edge between (odd, odd) node pair into the CIG in the case of "1" signature bit).
5. Furthermore, the generated fingerprint-based hardware security constraints are embedded into the design of the IP core (used in different IoT hardware) during the register allocation phase of the HLS to produce secured IoT hardware against various hardware threats (mentioned before). A CIG embeds the generated hardware security constraints in the design file. Two rules are followed to resolve the conflict raised due to embedding an extra edge between similar node colors. At first, swapping between the colors of storage variables is performed to meet the final requirement. Second, an extra-colored register is used if the first criterion is not satisfied. Based on these two rules, all the security

constraints are embedded, and the final CIG (security constraints embedded) and its corresponding register allocation table are obtained. The obtained register transfer level (RTL) structure (file) is transferred to the next level of the chip design process, known as RTL.

8.3.3 Advantages of the fingerprint (signature-based) biometric approach

The fingerprint biometric-based technique offers distinct advantages over steganography, which is a signature-free technique [8]. Unlike steganography, the fingerprint biometric approach generates a unique signature with stronger characteristics. The generated signature contains a larger number of bits and allows for different permutations based on various mapping criteria, concatenation orders, and the number of generated features.

The generated fingerprint-based signature adheres to the ISO/IEC Standard 24745, ensuring certain desirable properties. First, it satisfies the criterion of unlikability, meaning that multiple combinations of the signature can be generated from a single fingerprint image, and these combinations are completely unrelated to each other. This property adds an extra layer of security by making it challenging for attackers to identify the original fingerprint image from the generated signatures.

Second, the fingerprint-based signature is revocable. This means that if needed, the generated unique signature can be replaced with a new one derived from the same fingerprint image, but by varying different parameters such as the encoding rule, the number of generated features, the concatenation order of features, and the truncation size of the final signature. This revocability feature allows for the flexible management of the fingerprint-based signatures and provides an additional level of control over the security of the IoT hardware.

Furthermore, the fingerprint biometric-based technique ensures irreversibility. Reverse engineering the digital template to obtain the original fingerprint biometric data is virtually impossible without any prior knowledge of the specific parameters mentioned earlier. This irreversibility property guarantees that the fingerprint biometric data remains securely protected and reduces the risk of unauthorized access or misuse.

Moreover, the fingerprint biometric-based technique is nontransferable and spoof-proof. It is difficult to steal or forge the image of the fingerprint biometric approach or manipulate the generated features. This characteristic adds another layer of protection against unauthorized usage or fraudulent activities.

Additionally, the fingerprint biometric approach offers the advantage of being immune to aging. The image of the fingerprint and its generated features remain consistent over time, ensuring that the security and reliability of the IoT hardware are not compromised by changes in the fingerprint's appearance.

8.4   Facial biometric-based hardware security

The facial biometric is a highly recommended approach for ensuring robust hardware security in modern digital systems such as consumer electronics, IoT devices,

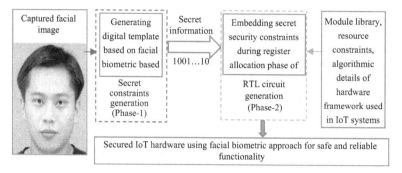

Figure 8.2   Overview of the facial biometric approach for enabling the security of IoT hardware

and cyber-physical systems, including liveness detection. The facial biometric approach also satisfies an ideal biometric technique's universality, permanence, collectability, and acceptability characteristics. The facial biometric approach incorporates unique facial features for generating the digital template; therefore, an adversary cannot replicate and reuse the digital facial template for authentication. The facial biometric approach for securing the IoT hardware against IP piracy and counterfeiting of their integrated hardware coprocessors is exploited in two phases—phase-1: covert security constraints generation using facial biometric approach and phase-2: RTL data path generation of corresponding integrated hardware embedded with facial biometric using HLS process as shown in Figure 8.2. The facial biometric approach depicts a robust security approach for crucial IoT hardware. It enables security by incorporating the unique facial features of IP vendors against IP piracy and counterfeited designs. The demonstration of the facial biometric approach for securing IPs used in IoT hardware is shown in Figure 8.3 [9].

In this approach, the process of generating secret constraints takes a facial image (captured using a high-resolution camera) as its input. Then, the captured facial image is subjected to specific grid size and spacing, which helps determine nodal points precisely and neutralizes face movement's impact during facial signature generation. Subsequently, nodal points are designated based on the designer's selected feature set (no. of features that impact the digital signature strength). Then, the naming conventions are assigned to each nodal point, which helps determine the feature dimensions. After that, a facial image with chosen features is generated (incorporating the details of nodal points with their coordinates and designer-selected features and their naming conventions). Subsequently, feature dimensions corresponding to each feature are evaluated and represented in their corresponding binarize form. The facial biometric-based digital template corresponding to the designer-selected feature set is generated based on the designer-selected feature order. At last, the facial signature is converted into covert secret constraints using the encoding rule specified by the IP designer.

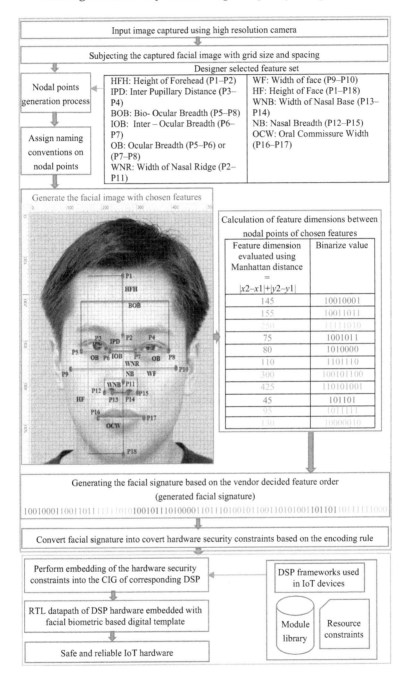

Figure 8.3   Demonstration of facial biometric approach for securing the IoT hardware

In the next phase of RTL data path generation, embedding the encoded covert secret constraints into the color interval graph corresponding to the DSP hardware framework is performed using the HLS process. The signature embedding process takes module library, resource constraints (hardware specification), and algorithmic description of hardware design as its input. Moreover, the HLS process transforms the algorithmic or behavioral description of the design into the RTL structure/data path. Finally, an RTL circuit is generated with a facial template corresponding to DSP hardware. These micro-IPs are responsible for safe and reliable IoT hardware that detects the counterfeited IPs and ensures design security against IP piracy.

8.4.1   Detection of counterfeited hardware using the facial biometric approach

Counterfeited IPs can be detected by matching the original facial signature of the IP vendor's facial image and extracting the register allocation information from the RTL design under test. Suppose the extracted facial biometric constraints from the regenerated signature are not matched with true secret constraints (belonging to true IP vendor facial image). In that case, the design is reported as counterfeited. Further, if the design is not counterfeited, the position of bits in the facial signature matches the embedded digital template. If matching is found, IP ownership is awarded to the true IP vendor, and also it nullifies the false claim of IP ownership.

8.5   Contactless palmprint biometric-based hardware security

8.5.1   Overview of the contactless palmprint biometric approach

The palmprint biometric-based methodology [10] uses a uniquely generated signature from an image of a palmprint to embed into the IP core design during HLS. This palmprint-based security methodology provides security from hardware threats like IP counterfeiting, cloning, piracy, and fraudulent claim of IP ownership. The overview of the palmprint biometric-based approach has been highlighted in Figure 8.4. In the first step, an image of the palmprint is captured with the help of a high-resolution camera. Then, a unique signature is generated with the help of the captured palmprint. Step 2 deals with the mapping of generated signature to its corresponding equivalent hardware security constraints on the basis of a predefined mapping rule. Finally, in step 3, the register allocation phase of the HLS framework is used to implant the generated hardware security constraints into the IP core design to provide immunity from the hardware security threats mentioned earlier. The final obtained palmprint-embedded IP core design protects IP core from IP counterfeiting, cloning, piracy, and the fraudulent claim of IP ownership and makes it easy to clearly demarcate between counterfeited and genuine IP during the counterfeit detection process [10].

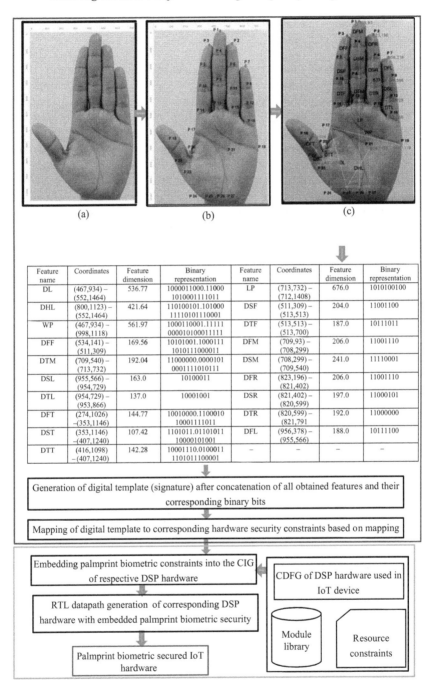

Figure 8.4   Palmprint biometric security approach for securing IoT hardware: (a) image of palmprint under grid size and spacing, (b) generation of nodal points on the palmprint image, and (c) feature generation on the basis of different nodal points

8.5.2 Details of the contactless palmprint biometric methodology [11]

1. First, the high-resolution image of the palmprint is placed under grid size and spacing to generate precise nodal points on the image. The palmprint image used to generate hardware security constraints is again used to generate the same nodal points during the authentication process. After that, each nodal point is assigned with different names to maintain uniqueness in deciding the feature set. For example, the DST feature (in Figure 8.4(c)) has two nodal points, P22 and P23, respectively.

2. After generating various features, dimensions corresponding to each feature are computed, and these decimal dimension values are converted into their equivalent binary values. Pythagoras theorem and Manhattan distance formulas are used to calculate the inclined line and straight-line distances, respectively, with the help of obtained each feature coordinates. Figure 8.4 illustrates all the generated nodal points and features.

3. The final palmprint-based digital signature is obtained after concatenating desired features. Thus, creating various permutations of concatenation order of feature set. For example, from Figure 8.4, the concatenated order and finally generated digital signature is $Z1+Z2+\cdots+Z18+Z19$ and $1000011\cdots111011$. Based on the maximum embedded value for a particular IP (given in the module library), initial that many bits from the signature are selected from the generated signature for embedding.

4. Finally, all the selected signature bits are mapped to their corresponding hardware security constraints on the basis of a predefined mapping rule, and then the hardware security constraints are embedded into the IP design (during the RTL phase of the HLS framework) [11]. The generation of hardware security constraints will depend on the number of storage variables (registers) required for a particular IP (given in the module library). For example, some of the generated hardware security constraints for the 8-point DCT IP core (having 23 storage variables) used in various IoT hardware devices are $\langle T0, T2\rangle$, $\langle T0, T4\rangle$, ..., $\langle T6, T14\rangle$, ..., $\langle T13, T17\rangle$, $\langle T13, T19\rangle$, and so on. These T0, T1, ..., and T23 are the storage variables (different registers) used in the IoT hardware design.

5. The final generated hardware security constraints are embedded in the design using CIG during the HLS framework.

8.5.3 Advantages of contactless palmprint biometric security [11] technique over various others

The palmprint biometric-based security approach [11] is more robust and provides higher security than compared to previous fingerprint [7] and facial-based biometric [9] techniques due to the following reasons: (a) the palmprint biometric-based security methodology facilitates a vast number of feature generation and various combinations of features to generate the final signature, thus increasing the uniqueness and robustness of the security mechanism. Compared to fingerprint and facial biometrics, it offers a lower probability of coincidence (*Pc*) and higher tamper tolerance due to the generation of many features, combinations, and encoding algorithms [11], (b) external factors, such as dirt and grease, do not affect this palmprint biometric approach as they are contactless (free from continuous use of optical scanner/camera). The high-resolution camera is only used in the beginning to capture the palmprint image, and the same image is stored and again used during the counterfeit detection process. Similarly, it is also immune to any injury. Any trusted employee/person in the company or IP vendors firm can be carefully selected (a person having a work bond for 5 years/average life cycle of a chip) to obtain the palmprint image and generate its corresponding signature. Suppose that person leaves the firm or meets with an unfortunate accident. In that case, it does not affect the authentication process due to the palmprint biometric security approach's contactless nature, (c) the contactless palmprint biometric technique facilitates an easier extraction of features than the fingerprint [7]-based biometric process. The generated features on the image of palmprint are also immune to aging. In contrast, features of facial biometrics [10] change from time to time, (d) due to its contactless, non-replicable, and non-vulnerable nature, unlike digital signature and stego-constraints, the palmprint biometric approach provides various benefits over the various state of the art [8,12,13]. This technique also satisfies all different ISO/IEC Standard 24745, such as irreversibility, unlikability, and revocability.

8.6 Other security techniques used for IoT security and identity authentication

There are various contemporary security techniques available for the security of IoT and identity authentication. For example, authors in Ref. [14] proposed a template protection scheme using fuzzy commitment and chaotic systems for multibiometrics. The scheme proposed in Ref. [14] uses a fusion of dual iris and thermal and visible facial images to generate a multibiometric template. In the first phase, forgery had been tackled using thermal face images. In the second phase, error-correcting code and fused binary features yield fuzzy commitment. Further, using a chaotic system, dual iris feature vectors are encrypted, and finally, performance is verified using score level fusion. Similarly, the authors in Ref. [15] also proposed a multibiometric fusion approach using dual iris, thermal, and visible face features. This chapter used a triangular norm to fuse matching scores of irises and facial features, which ultimately boosts the identification performance and protects the system against spoofing attacks. A security methodology based on electro-cardiograms (ECGs) had been proposed in Ref. [16], which uses convolution (CNN) tool of deep learning technique to validate ECG signals, subsequently providing security to IoT on the basis of signal acceptance and rejection. The input of CNN used in the proposed technique [16] accepts ECG signals and classifies them as accepted and rejected after analysis. In Ref. [16], all the processes, including preprocessing, feature extraction, and classification, are placed in only a single unit. A multi-algorithm feature level fusion-based iris verification was proposed in Ref. [17] to provide IoT security. An iris biometric authentication-based system was proposed in place of a normal text-based method using a broker server to increase authentication in IoT devices. Vectors of delta mean and multialgorithm mean were fused in the feature extraction phase, followed by the reduction method [17]. The classifier used in Ref. [17] uses the Euclidian mean for classifying. Various other biometric-based approaches are available in literature apart from those discussed earlier. Further, this chapter provides a novel comparison among fingerprint, facial, and palmprint-based biometric methodologies used to secure IP cores used in various IoT systems, as discussed in Section 8.1.

8.7   Comparative perspective and analysis

All three biometric approaches offer robust hardware security. However, a comparative perspective between each of them in terms of 12 unique parameters is provided in Table 8.1.

Figures 8.5–8.7 depict a comparison of the Pc among all three approaches [7,9,11]. The fingerprint biometric [7] shows a lower Pc than Refs. [9,11]. Facial biometric shows the highest value for the Pc due to a smaller number of features generation among all. The Pc indicates the proof of ownership. The higher the number of hardware security constraints embedded, the lower the Pc. Additionally, as evident from security analysis (from Figures 8.8–8.10), the palmprint biometric-based approach, among all three different biometric-based approaches, depicts more robust security strength due to higher tamper tolerance ability and contactless nature. The tamper tolerance depends on the encoding bits type (three bits in palmprint biometric, two bits in both facial and fingerprint biometric) and signature strength. Tamper tolerance is formulated as tamper tolerance=(encoding bits)$^{\text{signature size}}$. The signature bits used in palmprint, facial, and fingerprint biometrics are 231-, 81-, and 350-bit.

Furthermore, no adversary can regenerate the original digital template (for counterfeiting and piracy) as the final generated digital template depends on various crucial parameters such as minutiae points in the case of fingerprint biometrics, nodal points in the case of facial and palmprint biometrics, feature set, feature order (concatenation order), grid size and spacing, and so on. Moreover, fingerprint biometrics involves complex preprocessing steps, such as FFT enhancement, binarization, and thinning. The detection of counterfeited DSP hardware is complex in the case of fingerprint and palmprint biometrics compared to facial biometrics due to more detailed minutiae point generation and more accurate and a higher number of nodal point generations, respectively. The fingerprint biometric is prone to external factors like dirt, grease, and so on, while palmprint and facial do not. However, facial features may change due to aging, while palmprint and fingerprint features do not.

Figure 8.11 describes the comparison of design cost between facial [9] and palmprint biometric [11] approaches for embedding generated hardware security

Table 8.1 Comparative perspective among fingerprint, facial, and palmprint biometric approaches

S. no.	Characteristics/parameters	Fingerprint biometric approach [7]	Facial biometric approach [9]	Palmprint biometric approach [11]
1.	Dependence on external factors	Yes; grease and dirt may affect the fingerprint verification process	No	No
2.	Preprocessing	Image enhancement is required for extracting accurate minutiae points	Not required	Not required
3.	Implementation complexity	High	Less	Moderate
4.	Security approach	Depends on minutiae points generation on fingerprint image	Depends on nodal points generation on facial image	Depends on nodal points generation on palm image of IP vendor
5.	Security strength	More robust and unique security	Less unique than palmprint biometric	Most robust and unique security
6.	Cost overhead (due to embedded signature)	Higher	Almost negligible	Moderate
7.	Counterfeited DSP hardware detection	More complex	Robust and seamless	Complex than facial biometric
8.	Probability of coincidence	Lesser Pc value, indicating stronger digital evidence	Pc value higher than fingerprint and palmprint biometric approach	Pc value higher than fingerprint and lower than facial biometric
9.	Tamper tolerance capability	Moderate	Lower than palmprint and fingerprint-based approach	Higher
10.	Digital template regeneration by an adversary	Not possible (as the regeneration of digital template depends on minutiae points, feature set, feature order, grid size, etc.)	Not possible (as the regeneration of digital template depends on nodal points, feature set, feature order, grid size, etc.)	Not possible (as the regeneration of digital template depends on nodal points, feature set, feature order, grid size, etc.)
11.	Security approach type	Not contactless	Contactless	Contactless
12.	Permanence	Features independent of aging	Aging may impact the facial feature dimensions	Features independent of aging

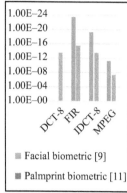

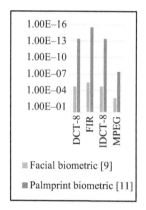

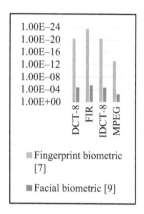

Figure 8.5   *Comparison of probability of coincidence between fingerprint [7] and palmprint biometrics [11]*

Figure 8.6   *Comparison of probability of coincidence between facial [9] and palmprint biometrics [11]*

Figure 8.7   *Comparison of probability of coincidence between fingerprint [7] and facial biometrics [9]*

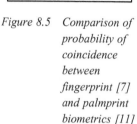

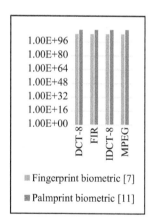

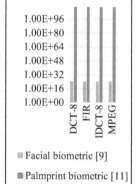

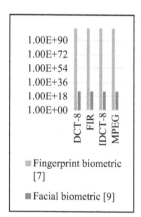

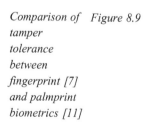

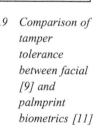

Figure 8.8   *Comparison of tamper tolerance between fingerprint [7] and palmprint biometrics [11]*

Figure 8.9   *Comparison of tamper tolerance between facial [9] and palmprint biometrics [11]*

Figure 8.10   *Comparison of tamper tolerance between fingerprint [7] and facial biometrics [9]*

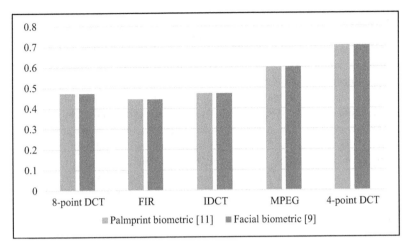

*Figure 8.11   Comparison of design cost between facial [9] and palmprint
biometrics [11]*

constraints into the IP hardware design file during HLS. The design cost includes design area and design latency in equal weightage. Design cost overhead to embed the hardware security constraints into the IP hardware design file is higher in the case of fingerprint biometrics [7] due to the generation and embedding of a large number of hardware security constraints than palmprint [11] and facial biometric [9]. Facial biometrics [9] shows the lowest design cost overhead among all [7,9,11]. IP core benchmarks (adopted from Refs. [18,19]) and the NanGate library based on a 15-nm technology scale [20] have been used to evaluate design cost. Palmprint biometric approach is contactless, while others are not. The implementation complexity of the fingerprint biometric [7] approach is more complex as compared to Refs. [9,11] due to the requirement of an external optical scanner and detailed minutiae point generation. Palmprint and facial images can be captured using a high-resolution camera or downloaded from standard databases like Ref. [21]. Similarly, a fingerprint image captured through an optical scanner can be used.

Apart from various advantages, biometric-based techniques have some limitations, such as requiring an additional biometric setup (increase in the cost). Sometimes biometrics databases can also be compromised (comprises the security) and are prone to external environments (like dirt, grease, etc.) if the approach is non-contactless. Unlike signature-free techniques (such as steganography), the biometric-based approach is complex in nature due to the involvement of extraction of the signature from biometric images.

8.8   Conclusion

This chapter discusses the three different biometric techniques (fingerprint-, facial-, and palmprint-based, respectively) to secure the IoT hardware against the various hardware security threats, such as counterfeiting, cloning, piracy, and fraudulent claim of IP ownership. As discussed earlier in this chapter, IoT hardware is a crucial element in this current IT environment, responsible for collecting, storing, and transferring essential and sensitive information across the globe. So, to protect the esteem and integrity of IP designers and SoC integrators and ensure the safety of end consumers, it is crucial to safeguard IoT hardware against the different hardware threats mentioned before. All of the discussed biometric-based techniques are capable of generating unique (non-replicable and non-vulnerable) signature satisfying all different ISO/IEC Standard 24745, such as irreversibility, unlikability, and revocability, which is implanted as security constraints in the design file of IoT hardware/ IP core to provide security against hardware threats mentioned before.

Acknowledgement

This work is technically and financially supported by CSIR grant no. 22/0856/23/ EMR-II.

References

[1]   A. A. Ateya, M. Mahmoud, A. Zaghloul, N. F. Soliman, and A. Muthanna, "Empowering the Internet of Things using light communication and distributed edge computing," *Electronics*, 11(9), 1511, 2022.

[2]   S. Bushelenkov, A. Paramonov, A. Muthanna, *et al.*, "Multi-story building model for efficient IoT network design," *Mathematics*, 11(6), 1403, 2023.

[3]   M. Hammad, A. A. Abd El-Latif, A. Hussain, *et al.*, "Deep learning models for arrhythmia detection in IoT healthcare applications," *Computers and Electrical Engineering*, 100, 108011, 2022.

[4]   B. Abd El-Rahiem and M. Hammad., "A multi-fusion IoT authentication system based on internal deep fusion of ECG signals," In: Abd El-Latif, A.A., Abd-El-Atty, B., Venegas-Andraca, S.E., Mazurczyk, W., Gupta, B.B. (eds), *Security and Privacy Preserving for IoT and 5G Networks. Studies in Big Data*, vol. 95, Springer, Cham, 2022.

[5]   A. Sengupta and S. Kundu, "Guest editorial securing IoT hardware: Threat models and reliable, low-power design solutions," *IEEE Transactions on Very Large Scale Integration (VLSI) Systems*, 25(12), 3265–3267, 2017.

[6]   R. Schneiderman, "DSPs evolving in consumer electronics applications [special reports]," *IEEE Signal Processing Magazine*, 27(3), 6–10, 2010.

[7]   A. Sengupta and M. Rathor, "Securing hardware accelerators for CE systems using biometric fingerprinting," *IEEE Transactions on Very Large Scale Integration (VLSI) Systems*, 28(9), 1979–1992, 2020.

[8]   A. Sengupta and M. Rathor, "IP core steganography for protecting DSP kernels used in CE systems," *IEEE Transactions on Consumer Electronics*, 65(4), 506–515, 2019.

[9] A. Sengupta and M. Rathor, "Facial biometric for securing hardware accelerators," *IEEE Transactions on Very Large Scale Integration (VLSI) Systems*, 29(1), 112–123, 2021.

[10] R. Chaurasia, A. Anshul, A. Sengupta, and S. Gupta, "Palmprint biometric versus encrypted hash based digital signature for securing DSP cores used in CE systems," *IEEE Consumer Electronics Magazine*, 11, 73–80, 2022, doi:10.1109/MCE.2022.3153276.

[11] A. Sengupta, R. Chaurasia, and T. Reddy, "Contact-less palmprint biometric for securing DSP coprocessors used in CE systems," *IEEE Transactions on Consumer Electronics*, 67(3), 202–213, 2021.

[12] A. Sengupta and S. Bhadauria, "Exploring low-cost optimal watermark for reusable IP cores during high-level synthesis," *IEEE Access*, 4, 2198–2215, 2016.

[13] B. L. Gal and L. Bossuet, "Automatic low-cost IP watermarking technique based on output mark insertions," *Design Automation for Embedded Systems*, 16(2), 71–92, 2012.

[14] N. Wang, Q. Li, A. A. Abd El-Latif, *et al.*, "A novel template protection scheme for multi biometrics based on fuzzy commitment and chaotic system," *Signal, Image and Video Processing,* 9, 99–109, 2015.

[15] N. Wang, Q. Li, A. A. Abd El-Latif, J. Peng and X. Niu, "Multibiometric fusion for identity authentication: Dual iris, visible and thermal face imagery," *International Journal of Security and its Applications*, 7, 33–44, 2013.

[16] M. Hammad, A. M. Iliyasu, I. A. Elgendy, and A. A. Abd El-Latif, "End-to-end data authentication deep learning model for securing IoT configurations," *Human-centric Computing and Information Sciences*, 12(4), 2022.

[17] R. Gad, A. A. Abd El-Latif, S. Elseuofi, H. M. Ibrahim, M. Elmezain, and W. Said, "IoT security based on iris verification using multi-algorithm feature level fusion scheme," In *2019 Second International Conference on Computer Applications & Information Security (ICCAIS)*, pp. 1–6, 2019.

[18] University of California Santa Barbara Express Group, accessed on March, 2022. [Online]. Available: http://express.ece.ucsb.edu/benchmark/

[19] R. Jain and P. R. Panda, "An efficient pipelined VLSI architecture for lifting based 2D-discrete wavelet transform," In *Proceedings IEEE International Symposium on Circuits and Systems (ISCAS)*, pp. 1377–1380, May, 2007.

[20] 15 nm open cell library, last accessed on January, 2022. [Online]. Available: https://si2.org/open-celllibrary/.

[21] CASIA Palmprint Database, NIST, Chinese Academy of Sciences, accessed on January, 2022. http://biometrics.idealtest.org/dbDetailForUser.do?id=5#/.

Chapter 9

Intelligent authentication system using graphical one-time passwords

Adarsha Sigdel[1], Kheng Cher Yeo[1], Yassine Maleh[2] and Mamoun Alazab[1]

Conventional alphanumerical passwords have been the most common authentication medium for years; however, it is plagued by a fundamental problem: secure strong passwords are hard to create and remember, leading to insecure practices. There have been several studies proposing alternatives to replace alphanumerical passwords. However, such alternatives have not reached mainstream usage or widespread application. Our study has reviewed several authentication schemes and found that graphical authentication can be an alternative solution, leveraging visual components instead of text and taking advantage of the human mind's ability to remember graphical and positional information. Our study conducts an in-depth analysis of the existing graphical passwords and presents a graphical one-time-password (OTP) scheme as a replacement for alphanumerical passwords. The proposed one-time graphical password is built upon the user remembering their four preselected picture passwords displayed on a random 4×4 matrix and entering the (x,y) coordinate of the picture password on the matrix. Several different categories of picture passwords are provided, with the authentication matrix displaying decoy images along with the picture passwords. An in-depth analysis of the security, memorability and usability aspects is presented to show that our graphical OTP scheme can successfully thwart common graphical password attacks (such as shoulder-surfing and dictionary attacks). We also demonstrate that the proposed graphical authentication system can protect against various known attacks and satisfies different criteria as a replacement for alphanumerical passwords.

9.1 Introduction

Cybercrime is a top concern for government, businesses and individuals today. Damages related to cybercrime are projected in Trillions globally by the end of 2022.

[1]Faculty of Science and Technology, Charles Darwin University, Australia
[2]LaSTI Laboratory, Sultan Moulay Slimane University, Morocco

Passwords are commonly compromised. Compromised passwords cause over 80% of all data breaches. Hackers are actively on the lookout for innovative ways to steal passwords to bypass security controls (e.g. social engineering [1]). A password attack is simply when a hacker attempts to steal the password. Most traditional systems use some form of authentication system-based around mostly three factors as follows:

- something you know (e.g. a personal identification number (PIN), password or response to a challenge);
- something you have (e.g. a physical token, smartcard or software certificate);
- something you are (e.g. a fingerprint or iris scan).

To make authentication systems secure, a combination of these factors is used, called multi-factor authentication [2]. Multi-factor authentication is considered to be the most effective controls to prevent an adversary from accessing sensitive information.

Alphanumeric passwords fall under the something you know factor and are the most common method of authentication method despite having various security issues, harder to remember and other secure alternatives available. Although alphanumeric passwords are widely used and easier to implement, it has some severe weaknesses. For example, users tend to create very short passwords that are easy to remember. A stronger password is longer in length and harder to guess, making it harder to remember. Due to this fact, users tend to create short and easy passwords. Moreover, an average person logs into eight or more systems in a day but remembering eight different passwords for each system is almost impossible to remember [3]. So, they tend to reuse passwords which are undesirable as one compromised password can compromise multiple accounts and systems.

Due to the inherent issues with alphanumerical password authentication, there is a need for a more secure alternative authentication method that replaces alphanumeric passwords. Several alternative authentication systems have been developed but are not used as widely as alphanumeric passwords [4]. Such alternatives include OTP (one-time password), certificate-based authentication systems, biometrics and graphical passwords. However, these authentication systems are not used widely as most of them require additional hardware and are expensive and complex to implement. There are several criteria that determine a good authentication system that is a viable replacement to alphanumerical passwords, such as improved security, easily memorable and ease of use and implementation.

9.2   Alphanumeric password-based authentication

Alphanumerical passwords have been widely used for authentication by operating systems, applications and websites despite their recognized vulnerabilities generally related to user behaviour. Several studies have found that the major vulnerabilities in the passwords are due to user behaviour, either by sharing passwords across or creating weak passwords that are easy to remember. The issue with secure passwords is that they are harder to remember, and easy-to-remember passwords are unsecure, which is famously referred to as the password problem [5]. Password problem arises due to the conflicting requirements that passwords should be easy to remember, but passwords must also be hard to guess and changed frequently. The password problem arises due to the limitations of human beings' memory on remembering things, and the fact that remembering multiple passwords makes it confusing and harder. The issue worsens when users are required to change their passwords periodically, usually every 90 days, creating new passwords that they need to remember. This leads to a scenario where the users write down their passwords to reduce the burden of remembering them, which causes additional security problems. In most cases, users tend to choose a single password across multiple systems and applications, which means if a password from one system is compromised, multiple systems can be compromised. Users also find their own ways of beating the system policies for periodic password changes by just adding one more letter to make it different. This leads to users creating predictable passwords that can easily be cracked using brute-force attacks and dictionary attacks.

Furthermore, there are also several security issues with alphanumeric password-based authentication systems, such as snooping, spying, social engineering attacks, brute-forcing passwords and dictionary attacks [4]. A user's password can be stolen by watching them during the authentication, which is also known as shoulder surfing. It can also be compromised by using spyware software to record sensitive information. Phishing email and spoofing are used to conduct social engineering attacks to steal sensitive information, including passwords. Passwords are also prone to brute-force attacks where the intruder tries all possible combinations of the password. Passwords are also prone to dictionary attacks where the attacker uses common words in a dictionary rather than trying all possibilities. Dictionary attacks are successful since common words are easier to remember than random letters, and users tend to use them in their passwords. Due to these reasons, it is essential to find alternatives to replace alphanumerical passwords.

9.3   Alternative authentication systems

Several extensive studies have been carried out to find alternative authentication to replace alphanumerical passwords [6]. OTP systems, certificate-based authentication systems, biometrics and non-alphanumerical passwords have great potential to replace alphanumerical passwords, and several studies have been done to prove their usefulness.

9.3.1   One-time passwords

One of the potential alternatives to an alphanumerical password is OTP. OTP falls under something you have category has two types: token-based systems and tokenless systems. Token-based systems synchronize with an authentication server and utilize the same hashing algorithm. Token-based OTP is of two types: TOTP (time-based OTP) and HOTP (HMAC-based OTP) [7]. The time-based algorithm is used to generate a six-digit token during a periodic interval and displayed on the token's screen, similar to Google Authenticator. HOTP uses an event-based algorithm to generate an OTP when the button on the token is pressed and increments the counter. Such OTPs do not expire until used. TOTP and HOTP both have their own strengths and weaknesses. TOTP has an advantage in the fact that there is a limited amount of time before the password expires, due to which there is a limited window of it being compromised. However, the authentication server and the token may be out of sync and need replacement. HOTP has its strength in that it does not require the clock to be synced. However, due to the OTP not expiring until used, the attacker has more chance to attack. The strength of token-based systems is that they require users to identify themselves using something they have and provides nonrepudiation since the OTP is only known to the user. Moreover, it is not vulnerable to shoulder surfing and keyloggers, unlike alphanumerical passwords. However, the token can be stolen, lost, or destroyed, which can lock the user out until a new token is issued. On the other hand, tokenless systems use an alternative communication medium such as SMS or email to deliver an OTP. The main advantage of a tokenless system is that you do not need a token. Despite all the benefits, a tokenless system can be limited to cellular reception or access to the email account as it relies on the out-of-band channel's security to receive the OTP.

9.3.2   Certificate-based authentication

Another alternative is certificate-based authentication which uses digital certificates to authenticate users based on the PKI (public key infrastructure) [8]. PKI is based on the principle of trust, where a computer verifies the identity of the certificate. The certificate allows the validation of the subject's identity, usually a person or machine. Certificates are issued by the certificate authority. These are trusted machines that issue and validate the certificates and are commonly trusted by operating systems and web browsers, thus making it possible for authentication to occur on the machine or over the Internet. Certificates are most commonly used to identify the validity of the websites on the browsers and provide a seamless single sign-on for various applications without the need for additional hardware. Similarly, smart cards are a typical example of a certificate-based authentication mechanism where digital signatures are loaded into the smart card, identifying the user. Smart cards can uniquely identify a particular user and can also be revoked and reissued easily if lost or stolen. Moreover, they are designed to be resistant to any tampering to extract the digital certificate. However, they require smart card readers and may not be suitable for widespread utilization.

9.3.3   Biometric authentication

Biometrics uses the 'something you are' factor and is based on a person's physical characteristics that do not change and are unique [9]. Common biometrics currently in use are finger and palm prints, iris, voice scans and retina scans. A significant advantage of a biometric system is the ease of use that does not require users to remember a password and carry a token. It is also tough to steal or replicate, unlike passwords. However, the biometric enrolment phase includes scanning of the biometric data to find distinct biometric features known as a trait which are stored as a digital representation called a biometric template [10]. It requires greater protection as they cannot be reissued simply like a password or token, which raises serious security concerns over biometric authentication. In addition to that, different applications might use the same biometric trait for authentication. If an attacker gains access to the biometric template stored in one application, it can be used to access other applications that use the same biometric traits. Furthermore, attackers can spoof the biometric system if it cannot differentiate between fake and genuine characteristics. Fingerprint sensors can be fooled by fake fingerprint films. In addition to that, the efficiency of the biometric systems under non-ideal conditions is an issue of concern. Biometric data, when read during authentication, is slightly different each time, and there is no exact match to the stored template, due to which there must be a threshold set for the near-identical match. This creates an issue for false-positive and false-negative matches. A false-positive match could allow an attacker through the authentication, and a false-negative could deny the genuine user access. In recent days, many smartphones use fingerprints or facial scans for authentication. However, its widespread use across different platforms has been limited by hardware requirements and its unsuitability for network authentication.

9.3.4 Graphical password authentication

Graphical password leverages graphical components instead of text and takes advantage of the human mind's ability to remember graphical and positional information. Graphical passwords can be categorized as recognition-based, recall-based, cued-recall-based and hybrid systems. Recognition-based graphical password involves recognizing previously seen images without any aid. On the contrary, recall-based is retrieval without any aids to the memory. In cued-recall graphical passwords, the user is asked to recall the visual cue in a previously selected image. There are also various graphical passwords that use a mixture of the three different types called hybrid systems. Graphical passwords have diverse nature and can be used widely compared to other authentication systems.

A comparison of the alternative authentication schemes to the alphanumerical password has been done below to analyse the security, memorability and usability aspects, as shown in Table 9.1.

Based on our comparison, graphical passwords seem to be a suitable replacement for alphanumeric passwords due to their strengths and versatility and will be discussed further in the next section.

9.4 Graphical passwords

There are various types of graphical passwords, which can be categorized into recognition-, recall-, cued-recall-based and hybrid systems. An in-depth review and analysis of different graphical passwords from different categories have been conducted to evaluate their security, memorability and usability aspects. Table 9.2 shows the different graphical password schemes (GPSs) from different categories.

Table 9.1   Comparison of alternative authentication schemes

	Alphanumerical password	One-time password systems	Certificate-based authentication systems	Biometrics	Graphical passwords
Security	Weak passwords are created. Passwords can be shared, stolen, guessed or reused	Two types: token-based and token-less. OTP is only known to the user. Tokens can be lost and misused	Requires users to authenticate with the use of digital certificates. Certificates can be revoked if stolen	Biometric template if stolen, cannot be revoked	Various secure password schemes are available
Memorability	Complex passwords are harder to remember so users create weak passwords	No need to remember the password. Authenticate using a one-time password	No need to remember the password. Authenticate using a certificate	Nothing to remember	Visual information is easy to remember for the human brain
Usability	Widely used as a primary authentication scheme	Easy to use	Commonly used in smart cards. Easy to use	Users do not need to remember a password or carry a token	Easy to remember and use. No token is required

Table 9.2   Graphical password schemes categories

Categories	Graphical password schemes
Recognition	WYSWY [11], Evo-pass [12], PassApp [13], Déjà vu [14], Passfaces [15], Convex Hull Click Scheme [16], LocPass [17]
Recall	PassShapes [18], Pass-Go [19], DRAW-A-PIN [20], gRAT [21], TMD [22]
Cued-recall	Passpoint [23], PassMatrix [24], PassBYOP [25], HapticPoints [26]
Hybrid	CD-GPS [27], GOTPass [28], CuedR [29], Jumbled PassSteps [30]

9.4.1   Recognition-based GPS

Several recognition-based GPSs have been developed over the last decades which have been compiled for our comparison based on their security, memorability and usability aspects, as shown in Table 9.3.

WYSWY (Where You See is What You Enter) [11] uses an authentication process where a user needs to map a pattern from a larger grid to a different grid. It is a complex process unsuitable for small-screened devices and suffers from intersection attacks.

Table 9.3 Comparison of recognition-based graphical password schemes

	Déjà vu [14]	Passfaces [15]	Convex Hull Click Scheme [16]	LocPass [17]	WYSWY [11]	Evo-pass [12]	PassApp [13]
Security	Prevents weak password creation Not resilient to brute-force and shoulder-surfing attacks	More secure than passwords Not resilient to brute-force, dictionary, and shoulder-surfing attacks	Uses pass icons as passwords Guards against shoulder-surfing attacks by human observation, video recording, or electronic capture	Prevents shoulder-surfing attacks No offset mechanism is used to confuse the attacker	One-time password scheme Complex and resistant against brute-force and shoulder-surfing attacks Vulnerability against intersection attacks	Personal images and pass sketches provide security Pass sketches evolve periodically Fewer chances of shoulder-surfing attackers to recognize pass sketches	Vulnerable to dictionary attacks. Robust against strong shoulder-surfing attack Utilizes installed apps as a shared secret for authentication
Memorability	Better memorability than PIN/Password	Easy to remember	Memorability is similar to other challenge-response graphical password systems	High memorability	High memorability	High memorability	Reduces additional memory burden
Usability	Higher login time	Easy to use	Easy to learn and use but time-consuming to enter	Need training Long execution time as it needs to follow an algorithm to find out the pass location	Higher login time	The average login time is 4.1 s, which is an acceptable range	Enhances the experience of the users PassApp (7.27 s) costs users slightly longer to unlock than the numeric PIN (4.7 s) and pattern lock (3.0 s)

Evo-pass [12] scheme requires users to recognize corresponding pass sketches from a collection of challenge images for authentication. Personal images and pass sketches provide greater security which also evolves periodically.

PassApp [13] is based on the user recalling the apps installed on the mobile phone to authenticate. Thus, eliminating the registration phase reduces the cognitive burden of remembering passwords. The study has also shown that it is resistant to shoulder-surfing attacks but vulnerable to dictionary attacks.

Déjà vu [14] requires users to recognize and select their pass images from a challenging set of images to authenticate. It uses random images, which makes it secure. It only uses a single authentication round, and the password size is very small.

Passfaces [15] was inspired by the human's ability to recognize faces. The authentication phase requires users to select pass faces from a grid and uses a multiple authentication round. However, the authentication scheme is not secure against shoulder-surfing, brute-force and dictionary attacks.

Convex Hull Click Scheme [16] authentication requires users to click inside the hull or region created by three pass icons. It also uses multiple authentications round and does not require users to click the pass image making it resistant to shoulder-surfing attacks.

LocPass [17] authentication scheme requires users to memorize the locations of the images. The user is prompted to select the pass location on a grid that has five types of images. Since meaningful images are used there are no issues with memorizing the images.

9.4.1.1   Recall-based GPS

A comparison of different recall-based GPS has been done based on their security, memorability and usability aspects.

PassShapes [18] requires users to draw geometric shapes to eight distinctive straight-line strokes regardless of the size or position on the screen. The straight lines of the shapes create and remember the shape easier.

Pass-Go [19] is inspired by the draw-a-secret scheme but uses grid intersection points instead of using grid cells to draw the password. This makes PassShapes more secure by increasing password space.

DRAW-A-PIN [20] requires users to draw a pin on the touchscreen rather than typing the PIN. The scheme uses drawing traits so that even if an attacker knows the PIN, they cannot log in.

gRAT [21] requires users to draw a pattern on the same set of images selected during the registration phase from a random set of images. It is similar to a lock screen on Android phones but uses an image for the patterns.

TMD [22] uses a multi-layered scheme for touchscreen devices where the user needs to select cells from a grid without lifting a finger in a single motion (Table 9.4).

9.4.1.2   Cued-recall-based GPS

A comparison of different cued-recall-based GPS has been done based on their security, memorability and usability aspects.

Table 9.4 Comparison of recall-based graphical password scheme

	PassShapes [18]	Pass-Go [19]	DRAW-A-PIN [20]	gRAT [21]	TMD [22]
Security	PassShapes are drawn on the screen of any size and in any location. Password space is reduced with the shapes and can be vulnerable to shoulder-surfing attacks	Large password space Using grid intersection to make it more secure Error tolerance mechanism is used. Not resistant to dictionary attack, shoulder-surfing attacks	Even if the PIN is known, it is difficult for attackers to emulate Behavioural biometrics Pins are drawn one at a time to guard against smudge attacks	Resistant against shoulder-surfing attack and smudge attack Images are randomized in the login phase. The user needs to select the password image in the same pattern	The password space is increased with layers Eliminated the fuzzy boundary problem
Memorability	Shapes are easier to remember than a PIN	Memorability aspects not studied thoroughly	Easy to remember the pin	Easy to recognize images and pattern	High password memorability
Usability	Easy to use	Simple method of use	Can be used only on touch-based devices. Easy to use	Easy to use	It is difficult to draw a pattern using only one line for some users

Passpoint [23] requires users to select five clickpoints on the displayed image within an acceptable distance from the clickpoint selected by the user in the registration phase. The user can also use their choice of image, creating a large password space.

PassMatrix [24] uses a complex method to divide a single image into several different squares. When the user logs in, the user needs to draw a circle through a touchscreen and in the next phase, the user needs to respond to a challenge where the first pass image is shown with a vertical and horizontal bar across it. The user needs to drag the bars and align the selected pass-square with the login indicator. This process runs for several rounds, causing longer login times.

PassBYOP [25] scheme uses a physical image to be presented to the camera and uses the live video to select the pass locations on the image. This system requires a touchscreen and a camera to select the pass locations on the image. The pass image is like a token, and the user cannot log in if it is lost.

HapticPoints [26] authentication scheme is similar to Passpoints [23] but adds haptic feedback to the Passpoints as decoy points (Table 9.5). This makes it harder for an attacker to eavesdrop or guess the password.

9.4.1.3   Hybrid GPS

A comparison of different Hybrid GPS has been done based on their security, memorability and usability aspects.

CD-GPS [27] during the registration phase requires users to select a sequence of images from a collection in order then use one or a few images and draw a secret picture with a series of clicks on the image. The user must select the picture in order and reproduce the secret picture in the selected picture.

GOTPass [28] requires users to draw a pattern given in the registration phase during the first phase. In the second phase, the users are presented with pass images with an OTP code that needs to be entered to login successfully. The password space is not large, but the multi-step authentication increases the security of the scheme.

CuedR [29] requires users to identify a keyword of each portfolio and enter the key corresponding to the keyword. The keyword is assigned randomly to the user during the registration phase. It has a large password size but has a higher login time.

Jumbled PassSteps [30] is a complex authentication process where the user must remember an audio output that has a random number and traversal direction (Table 9.6). During the authentication process, the random is required along with the user to identify the pass images from the image pool. The user then uses the pass image as a starting point and must click the decoy image.

9.5   Graphical OTP system

Graphical passwords are one of the most popular widely researched fields as an alternative to an alphanumerical password. Our systematic literature review of

Table 9.5 Comparison of cued-recall-based graphical password scheme

	Passpoint [23]	PassMatrix	PassBYOP [25]	HapticPoints [26]
Security	Allows any image to be used	No need to touch the password directly	Multi-factor authentication system	Mitigates dictionary attacks
	Large password space	Random login indicator	There needs an extra camera-based device to log in with desktop	Susceptible to dictionary attacks
	Recording the user's mouse motion can be used to reproduce a password	Users can upload images	It will be hard to log in if the user loses the physical token	Adds haptic feedback to Passpoints as decoy clickpoints
	It is difficult to ensure tolerable clickpoints	Susceptible to guessing attack and brute-force attack	Image token used	Similar memorability of Passpoints
	Vulnerable to shoulder-surfing			Can be used on smartphones only
Memorability	Memorability similar to other cued-recall GPSs	User can upload their own image to improve memorability		
Usability	Login takes a longer time for graphical password users	Friendly interface but a longer login time	Less login times	

Table 9.6 Comparison of hybrid graphical password scheme

Criteria	CD-GPS [27]	GOTPass [28]	CuedR [29]	Jumbled PassSteps [30]
Security	Large password space	Multiple authentication mechanisms (graphical and one-time password) combined	System assigned password	Hard to guess even if the login session is observed
	Increased entropy	No need to click on pass images	Large password size	
		Password space is not long	Provides implicit feedback	
Memorability	Hard to remember additional images in an ordered sequence	Easy-to-remember images from different categories	Easy to remember	Several independent images
				Easy to remember
Usability	Authentication time is longer	High registration time	Deployment of cuedR required more effort	User needs an earphone or headset to hear the audio
			High login time	Not suitable for defaced people

various graphical password authentication schemes based on their security mem-orability and usability aspects in the earlier section has given us valuable insight into the strengths and weaknesses of each scheme. With that in-depth under-standing, we have proposed a graphical OTP scheme that is easy to use, easy to remember and also can provide different levels of security. Our proposed authen-tication scheme is resistant to several known attacks that include shoulder surfing and brute force. The proposed authentication schemes rely on the user to recall the pass images selected in the registration phase and enter the one-time PIN associated with the pass image in the authentication phase. The research also provides a detailed study on various levels of security that can be attained by utilizing an increased number of pass images, a larger authentication matrix and larger range of the OTP number. The authentication combines the benefits of an OTP and gra-phical password to create a secure and easy-to-use authentication scheme.

9.5.1   Registration phase

In this phase, the user selects a username and passes images. As depicted in Figure 9.1 registration, in the first step, the user enters a unique username. If the

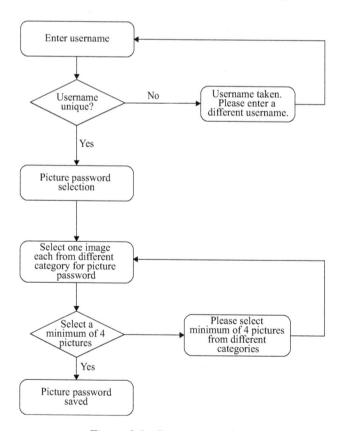

Figure 9.1   Registration phase

username is not unique, the user is asked to re-enter a unique username. In the second step, the user selects a minimum of four pass images, each from a different category of images. There are hundreds of categories of images to choose from. These pass images later form the password in the authentication phase.

9.5.2 Authentication phase

As depicted in Figure 9.2 authentication phase, the first step requires you to enter the unique username that you set during the registration phase.

If the username is valid, the user is shown a graphical OTP authentication matrix as shown in Figure 9.3.

The user then enters the (x,y) coordinate of the pass image the user has set in the registration phase. The user enters the coordinate in the order of left to right and top to bottom. If the user enters an incorrect OTP, the authentication matrix

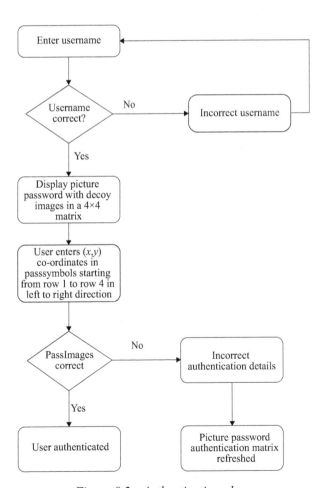

Figure 9.2 Authentication phase

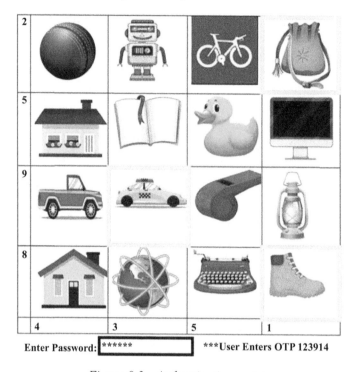

Figure 9.3   Authentication matrix

refreshes. If the OTP is correct, the user is authenticated. The OTP coordinates are generated randomly, and numbers are not repeated in the coordinate. The size of the authentication matrix, the number of pass images and the number range in the (*x,y*) coordinates can be increased to increase the security.

9.6 Measurements

To calculate the security aspects of the authentication scheme, we calculate the password strengths using permutations of the OTP:

$$\text{Password permutation} = \frac{N!}{(N - I)!}$$

where *N* is the number range (0–9 equals 10 numbers, 0–99 equals 100 numbers), *I* is the number of pass images.

To calculate the permutations for both (*x,y*) coordinates, we simply square the permutations.

Table 9.7 shows the permutations for different numbers of pass images and a different range of numbers for the OTP.

9.7   Analysis and discussion of results

Based on our measurement, we can clearly see that increasing the number of pass images to be selected increases password permutations. It can also be increased by increasing the range of the OTP coordinate, for example 0–9 and 0–99. A higher range number has higher password permutations.

We can clearly see from Figure 9.4 that the permutations of passwords increase greatly when the number range is increased. The permutations of passwords for four pass images with a number range of 0–99 used are still higher than six pass images with a number range of 0–9 used. This is because increasing the range of numbers increases the password space.

In addition to that, since the images are not clicked, and only the coordinate numbers are entered, the attacker will not be able to carry out a shoulder-surfing

Table 9.7   Password permutations

Number range	Three images	Four images	Five images	Six images
0–9	5.18E+05	2.54E+07	9.14E+08	2.29E+10
0–99	9.41E+11	8.86E+15	8.16E+19	7.37E+23

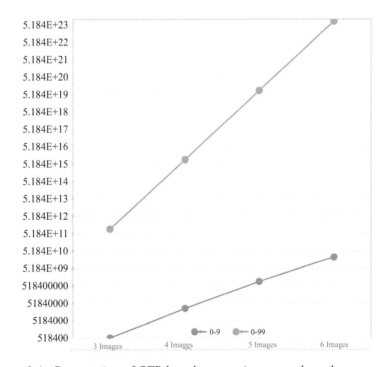

Figure 9.4   Permutation of OTP based on pass images and number range used

attack as they will have no idea on which is the picture password. This is a great advantage as several graphical passwords are prone to shoulder-surfing attacks, as identified in our in-depth analysis of graphical passwords. The OTP coordinate changes on every authentication attempt and eliminates the chances of the attacker using the old OTP coordinate. Brute forcing the password is also very hard due to the large password space and use of account lockout policies. Thus, our proposed scheme fares well in terms of security.

Since the user only needs to recall four to six images, it is not burdensome on the memory, and the user can easily recall the images. Thus, the authentication scheme rates highly in the memorability aspect.

Additionally, the user does not need to carry any token to generate the OTP, which highly promotes usability.

9.8　Conclusion

The proposed authentication method fares well against the memorability, usability and security aspects, making it a suitable replacement for an alphanumerical password. Using a recall-based graphical password is easier to remember, and we have also demonstrated mathematically that it can be used at different security levels with very high password strengths. We have also determined that brute forcing and shoulder surfing are very hard due to the OTP elements in the authentication scheme.

9.9　Future work

Future works for the research can be carried out in the real-world implementation of the authentication scheme and an assessment of the security scheme with various real-time attacks.

References

[1] Alazab, M., Layton, R., Broadhurst, R., and Bouhours, B. (2013, November). Malicious spam emails developments and authorship attribution. In *2013 Fourth Cybercrime and Trustworthy Computing Workshop* (pp. 58–68), IEEE.
[2] Whitman, M. and H. J. Mattord (2012). "Legal, ethical, and professional issues in information security." *Principles of information security*. Course Technology, Cengage Learning, Boston, MA. Retrieved from http://www.cengage.com/resource_uploads/downloads/1111138214_259148.pdf.
[3] Florencio, D. and C. Herley (2007). A large-scale study of web password habits. In *Proceedings of the 16th International Conference on World Wide Web*.

[4] Elftmann, P. (2006). "Secure alternatives to password-based authentication mechanisms." Lab. for Dependable Distributed Systems, RWTH Aachen Univ. Diploma thesis, Aachen, Germany.

[5] Walkup, E. (2016). *The password problem*, Sandia National Lab. (SNL-NM), Albuquerque, NM.

[6] O'Gorman, L. (2003). "Comparing passwords, tokens, and biometrics for user authentication." *Proceedings of the IEEE* 91(12): 2021–2040.

[7] Dobreva, J., Lumburovska, L., Trpcheska, H. M. and Dimitrova, V. (2021). "A comparative analysis of HOTP and TOTP authentication algorithms. Which one to choose?" *Security & Future* 5(4): 131–136.

[8] Mandal, S. K. and A. R. Deepti (2017). "A general approach of authentication scheme and its comparative study." *International Journal of Computer (IJC)* 26(1): 15–22.

[9] Weaver, A. C. J. C. (2006). "Biometric authentication." *Computer* 39(2): 96–97.

[10] Sarkar, A. and Singh, B. K. (2020). "A review on performance, security and various biometric template protection schemes for biometric authentication systems." *Multimedia Tools and Applications* 79(37): 27721–27776.

[11] Khot, R. A., Kumaraguru, P. and Srinathan, K. (2012). WYSWYE: Shoulder surfing defense for recognition based graphical passwords. In *Proceedings of the 24th Australian Computer-Human Interaction Conference*.

[12] Yu, X., Wang, Z., Li, Y., Li, L., Zhu, W. T. and Song, L. (2017). "EvoPass: Evolvable graphical password against shoulder-surfing attacks." *Computers & Security* 70: 179–198.

[13] Sun, H., Wang, K., Li, X., Qin, N. and Chen, Z. (2015). PassApp: My app is my password! In *Proceedings of the 17th International Conference on Human-Computer Interaction with Mobile Devices and Services*.

[14] Dhamija, R. and A. Perrig (2000). Déjà {Vu–A} user study: Using images for authentication. In *9th USENIX Security Symposium (USENIX Security 00)*.

[15] Brostoff, S. and M. A. Sasse (2000). Are Passfaces more usable than passwords? A field trial investigation. *People and computers XIV—Usability or else!*, Springer: Berlin 405–424.

[16] Wiedenbeck, S., Waters, J., Sobrado, L. and Birget, J. C. (2006). Design and evaluation of a shoulder-surfing resistant graphical password scheme. In *Proceedings of the Working Conference on Advanced Visual Interfaces*.

[17] Por, L. Y., Adebimpe, L. A., Idris, M. Y. I., Khaw, C. S. and Ku, C. S. (2019). "LocPass: A graphical password method to prevent shoulder-surfing." *Symmetry* 11(10): 1252.

[18] Weiss, R. and A. De Luca (2008). PassShapes: Utilizing stroke based authentication to increase password memorability. In *Proceedings of the Fifth Nordic Conference on Human-Computer Interaction: Building Bridges*.

[19] Tao, H. and C. Adams (2008). "Pass-go: A proposal to improve the usability of graphical passwords." *International Journal of Network Security* 7(2): 273–292.

[20] Van Nguyen, T., Sae-Bae, N. and Memon, N. (2017). "DRAW-A-PIN: Authentication using finger-drawn PIN on touch devices." *Computers & Security* 66: 115–128.

[21] Khan, M. A., Din, I. U., Jadoon, S. U., Khan, M. K., Guizani, M. and Awan, K. A. (2019). "G-RAT| a novel graphical randomized authentication technique for consumer smart devices." *IEEE Transactions on Consumer Electronics* 65(2): 215–223.

[22] Chiang, H.-Y. and S. Chiasson (2013). Improving user authentication on mobile devices: A touchscreen graphical password. In *Proceedings of the 15th International Conference on Human-Computer Interaction with Mobile Devices and Services*.

[23] Wiedenbeck, S., Waters, J., Birget, J. C., Brodskiy, A. and Memon, N. (2005). "PassPoints: Design and longitudinal evaluation of a graphical password system." *International Journal of Human-Computer Studies* 63 (1–2): 102–127.

[24] Tabrez, S. and D. J. Sai (2017). Pass-matrix authentication a solution to shoulder surfing attacks with the assistance of graphical password authentication system. In *2017 International Conference on Intelligent Computing and Control Systems (ICICCS)*, IEEE.

[25] Bianchi, A., Oakley, I. and Kim, H. (2015). "PassBYOP: Bring your own picture for securing graphical passwords." *IEEE Transactions on Human-Machine Systems* 46(3): 380–389.

[26] Wiangsripanawan, R. (2018). "HapticPoints: The extended PassPoints graphical password." In *International Workshop on Information Security Applications*, Springer.

[27] Meng, Y. (2012). Designing click-draw based graphical password scheme for better authentication. In *2012 IEEE Seventh International Conference on Networking, Architecture, and Storage*. IEEE.

[28] Alsaiari, H., Papadaki, M., Dowland, P. and Furnell, S. (2015). "Secure graphical one time password (GOTPass): An empirical study." *Information Security Journal: A Global Perspective* 24(4–6): 207–220.

[29] Al-Ameen, M. N., Wright, M. and Scielzo, S. (2015). Towards making random passwords memorable: Leveraging users' cognitive ability through multiple cues. In *Proceedings of the 33rd Annual ACM Conference on Human Factors in Computing Systems*.

[30] Songcuan, J. P., Sison, A. M. and Medina, R. P. (2019). "Towards usability evaluation of jumbled PassSteps." *International Journal of Advanced Trends in Computer Science and Engineering* 8(4): 1032–1037.

Chapter 10

Role of AI in social cybersecurity: real-world case studies

*Mudasir Ahmad Wani[1], Mohamed Hammad[1,2]
and Ahmed A. Abd El-Latif[1,3]*

The rapid advancement of artificial intelligence (AI) has significantly influenced the field of social cybersecurity, addressing the challenges of protecting individuals and communities in the digital realm. This chapter explores the role of AI in social cybersecurity through real-world case studies, showcasing its application and impact in various contexts. The abstract delves into the practical implementations of AI technologies, such as machine learning and natural language processing, to detect and prevent cyber threats, identify malicious activities, and safeguard sensitive information. The case studies highlight how AI-powered solutions have improved the efficiency and effectiveness of cybersecurity measures, leading to enhanced threat intelligence, faster incident response, and proactive defense mechanisms. Moreover, ethical considerations and privacy concerns associated with AI in social cybersecurity are examined, emphasizing the need for responsible and transparent practices. This chapter concludes by discussing the potential future developments and challenges in the field, calling for continuous innovation, collaboration, and adaptation to ensure the resilient protection of individuals and societies in the face of evolving cyber threats.

10.1 Introduction

The notion of social cybersecurity has become increasingly significant in contemporary times, given the interconnectivity of the world and the integral role that social media platforms play in communication, information dissemination, and online interactions [1]. Social cybersecurity pertains to safeguarding individuals,

[1]EIAS Data Science Lab, College of Computer and Information Sciences, Prince Sultan University, Saudi Arabia
[2]Department of Information Technology, Faculty of Computers and Information, Menoufia University, Egypt
[3]Department of Mathematics and Computer Science, Faculty of Science, Menoufia University, Egypt

institutions, and communities against cyber hazards and vulnerabilities that stem from the utilization of social media platforms and virtual communities [2]. The present chapter offers a comprehensive analysis of the context and importance of social cybersecurity, emphasizing the difficulties and consequences linked to this swiftly developing domain.

10.2   The rise of social media and its implications

The advent of social media platforms, such as Facebook, Twitter, Instagram, and LinkedIn, has transformed the way people connect, share information, and engage with each other [3]. These platforms have revolutionized communication, enabling individuals to reach a global audience instantaneously. However, this widespread adoption of social media has also introduced new risks and vulnerabilities. The proliferation of personal data shared on these platforms, in conjunction with the possibility of nefarious activities, has engendered a propitious environment for cyber hazards [4].

10.2.1   Social media and cybersecurity challenges

The widespread use of social media platforms has given rise to several cybersecurity challenges that need to be addressed effectively [5]. These challenges include the following:

Privacy and data protection: Social media platforms collect and store vast amounts of personal data, including personal information, photographs, and user preferences. The protection of this data is crucial to safeguard individuals' privacy and prevent unauthorized access or misuse [5].

Identity theft and impersonation: Cybercriminals exploit social media platforms to steal identities and impersonate individuals, leading to financial fraud, reputation damage, and other malicious activities [6].

Online harassment and cyberbullying: Social media platforms have become hotspots for cyberbullying and online harassment, affecting individuals emotionally, psychologically, and socially. The impact of such activities can be severe and long-lasting [7].

Spread of misinformation and fake news: Social media platforms are often used as channels for spreading misinformation and fake news, which can have significant consequences on public opinion, social cohesion, and democratic processes [8].

Social engineering attacks: Cybercriminals employ social engineering techniques to manipulate and deceive individuals into revealing sensitive information or performing malicious actions. These attacks can lead to financial losses, data breaches, or unauthorized access to critical systems [9].

10.2.2   Implications of social cybersecurity

The implications of social cybersecurity extend beyond individual users and organizations [10]. They have broader societal, economic, and political implications. Several significant consequences arise from this situation, including the following:

Trust and reputation: Cybersecurity incidents, such as data breaches or the spread of fake news, erode trust in social media platforms and online communities. The sustained growth and adoption of these platforms is contingent upon the imperative task of rebuilding trust.

Information integrity: Maintaining the integrity of information shared on social media platforms is critical for the proper functioning of democratic processes, public discourse, and decision-making. The widespread dissemination of fabricated news articles represents a considerable menace to the veracity of information and has the potential to influence the views held by the general populace.

The economic ramifications of cybersecurity incidents can be significant. Data breaches can have significant consequences for businesses, including financial losses, damage to reputation, and legal liabilities. Furthermore, the erosion of consumer trust in online platforms can have significant implications for the e-commerce and digital economies.

Social media platforms have a significant impact on public discourse and societal interactions, which in turn affect social cohesion and well-being. Cyberbullying, harassment, and the spread of hate speech undermine social cohesion, well-being, and inclusivity.

10.2.3 The necessity of implementing social cybersecurity measures

Given the complex and evolving nature of social cybersecurity threats, it is crucial to implement effective measures to mitigate risks and protect users [11]. This includes the following:

Awareness and education: Promoting cybersecurity awareness and educating users about safe practices, privacy settings, and the identification of potential threats can empower individuals to protect themselves online [12].

Robust security frameworks: Social media platforms and online communities must implement robust security frameworks to ensure the confidentiality, integrity, and availability of user data. This involves implementing strong authentication mechanisms, encryption protocols, and proactive monitoring systems to detect and respond to security incidents promptly [13].

Collaboration and information sharing: Collaboration among social media platforms, cybersecurity organizations, law enforcement agencies, and governments is essential to exchange information, share best practices, and coordinate efforts in combating social cybersecurity threats. This collaboration can lead to the development of standardized protocols and frameworks to enhance security across platforms [14].

The provision of strong privacy controls and customizable sharing preferences by social media platforms is imperative in enabling user empowerment. This allows individuals to have greater control over their personal data and reduces the risk of unauthorized access or misuse.

Continuous monitoring and incident response are essential in detecting and addressing security incidents in a timely manner through proactive monitoring of social media platforms. This includes the use of advanced threat detection mechanisms, real-time monitoring tools, and automated incident response systems to mitigate risks and minimize the impact of cybersecurity incidents.

Ethical use of artificial intelligence (AI) and machine learning (ML): AI and ML technologies can play a significant role in enhancing social cybersecurity [15]. However, the ethical use of these technologies is paramount. Ensuring transparency, fairness, and accountability in AI algorithms and models can help address concerns related to bias, privacy violations, and unintended consequences.

Educating users on the diverse range of social cybersecurity threats, including but not limited to phishing, social engineering, and fake news, is a crucial aspect of user education on threats and risks. Equipping individuals with the necessary knowledge and competencies to recognize and alleviate these hazards can enable them to make a meaningful contribution toward establishing a more secure digital milieu [16].

The development of comprehensive regulatory frameworks and legal protections is recommended by governments and regulatory bodies to effectively address social cybersecurity challenges. This includes legislation on data protection, privacy rights, and cybersecurity standards to hold both individuals and organizations accountable for their actions [17].

International cooperation: Social cybersecurity is a global issue that requires international cooperation and collaboration. It is imperative for governments, organizations, and stakeholders to collaborate in order to establish global standards, exchange threat intelligence, and jointly address cyber threats that surpass geographical borders [18].

AI is a discipline within the realm of computer science that centers on the advancement of intelligent machinery with the ability to execute tasks that conventionally necessitate human intelligence [19]. AI is a field that involves a diverse set of techniques, algorithms, and methodologies that allow computers to emulate cognitive functions, including, but not limited to, learning, problem-solving, reasoning, perception, and decision-making [20]. AI has attracted considerable interest and has emerged as a disruptive influence in diverse fields, such as healthcare, finance, transportation, and entertainment [21–25].

The principal objective of AI is to develop systems that can demonstrate intelligent conduct, adjust to novel circumstances, and enhance their performance independently as time progresses [26]. AI can be classified into two main categories: narrow and general. The term "narrow AI" or "weak AI" pertains to computer systems that are specifically developed to perform particular tasks and are trained using specific datasets [27]. These systems demonstrate exceptional performance in executing particular tasks, such as identifying images, processing natural language, and providing voice-based assistance. Conversely, artificial general intelligence, commonly referred to as general AI or strong AI, pertains to systems that exhibit the capacity to comprehend, acquire, and utilize knowledge across diverse domains, akin to human intelligence [28].

In recent years, the field of AI has experienced notable progress, largely attributable to the accessibility of extensive data, enhanced computational capabilities, and innovative algorithms [29]. ML is a significant subfield of AI that concentrates on facilitating machines to acquire knowledge from data and generate forecasts or decisions without the need for explicit programming [30]. ML algorithms are specifically developed to examine patterns and extract valuable insights from data, thereby facilitating the enhancement of system performance through experiential learning [31].

The subfield of ML known as deep learning has garnered significant attention owing to its capacity to acquire hierarchical data representations via neural networks [32]. Deep neural networks comprise numerous interconnected layers of artificial neurons, which possess the ability to capture complex features and relationships within data. The aforementioned advancements have resulted in notable progressions in domains such as visual perception, computational linguistics, and self-driving vehicles.

AI exhibits a wide range of potential applications across diverse industries. AI is currently being employed in the healthcare sector to aid in the identification of diseases, the exploration of new drugs, and the development of personalized medical treatments. AI algorithms are used in the field of finance for purposes such as detecting fraudulent activities, conducting algorithmic trading, and assessing risks. Transportation industries are leveraging AI for autonomous vehicles, traffic management, and route optimization. AI is employed by entertainment platforms to facilitate recommendation systems, generate content, and enhance user engagement.

The significance of AI lies in its potential to revolutionize industries, enhance efficiency, and address complex challenges. AI systems can process vast amounts of data, identify patterns, and extract valuable insights, leading to informed decision-making. Automating tedious and repetitive tasks can result in the liberation of human resources, allowing them to engage in more creative and strategic pursuits. AI possesses the capability to address societal predicaments, including climate change, healthcare accessibility, and resource optimization, through the facilitation of data-driven solutions and predictive modeling [33].

However, AI also presents several challenges and considerations. The responsible development and deployment of AI necessitates the resolution of ethical considerations, including, but not limited to, issues of privacy, bias, and transparency. The ramifications of AI on the labor force and subsequent displacement of jobs represent a crucial area necessitating careful consideration. Achieving a harmonious equilibrium between the competencies of AI systems and human supervision is imperative to avert inadvertent ramifications and guarantee that the technology operates in the optimal welfare of the community.

The advent of AI has yielded noteworthy progress and transformative potentialities in the realm of cybersecurity. The field of social cybersecurity is concerned with safeguarding individuals, organizations, and societies against cyber threats that leverage human behavior and social engineering tactics. The convergence of AI and social cybersecurity presents significant opportunities for improving the identification, mitigation, and remediation of cyber threats in an interconnected global landscape [33].

AI technologies have the potential to significantly contribute to the mitigation of the constantly changing social cyber threats. The domain of threat detection and analysis is considered a crucial area where AI can potentially exert a substantial influence. Conventional cybersecurity systems frequently depend on rule-based methodologies that necessitate preestablished patterns or signatures of recognized attacks. Notwithstanding, given the dynamic and ever-changing landscape of cyber threats, these fixed techniques may prove inadequate in identifying novel and intricate assaults.

AI methodologies, including ML and deep learning, have the potential to enhance cybersecurity measures by allowing systems to assimilate extensive quantities of data and detect patterns that signify cyber assaults. ML algorithms have the capability to analyze various forms of data such as network traffic, user behavior, and system logs in order to identify anomalous activities that could potentially signify a security breach or intrusion. Deep learning algorithms possess the capability to effectively handle intricate and disorganized data, thereby enabling them to offer more precise and sophisticated threat detection capabilities. This includes the ability to identify attack patterns that were previously unknown [33].

Moreover, AI can be utilized in the creation of preemptive and flexible security protocols. Through the examination of past data and the recognition of patterns in cyber threats, AI systems have the capability to predict and avert potential attacks. The utilization of predictive analytics can facilitate the detection of nascent hazards and the execution of preemptive strategies to alleviate potential perils. AI-enabled systems have the capability to learn and adjust their defensive mechanisms on a continuous basis by utilizing real-time data. This feature enhances their efficacy in mitigating the impact of constantly evolving cyber threats.

AI plays a significant role in enhancing social cybersecurity through its application in user authentication and access control [34–39]. Conventional means of authentication, such as passwords or personal identification numbers, are frequently susceptible to security breaches, encompassing password cracking and phishing. AI techniques, such as behavioral biometrics, have the potential to offer stronger and more secure methods of authentication. The aforementioned methodologies scrutinize distinctive user conduct patterns, encompassing keystrokes, mouse movements, or touchscreen interactions, for the purpose of ascertaining user identities with a notable level of precision and resilience against spoofing attacks.

In addition, AI has the potential to aid in the detection and reduction of social engineering attacks, which leverage human psychology and trust to coerce individuals into divulging confidential data or engaging in harmful behaviors. AI-based systems possess the capability to scrutinize communication patterns, content, and context in order to identify instances of social engineering, including, but not limited to, phishing emails, impersonation, and online scams. AI systems can detect potentially harmful intentions in communications by using natural language processing (NLP) and sentiment analysis techniques. This capability enables the AI systems to issue timely alerts and implement precautionary measures [40].

The convergence of AI and social cybersecurity presents certain ethical and practical challenges. The utilization of AI algorithms gives rise to plausible susceptibilities, including adversarial attacks, which entail the malevolent efforts of actors to deceive or manipulate AI systems. The susceptibility of AI models to adversarial attacks can result in the misclassification of threats, thereby generating false positives or negatives in threat detection. The maintenance of social cybersecurity systems' effectiveness is contingent upon the crucial task of ensuring the robustness and security of AI algorithms against potential attacks.

Furthermore, it is imperative to meticulously consider the ethical ramifications of AI in the realm of social cybersecurity. The utilization of AI algorithms for the purposes of surveillance, profiling, or decision-making has elicited apprehension with respect to issues of privacy, impartiality, and partiality [41]. The implementation of AI systems that are transparent and accountable, and that incorporate mechanisms for explainability and interpretability, is imperative in order to establish trust and guarantee the responsible and ethical use of AI.

The utilization of AI within the realm of social cybersecurity has brought about a significant transformation in the approach adopted by organizations toward the identification, mitigation, and remediation of cyber risks. Case studies from real-world scenarios offer valuable insights into the practical application of AI technologies and their effectiveness in improving security measures across different domains. The aforementioned case studies serve to showcase the efficacy, obstacles, and insights gained from the implementation of AI in the realm of social cybersecurity.

A noteworthy practical example pertains to the application of AI in identifying and addressing cyber threats that originate from social media platforms, including, but not limited to, fabricated news, disinformation initiatives, and virtual propaganda. The challenge of addressing these threats has been compounded by the widespread availability of social media platforms. The limitations of conventional manual monitoring and analysis techniques are attributed to the vast amount of data and the rapid propagation of malicious content.

This chapter describes the development of an AI-based system by an organization that employed NLP techniques and ML algorithms to perform real-time analysis of social media data. The automated system identified and marked potentially dubious material by using a range of criteria, including source reliability, sentiment analysis, and semantic coherence. Through the utilization of a comprehensive dataset of established malevolent content and the ongoing integration of novel patterns, the AI model underwent training to enhance its precision in detecting and eliminating injurious information.

The social media monitoring system that utilizes AI exhibited noteworthy efficacy in detecting and addressing cyber threats. The measure aided in curtailing the dissemination of false information and propaganda efforts, thus preserving the integrity of public sentiment and reducing the likelihood of adverse outcomes stemming from manipulated data. The system furnished significant insights to security analysts, facilitating their ability to expeditiously investigate and address emerging threats.

An additional noteworthy case study centers on the implementation of AI-based threat intelligence and incident response. Conventional cybersecurity methodologies frequently depend on predetermined regulations and identifying markers to identify and counteract established hazards. It is imperative for organizations to possess proactive and adaptive security measures due to the constant evolution of cyber attackers' techniques.

The present case study highlights the use of AI technologies, such as ML and data analytics, by an organization to scrutinize extensive security data and detect patterns that signify novel and developing threats. Through the acquisition and examination of data from diverse origins, including network logs, system events, and threat intelligence feeds, the AI system acquired the capability to identify abnormal patterns of behavior and signs of prospective cyber assaults.

The utilization of an AI-powered threat intelligence system equipped security teams with prompt notifications and practical knowledge, enabling them to promptly and efficiently address cyber threats. The implementation of this technology facilitated timely identification and preemptive resolution of security breaches, resulting in decreased consequences and limited harm stemming from intricate hazards, including advanced persistent threats and zero-day vulnerabilities.

Moreover, AI has been implemented in the domain of identifying and averting fraudulent activities. Financial institutions encounter persistent obstacles in identifying instances of fraudulent behavior, including, but not limited to, credit card fraud, identity theft, and money laundering. Conventional rule-based systems encounter difficulties in keeping up with the constantly evolving fraud techniques and patterns.

10.3 Current scenario of AI in social cybersecurity

The current scenario of AI in social cybersecurity involves the application of AI techniques and technologies to address security challenges related to social media platforms, online communities, and other social networks. AI plays a vital role in social cybersecurity. Figure 10.1 shows some of the domains of social cyber security, where AI has achieved promising results. Each of these domains is briefly discussed in the following subsections.

- Threat detection and prevention: AI is used to detect and prevent various types of threats on social media platforms, including malicious activities such as phishing attacks, spamming, account takeovers, and fake news propagation. ML algorithms analyze large volumes of data and patterns to identify suspicious behaviors and potential threats.
- Content moderation: Social media platforms employ AI-powered content moderation systems to automatically identify and remove harmful or inappropriate content, including hate speech, harassment, and graphic violence. NLP models help analyze text-based content, while computer vision techniques are used for analyzing images and videos.

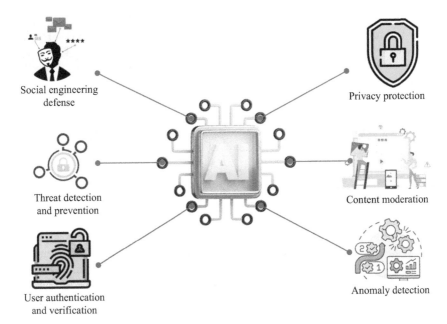

Figure 10.1   Domains of social cyber security where AI has achieved promising results

- User authentication and verification: AI technologies such as facial recognition and biometric authentication play a role in verifying user identities on social media platforms. These technologies help prevent impersonation, identity theft, and unauthorized account access.
- Anomaly detection: AI-powered anomaly detection systems monitor user activities and network traffic to identify unusual or suspicious behavior. This helps in detecting and mitigating cybersecurity threats, such as account compromise or bot-driven attacks, in real time.
- Privacy protection: AI can assist in enhancing privacy controls and protecting user data on social media platforms. ML algorithms can analyze user preferences, behaviors, and past activities to provide personalized privacy recommendations and detect potential privacy breaches.
- Social engineering defense: AI can help in identifying and mitigating social engineering attacks, where attackers manipulate users into divulging sensitive information. NLP techniques can be used to analyze text-based conversations and detect signs of manipulation or phishing attempts [42,43].

However, it is important to note that AI in social cybersecurity is not without its challenges. There are concerns related to algorithmic bias, privacy implications, and potential limitations in accurately identifying and addressing complex social engineering attacks. Striking the right balance between security and user privacy is crucial, and ongoing research and development are needed to enhance the effectiveness and ethical implementation of AI in social cybersecurity.

The focus of the study is to highlight the impact of AI pure social cybersecurity. We refer to social cybersecurity as the protection of individuals, organizations, and society as a whole from cyber threats and risks originating from social media platforms. These threats include identity theft, data breaches, fake profiles, bots, and online sexual predators. AI has the potential to significantly enhance social cybersecurity by leveraging ML algorithms, NLP, and image analysis techniques. AI algorithms can help detect and mitigate threats in real time, improving the security and privacy of social media users. In the following sections, our emphasis will be on discussing the role of AI in detecting fake and bot accounts on different social media platforms.

10.4   AI fake profile and bot detection

A fake profile refers to an online social media account that has been created with false information and deceptive intentions. Such profiles are commonly found on various social networking platforms, including Facebook, Twitter, and LinkedIn. While each platform may have specific policies and guidelines regarding fake profiles, the general concept remains consistent across these platforms. Facebook defines fake profiles as accounts that are created by someone pretending to be someone else or by using false information [44]. These accounts often violate Facebook's Community Standards, which aim to ensure authenticity and integrity on the platform. Facebook actively monitors and removes fake profiles to maintain a safe and trustworthy environment for its users [45].

Twitter also acknowledges the presence of fake profiles, commonly known as "bots" or "bot accounts." These accounts are typically automated and controlled by software, not real individuals. Twitter has strict rules against the use of bots for spamming, manipulation, or the dissemination of false information. The platform actively works to identify and suspend fake accounts to prevent misuse.

LinkedIn, being a professional networking platform, aims to maintain genuine user profiles. Fake profiles on LinkedIn are generally created with the intention of spreading false information, impersonating professionals, or engaging in fraudulent activities. LinkedIn has policies in place to detect and remove fake profiles to protect the credibility and professionalism of its platform.

In summary, a fake profile refers to an online social media account that uses false information or impersonates someone else. These profiles violate the terms and policies of social media platforms like Facebook, Twitter, and LinkedIn, and the platforms take measures to detect and remove such profiles to maintain a safe and trustworthy environment for their users.

10.4.1   *The rise of fake profiles and bots*

Fake profiles and bots are prevalent in social media platforms, and they pose various risks such as spreading misinformation, conducting phishing attacks, and influencing public opinion. According to a study by the University of Southern California, it was estimated that up to 15% of Twitter accounts are bots. In the

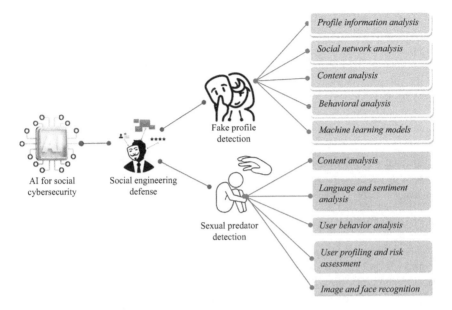

Figure 10.2   The role of AI in pure social cybersecurity (social engineering)

following sections, we will discuss the different features which are being employed by researchers around the globe to assure social cybersecurity using AI. The features are mainly used to identify and detect fake profiles and sexual predators on different social media platforms, including Facebook and YouTube. Figure 10.2 gives a clear picture of the upcoming sections in this study.

10.4.2   AI-based fake profile detection

AI-based fake profile detection refers to the use of AI techniques and algorithms to identify and detect fake profiles on social media platforms. With the increasing prevalence of fake profiles and their potential negative impacts, AI-based detection systems have become crucial in maintaining the integrity and trustworthiness of online communities. These systems leverage ML, NLP, and data analysis techniques to analyze various aspects of user profiles, activities, and behavior patterns to determine the likelihood of a profile being fake. Some common approaches and features used in AI-based fake profile detection include the following:

- *Profile information analysis*: AI algorithms analyze the profile information provided by users, such as profile pictures, names, biographies, and other details, to identify suspicious patterns or inconsistencies.
- *Social network analysis*: By examining the connections, interactions, and network structure of users, AI algorithms can identify unusual or abnormal behavior that may indicate the presence of fake profiles. This can include analyzing the network topology, detecting clusters of interconnected fake accounts, and identifying patterns of spamming or bot-like activities.

- *Content analysis*: AI models can analyze the content posted by users, including text, images, and links, to identify suspicious or deceptive behavior. This can involve detecting spam messages, inappropriate content, or repetitive patterns indicative of automated or scripted activity.
- *Behavioral analysis*: AI algorithms can analyze user behavior patterns, such as posting frequency, timing, engagement levels, and response patterns, to identify deviations from normal user behavior. This helps in identifying accounts that exhibit characteristics commonly associated with fake profiles.
- *ML models*: AI-based fake profile detection systems often employ ML models trained on labeled datasets to identify patterns and characteristics of fake profiles. These models can learn from a large volume of data and improve their accuracy over time.

It is important to note that AI-based fake profile detection is an ongoing field of research and development. Different platforms and organizations may employ varying techniques and algorithms tailored to their specific needs and requirements. AI plays a crucial role in identifying and combating automated bot accounts on social media platforms. Techniques such as behavioral analysis, sentiment analysis, and network analysis are employed to detect bot activities. A notable example is the Botometer [46] tool developed by the Indiana University, which uses ML to analyze Twitter accounts and assign a bot score.

10.4.3   Challenges and limitations

AI-based fake profile detection systems face several challenges and limitations. While they can be effective in identifying certain types of fake profiles, there are inherent complexities and evolving techniques employed by malicious actors that pose challenges to detection methods (Figure 10.3). Some of the key challenges and limitations include the following:

Adversarial techniques: Malicious actors continuously adapt their strategies to evade detection algorithms. They may employ sophisticated techniques such as mimicking human behavior, using AI-generated profile pictures, or obfuscating patterns to make fake profiles appear more genuine.

Data availability and quality: The availability and quality of training data can significantly impact the accuracy of AI-based detection systems. Obtaining labeled data that accurately represents a diverse range of fake profiles is challenging, as it requires access to known fake profiles and the cooperation of social media platforms.

Privacy concerns: Analyzing user data to detect fake profiles raises privacy concerns. Balancing the need for effective detection with user privacy rights and data protection regulations is an ongoing challenge. Striking the right balance is crucial to maintain user trust and comply with legal and ethical considerations.

False positives and false negatives: AI algorithms may occasionally misclassify genuine profiles as fake (false positives) or fail to detect sophisticated fake profiles (false negatives). Striking the right balance between accuracy and minimizing these errors is a continuous challenge.

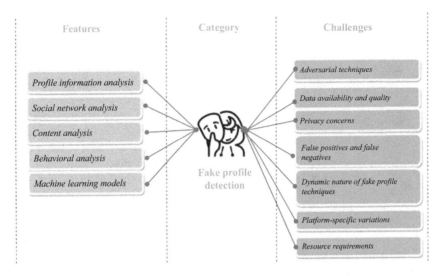

Figure 10.3   Fake profile detection (social cybersecurity) features and challenges

Dynamic nature of fake profile techniques: Fake profile creation techniques evolve rapidly, making it difficult for AI-based detection systems to keep up with emerging trends. Constant monitoring and updating of detection algorithms are necessary to address new strategies employed by malicious actors.

Platform-specific variations: Different social media platforms have unique characteristics and user behaviors, requiring tailored approaches for each platform. Detection algorithms developed for one platform may not be as effective or transferable to another, requiring additional customization and fine-tuning.

Resource requirements: AI-based detection systems often require significant computational resources and processing power. Implementing and maintaining such systems can be costly, especially for smaller platforms or organizations with limited resources.

Addressing these challenges requires ongoing research, the collaboration between researchers and platform providers, and continuous adaptation of AI algorithms to stay ahead of evolving fake profile creation techniques.

10.5   AI in sexual predator detection

AI in sexual predator detection refers to the use of AI techniques and algorithms to identify and mitigate the risks posed by sexual predators in online environments. It involves leveraging AI technologies to analyze various data sources, patterns, and behaviors associated with potential sexual predators to enhance the safety and security of online platforms [47]. The application of AI in sexual predator detection can have several components:

Content analysis: AI algorithms can analyze text, images, videos, and other forms of content to identify explicit or inappropriate materials that may be associated with sexual predators. NLP and computer vision techniques can be used to flag and categorize such content.

Language and sentiment analysis: AI models can analyze the language used in online conversations, comments, or private messages to identify patterns associated with grooming, exploitation, or predatory behavior [48]. Sentiment analysis can help identify suspicious or inappropriate communication patterns.

User behavior analysis: AI algorithms can analyze user behavior patterns, such as frequency of interactions, communication patterns, and online activities, to identify potential sexual predators. Deviations from normal behavior or interactions with vulnerable individuals can raise red flags for further investigation.

Image and face recognition: AI-powered facial recognition technologies can be used to detect and match images of known sexual predators, aiding in their identification across various online platforms. This can assist in identifying repeat offenders or individuals using multiple identities.

User profiling and risk assessment: AI models can build profiles of users based on their behavior, interests, and engagement patterns. By comparing these profiles against known characteristics of sexual predators, AI systems can assess the risk level associated with specific individuals.

It is important to note that the use of AI in sexual predator detection is a complex and sensitive area. Privacy concerns, ethical considerations, and the need for human oversight in decision-making are crucial aspects to address. AI algorithms should be developed and implemented with transparency, accountability, and fairness in mind, ensuring the protection of user privacy and the prevention of false accusations.

10.6   Case study on Facebook and Twitter

10.6.1   Case study 1: *Twitter's AI-powered fake profile identification*

Twitter has recognized the importance of addressing the presence of fake profiles on its platform and has invested in leveraging AI techniques to combat this issue. By using a combination of ML algorithms, NLP models, network analysis, and deep learning for image analysis, Twitter aims to detect and identify suspicious accounts in order to maintain platform integrity and user trust. Twitter's AI system employs ML algorithms to differentiate between human-operated accounts and automated bot accounts, which are commonly used for spreading misinformation and manipulating discussions. These algorithms analyze various account activities, such as posting frequency, retweet patterns, content similarity, and engagement metrics, to accurately classify and identify bots. Supervised learning techniques, including support vector machines and random forests, are trained on labeled datasets containing both genuine and bot accounts to improve detection accuracy.

NLP techniques play a crucial role in analyzing the textual content within tweets, profile descriptions, and user interactions. Sentiment analysis, topic modeling, and language coherence analysis are used to identify patterns indicative of fake profiles. By analyzing language usage, excessive use of certain keywords, repetitive content, and incoherent or misleading narratives, NLP models can help flag potentially fake profiles. These models contribute to the early detection of suspicious accounts and assist in minimizing the spread of misinformation.

Network analysis is another important aspect of Twitter's AI-powered fake profile identification system. Graph-based algorithms, such as community detection and centrality analysis, are used to identify clusters of fake profiles operating in coordinated campaigns. By examining the connections, interactions, and propagation patterns of Twitter accounts, these algorithms can uncover suspicious behaviors and associations. Anomaly detection algorithms also play a role in identifying accounts with abnormal network behaviors, such as rapid follower acquisition or highly retweeted content, which may indicate potential manipulation or fake profiles.

Additionally, deep learning models are employed to analyze images shared within profiles and tweets. Convolutional neural networks (CNNs) are used to identify manipulated or stolen images and recognize patterns of image-based misinformation. By detecting visual inconsistencies, image modifications, or signs of stock photos, these models can assist in flagging accounts associated with fake profiles.

User reports and feedback are valuable sources of information for improving the accuracy and effectiveness of Twitter's AI algorithms. By incorporating user input, Twitter can continuously refine its AI system and adapt to new patterns and emerging threats.

Overall, Twitter's AI-powered approach for fake profile identification combines multiple techniques, including ML, NLP, network analysis, and deep learning, to detect and combat fake profiles effectively. By proactively identifying and removing suspicious accounts, Twitter aims to provide users with a safer and more reliable platform for engaging in discussions and accessing trustworthy information. Appendix A provides the source code for analyzing the detecting fake profiles on the Twitter network.

10.6.2   Case study 2: *Facebook's AI-powered fake profile detection*

In addition to ML algorithms, Facebook leverages NLP techniques to analyze the textual content associated with user profiles. NLP enables the system to detect patterns, anomalies, and inconsistencies in the language used by fake profiles. This includes analyzing the profile descriptions, posts, comments, and messages for indications of spam, promotional content, or malicious intent.

Facebook's AI-powered fake profile detection system also incorporates deep learning models, such as CNNs and recurrent neural networks. These models are designed to extract complex features from profile pictures, enabling the system to detect manipulated or stolen images commonly used by fake profiles. By comparing profile pictures across different accounts and cross-referencing them with publicly available images, the system can identify instances where the same image is used across multiple profiles, a characteristic often associated with fake accounts.

To ensure the effectiveness of the AI system, Facebook continuously collects feedback from users through reporting mechanisms. This feedback is invaluable in training the algorithms to improve their accuracy and keep up with emerging techniques used by malicious actors. The data collected from user reports is carefully analyzed to identify common characteristics or patterns that distinguish fake profiles from genuine ones.

Upon detecting a potentially fake profile, Facebook employs a multistep verification process before taking action. This process may involve additional checks, such as requesting additional identification documents, phone number verification, or CAPTCHA challenges. By implementing these measures, Facebook aims to minimize false positives and false negatives, striking a balance between detecting and removing fake profiles while not inconveniencing legitimate users.

The impact of Facebook's AI-powered fake profile detection system is substantial. It helps protect users from scams, phishing attempts, and identity theft by reducing the presence of fake accounts. This, in turn, enhances the overall trust and credibility of the platform, leading to a better user experience. By proactively identifying and removing fake profiles, Facebook can also prevent the spread of misinformation, hate speech, and other harmful content that malicious actors often propagate through such accounts.

It is important to note that while Facebook's AI-powered system is highly effective, it is not infallible. Some sophisticated fake profiles may still evade detection, necessitating a combination of user reports, human moderation, and ongoing improvements to the AI algorithms. Facebook remains committed to investing in research and development to stay ahead of evolving techniques used by individuals attempting to deceive the system.

In conclusion, Facebook's AI-powered fake profile detection system combines ML algorithms, NLP techniques, and deep learning models to identify and remove fake profiles from its platform. By leveraging these technologies, Facebook aims to protect user privacy, security, and trust by combating scams, misinformation, and other malicious activities associated with fake accounts. Appendix A provides the source code for analyzing the detecting fake profiles on the Instagram/Facebook Social network.

10.7 Conclusion

The chapter has delved into the role of AI in social cybersecurity through real-world case studies, shedding light on the significant implications of AI technologies in safeguarding individuals and combating threats in the realm of social media. Section 10.1 highlights the growing influence of social media platforms and the need to address the associated cybersecurity challenges. The rise of social media has provided opportunities for cybercriminals, necessitating advanced techniques and solutions to protect users' privacy, integrity, and overall digital well-being. The current scenario of AI in social cybersecurity was discussed, showcasing the wide range of applications and benefits offered by AI-powered solutions. From detecting and combating fake profiles and bots to identifying sexual predators, AI has emerged as a valuable tool in enhancing security and mitigating risks in social media environments. The case study on Facebook and Twitter exemplified the practical implementation of AI in addressing social cybersecurity concerns. These platforms have leveraged AI algorithms to identify and remove fake profiles, detect malicious activities, and protect users from harmful content. The success of these case studies highlights the effectiveness of AI in improving the overall security posture of social media platforms.

Appendix A

Source Python code for analyzing the detecting fake profiles on the Facebook Social network:

Extracting the data:

```python
#Load the data
import pandas as pd
import csv
import os
import xml.etree.ElementTree
import json
#from google.colab import drive
#drive.mount('/content/gdrive')

path_folder ="folder_path_for_dataset"
print(path_folder)

import json
print('tes')
i=0
for line in open(path_folder+'negative_conv.json', 'r'):
 i=i+1
 if(i>64900):
 print(i)
 #print(line)
 data = json.loads(line)
 #for p in data['msg']:
  #print(p['text'])
 data2=""
 for p in data['msg']:
 #print(p['text'])
  if(p['text']):
  data2=data2+" "+p['author']+":"+p['text'].replace
     ('\r', '').replace('\n', '')
  #print(data2)
  with open(path_folder+'predator-victim_conversations_
     text.csv', 'a') as csvFile:
```

```
writer = csv.writer(csvFile)
writer.writerow(['1',[data2]])

#print(data2)

import warnings
warnings.filterwarnings("ignore")
Source Python code for analyzing the detecting fake profiles
on the Instagram:

Import data and bibliography
import pandas as pd
import matplotlib.pyplot as plt
import numpy as np
import seaborn as sns

sns.set_style("darkgrid")
sns.set_palette("pastel")
plt.rcParams.update({'font.size': 20})

import tensorflow as tf
from tensorflow.keras.layers import Dense, Dropout

from sklearn.preprocessing import StandardScaler
from sklearn.metrics import classification_report,accuracy_
score,roc_curve,confusion_matrix

from tensorflow.keras.models import Sequential
from tensorflow.keras.layers import Dense, Dropout
```

```
# Load the training dataset # Load data for testing
train = pd.read_csv("train.csv")
test = pd.read_csv("test.csv")
```

```
Conducting exploratory data analysis
# Getting information about the dataframe
train.info()
```

```
# Get a statistical summary for a dataframe
train.describe()
```

```
Performing data visualization
# Visualize data
plt.figure(figsize=(20,10))
sns.countplot(train["fake"])
plt.show("png")
```

```
# Data visualization of the private column
plt.figure(figsize=(20,10))
```

```
sns.countplot(train["private"])
plt.show("png")
```

```
# Visualize the data of the "profile pic" column
plt.figure(figsize=(20,10))
sns.countplot(train["profile pic"])
plt.show("png")
```

```
# Data visualization
fake = train[train["fake"] == 1]
not_fake = train[train["fake"] == 0]
fig = plt.figure(figsize = (20, 10))
sns.distplot(fake["nums/length username"], label =
"fake")
sns.distplot(not_fake["nums/length username"], label =
"not fake")
fig.legend()
plt.show("png")
```

```
# Plot Correlation
plt.figure(figsize=(20, 20))
cm = train.corr()
ax = plt.subplot()
sns.heatmap(cm, annot = True, ax = ax)
plt.show("png")
```

```
Preparing data for modeling
# Training and testing dataset (input)
X_train = train.drop(columns = ['fake'])
X_test = test.drop(columns = ['fake'])
# Training and testing dataset (output)
y_train = train['fake']
y_test = test['fake']
X_train.shape, y_train.shape, X_test.shape, y_test.shape
```

```
# Scale the data before training the model
scaler_x = StandardScaler()
X_train = scaler_x.fit_transform(X_train)
X_test = scaler_x.transform(X_test)
```

```
y_train = tf.keras.utils.to_categorical(y_train, num_
classes = 2)
y_test = tf.keras.utils.to_categorical(y_test, num_
classes = 2)
```

```
Building and training a simple deep learning model
model = Sequential()
```

```
model.add(Dense(50, input_dim = 11, activation = 'relu'))
model.add(Dense(150, activation = 'relu'))
model.add(Dropout(0.3))
model.add(Dense(25, activation = 'relu'))
model.add(Dropout(0.3))
model.add(Dense(2, activation = 'softmax'))
model.summary()
```

```
model.compile(optimizer = 'adam', loss = 'categorical_-
crossentropy', metrics = ['accuracy'])
```

```
epochs_hist = model.fit(X_train, y_train, epochs = 20,
verbose = 1, validation_split = 0.1)
```

References

[1]   Cammaerts, B. (2015). Social media and activism. In R. Mansell and P. Hwa (Eds.), *The International Encyclopedia of Digital Communication and Society* (pp. 1027–1034), Oxford: Wiley-Blackwell. http://eprints.lse.ac.uk/62090/

[2]   Herath, T. B., Khanna, P., and Ahmed, M. (2022). Cybersecurity practices for social media users: A systematic literature review. *Journal of Cybersecurity and Privacy*, 2(1), 1–18.

[3]   Kross, E., Verduyn, P., Sheppes, G., Costello, C. K., Jonides, J., and Ybarra, O. (2021). Social media and well-being: Pitfalls, progress, and next steps. *Trends in Cognitive Sciences*, 25(1), 55–66.

[4]   Levine, I. T. (2022). Modeling sovereignty: Towards a legal philosophy for platforms in the People's Republic of China. *Peking University Law Journal*, 10(1), 25–73.

[5]   Krishnamurthy, B. and Wills, C. E. (2009, August). On the leakage of personally identifiable information via online social networks. In *Proceedings of the Second ACM Workshop on Online Social Networks* (pp. 7–12).

[6]   Alkhalil, Z., Hewage, C., Nawaf, L., and Khan, I. (2021). Phishing attacks: A recent comprehensive study and a new anatomy. *Frontiers in Computer Science*, 3, 563060.

[7]   Festl, R. and Quandt, T. (2013). Social relations and cyberbullying: The influence of individual and structural attributes on victimization and perpetration via the internet. *Human Communication Research*, 39(1), 101–126.

[8]   McKay, S. and Tenove, C. (2021). Disinformation as a threat to deliberative democracy. *Political Research Quarterly*, 74(3), 703–717.

[9]   Alzahrani, A. (2020). Coronavirus social engineering attacks: Issues and recommendations. *International Journal of Advanced Computer Science and Applications*, 11(5).

[10] Von Solms, R. and Van Niekerk, J. (2013). From information security to cyber security. *Computers & Security*, 38, 97–102.

[11]   Ganin, A. A., Quach, P., Panwar, M., *et al.* (2020). Multicriteria decision framework for cybersecurity risk assessment and management. *Risk Analysis*, 40(1), 183–199.

[12]   Chang, L. Y. and Coppel, N. (2020). Building cyber security awareness in a developing country: Lessons from Myanmar. *Computers & Security*, 97, 101959.

[13]   Masinde, N. and Graffi, K. (2020). Peer-to-peer-based social networks: A comprehensive survey. *SN Computer Science*, 1(5), 299.

[14]   Ruefle, R., Dorofee, A., Mundie, D., Householder, A. D., Murray, M., and Perl, S. J. (2014). Computer security incident response team development and evolution. *IEEE Security & Privacy*, 12(5), 16–26.

[15]   Samtani, S., Zhao, Z., and Krishnan, R. (2023). Secure knowledge management and cybersecurity in the era of artificial intelligence. *Information Systems Frontiers*, 25(2), 425–429.

[16]   Mutula, S. M. (2005). Peculiarities of the digital divide in sub-Saharan Africa. *Program*, 39(2), 122–138.

[17]   Bertot, J. C., Jaeger, P. T., and Hansen, D. (2012). The impact of polices on government social media usage: Issues, challenges, and recommendations. *Government Information Quarterly*, 29(1), 30–40.

[18]   Al Sabbagh, B. and Kowalski, S. (2012, June). ST (CS) 2-Featuring socio-technical cyber security warning systems. In *2012 International Conference on Cyber Security, Cyber Warfare and Digital Forensic (CyberSec)* (pp. 312–316). IEEE.

[19]   Wirkuttis, N. and Klein, H. (2017). Artificial intelligence in cybersecurity. *Cyber, Intelligence, and Security*, 1(1), 103–119.

[20]   Smith, T. R. (1984). Artificial intelligence and its applicability to geographical problem solving. *The Professional Geographer*, 36(2), 147–158.

[21]   Hammad, M. (2023). The impact of artificial intelligence (AI) programs on writing scientific research. *Annals of Biomedical Engineering*, 51, 459–460.

[22]   Salankar, N., Qaisar, S. M., Pławiak, P., Tadeusiewicz, R., and Hammad, M. (2022). EEG based alcoholism detection by oscillatory modes decomposition second order difference plots and machine learning. *Biocybernetics and Biomedical Engineering*, 42(1), 173–186.

[23]   Hammad, M., Bakrey, M., Bakhiet, A., Tadeusiewicz, R., Abd El-Latif, A. A., and Pławiak, P. (2022). A novel end-to-end deep learning approach for cancer detection based on microscopic medical images. *Biocybernetics and Biomedical Engineering*, 42(3), 737–748.

[24]   Dwivedi, Y. K., Hughes, L., Ismagilova, E., *et al.* (2021). Artificial intelligence (AI): Multidisciplinary perspectives on emerging challenges, opportunities, and agenda for research, practice and policy. *International Journal of Information Management*, 57, 101994.

[25]   Wamba-Taguimdje, S. L., Fosso Wamba, S., Kala Kamdjoug, J. R., and Tchatchouang Wanko, C. E. (2020). Influence of artificial intelligence (AI) on firm performance: The business value of AI-based transformation projects. *Business Process Management Journal*, 26(7), 1893–1924.

[26] Oudeyer, P. Y., Kaplan, F., and Hafner, V. V. (2007). Intrinsic motivation systems for autonomous mental development. *IEEE Transactions on Evolutionary Computation*, 11(2), 265–286.

[27] Hogarty, D. T., Su, J. C., Phan, K., *et al.* (2020). Artificial intelligence in dermatology—Where we are and the way to the future: A review. *American Journal of Clinical Dermatology*, 21, 41–47.

[28] Voss, P. (2007). Essentials of general intelligence: The direct path to artificial general intelligence. *Artificial General Intelligence*, 131–157.

[29] Khan, A., Sohail, A., Zahoora, U., and Qureshi, A. S. (2020). A survey of the recent architectures of deep convolutional neural networks. *Artificial Intelligence Review*, 53, 5455–5516.

[30] Sil, R., Roy, A., Bhushan, B., and Mazumdar, A. K. (2019, October). Artificial intelligence and machine learning based legal application: The state-of-the-art and future research trends. In *2019 International Conference on Computing, Communication, and Intelligent Systems (ICCCIS)* (pp. 57–62). IEEE.

[31] Kavakiotis, I., Tsave, O., Salifoglou, A., Maglaveras, N., Vlahavas, I., and Chouvarda, I. (2017). Machine learning and data mining methods in diabetes research. *Computational and Structural Biotechnology Journal*, 15, 104–116.

[32] Chen, X. W. and Lin, X. (2014). Big data deep learning: Challenges and perspectives. *IEEE Access*, 2, 514–525.

[33] Schwab, K. (2017). *The Fourth Industrial Revolution*. Currency. New York, Crown Business.

[34] Saber, S., Amin, K., Pławiak, P., Tadeusiewicz, R., and Hammad, M. (2022). Graph convolutional network with triplet attention learning for person re-identification. *Information Sciences*, 617, 331–345.

[35] Abd El-Rahiem, B. and Hammad, M. (2022). A multi-fusion IoT authentication system based on internal deep fusion of ECG signals. *Security and privacy preserving for IoT and 5G networks: Techniques, challenges, and new directions*, Springer (pp. 53–79).

[36] Prakash, A. J., Patro, K. K., Samantray, S., Pławiak, P., and Hammad, M. (2023). A deep learning technique for biometric authentication using ECG beat template matching. *Information*, 14(2), 65.

[37] Prakash, A. J., Patro, K. K., Hammad, M., Tadeusiewicz, R., and Pławiak, P. (2022). BAED: A secured biometric authentication system using ECG signal based on deep learning techniques. *Biocybernetics and Biomedical Engineering*, 42(4), 1081–1093.

[38] Sakr, A. S., Pławiak, P., Tadeusiewicz, R., and Hammad, M. (2022). Cancelable ECG biometric based on combination of deep transfer learning with DNA and amino acid approaches for human authentication. *Information Sciences*, 585, 127–143.

[39] Hammad, M., Iliyasu, A. M., Elgendy, I. A., and Abd El-Latif, A. A. (2022). End-to-end data authentication deep learning model for securing IoT configurations. *Human-Centric Computing and Information Sciences*, 12(4).

[40] Campbell, C. C. (2019). Solutions for counteracting human deception in social engineering attacks. *Information Technology & People*, 32(5), 1130–1152.

[41] Veale, M., Van Kleek, M., and Binns, R. (2018, April). Fairness and accountability design needs for algorithmic support in high-stakes public sector decision-making. In *Proceedings of the 2018 chi conference on human factors in computing systems* (pp. 1–14).

[42] Wani, M. A. and Jabin, S. (2022). Mutual clustering coefficient-based suspicious-link detection approach for online social networks. *Journal of King Saud University—Computer and Information Sciences*, 34(2), 218–231.

[43] Wani, M. A., Agarwal, N., Jabin, S., and Hussai, S. Z. (2018). Design and implementation of iMacros-based data crawler for behavioral analysis of Facebook users. Computer Science: Social and Information Networks.

[44] Wani, M. A., Agarwal, N., Jabin, S., and Hussain, S. Z. (2019). Analyzing real and fake users in Facebook network based on emotions. In *2019 11th International Conference on Communication Systems & Networks (COMSNETS), Bengaluru, India* (pp. 110–117). doi: 10.1109/ COMSNETS.2019.8711124.

[45] Wani, M. A. and Jabin, S. (2017). A sneak into the Devil's colony-fake profiles in online social networks. arXiv preprint arXiv:1705.09929.

[46] Yang, K. C., Varol, O., Davis, C. A., Ferrara, E., Flammini, A., and Menczer, F. (2019). Arming the public with artificial intelligence to counter social bots. *Human Behavior and Emerging Technologies*, 1(1), 48–61.

[47] Wani, M. A., Sofi, M. A., and Wani, S. Y. (2017). Why fake profiles: A study of anomalous users in different categories of online social networks. *International Journal of Engineering Science Technology and Research*, 4, 320–329.

[48] Wani, M. A., Agarwal, N., and Bours, P. (2021). Sexual-predator detection system based on social behavior biometric (SSB) features. *Procedia Computer Science*, 189, 116–127.

Chapter 11

Ethical and privacy concerns and challenges

Mohamed Hammad[1,2], Mudasir Ahmad Wani[1]
and Ahmed A. Abd El-Latif [1,3]

The chapter on "Ethical and privacy concerns and challenges" delves into the critical aspects of ethics and privacy in the context of artificial intelligence (AI) in social cybersecurity. In today's digital age, where AI technologies are increasingly integrated into various aspects of our lives, including cybersecurity practices, it is essential to recognize the potential ethical and privacy implications that accompany their use. This chapter aims to provide an in-depth exploration of these concerns and their significance in shaping responsible and sustainable AI deployment in the realm of social cybersecurity.

11.1 Introduction

The importance of acknowledging ethical and privacy considerations within the realm of artificial intelligence (AI) in the domain of social cybersecurity is of utmost significance [1]. With the increasing sophistication and autonomy of AI systems, there is a significant potential for their profound impact on individuals, organizations, and society at large. It is imperative to take a proactive approach in contemplating the ethical dimensions and privacy implications that are linked with these technologies, in order to guarantee their deployment in a manner that preserves fundamental rights, values, and societal norms.

The safeguarding of individual rights constitutes a key rationale for addressing these aforementioned concerns [2]. The domain of social cybersecurity involving AI pertains to the management of extensive quantities of confidential data, encompassing personal details, communication trends, and behavioral attributes [3]. Neglecting to tackle ethical and privacy issues may lead to the degradation of privacy entitlements, probable prejudicial treatment, or improper utilization of

[1]EIAS Data Science Lab, College of Computer and Information Sciences, Prince Sultan University, Saudi Arabia
[2]Department of Information Technology, Faculty of Computers and Information, Menoufia University, Egypt
[3]Department of Mathematics and Computer Science, Faculty of Science, Menoufia University, Egypt

personal data. Through the acknowledgement and resolution of these issues, stakeholders can strive to uphold personal autonomy, privacy, and dignity amidst the progression of AI technologies.

It is imperative to consider ethical and privacy concerns when developing AI-based social cybersecurity solutions in order to establish trust and promote positive public perception [4]. The establishment of trust is a crucial element in ensuring the successful integration and efficacy of said technologies. The implementation of ethical protocols and privacy measures fosters trust among users, institutions, and the broader community. Through proactive measures to tackle these issues, stakeholders can foster a favorable perception of AI systems, resulting in heightened levels of receptivity, collaboration, and enduring viability [5].

The ethical and privacy implications of AI are congruent with the legal and regulatory frameworks that oversee data protection and privacy. Adherence to legal statutes and regulations, such as the General Data Protection Regulation (GDPR), is not solely a legal mandate but also a moral imperative. Mitigating these concerns can enable organizations to circumvent legal infractions, reputational harm, and monetary sanctions [6]. Furthermore, the observance of ethical and privacy principles signifies a dedication to conscientious and answerable methodologies in the creation and implementation of social cybersecurity solutions based on AI [7].

The circumvention of bias and discrimination is a pivotal element in tackling ethical and privacy apprehensions [8]. AI systems acquire knowledge from data and subsequently render decisions that have implications for individuals. It is crucial to guarantee that these systems are formulated and educated to exhibit impartiality, lack of prejudice, and absence of discrimination. Mitigating privacy concerns is crucial in preventing the unauthorized utilization or revelation of confidential information, thereby minimizing the likelihood of discriminatory actions and upholding the fundamental values of fairness and impartiality [9].

Furthermore, ethical and privacy concerns exert a significant influence on social justice and the wider societal ramifications of AI systems [10]. Stakeholders can endeavor to achieve equitable access to AI-based social cybersecurity solutions by addressing issues pertaining to fairness, transparency, and accountability. This facilitates the reduction of the digital divide, fosters inclusiveness, and mitigates the potential adverse effects of AI implementation, particularly for underprivileged groups [11].

Ultimately, the consideration of ethical and privacy implications within AI-driven social cybersecurity initiatives promotes conscientious and enduring progress. Through the incorporation of these factors during the initial phases of the development process, stakeholders can take a proactive approach to recognizing and addressing potential hazards, thereby guaranteeing the ethical implementation of AI. The aforementioned methodology facilitates the sustainable endurance and endorsement of AI technologies, cultivating originality that conforms to communal principles and ambitions [12].

AI has become a potent instrument in augmenting social cybersecurity measures by aiding in the identification of potential threats, responding to incidents, and conducting vulnerability assessments. This development has occurred in recent times. As AI systems advance in complexity and independence, it is imperative to contemplate the ethical and privacy implications that come with their integration [13]. There are several factors that underscore the significance of addressing these concerns.

1. The safeguarding of individual rights and dignity is a matter of ethical consideration and privacy concern. The application of AI in the realm of social cybersecurity pertains to the handling of confidential information, such as personally identifiable data, communication trends, and behavioral attributes. Neglecting to attend to ethical and privacy issues may lead to violations of privacy entitlements, probable prejudicial treatment, or improper handling of personal data [14].

2. The establishment of trust in AI-based social cybersecurity solutions is a crucial factor for their efficacy and broad acceptance among the public. The implementation of ethical protocols and privacy measures fosters trust among users, institutions, and the wider community. Through the resolution of these issues, stakeholders have the potential to cultivate a favorable perception of AI systems, thereby resulting in heightened levels of receptivity and collaboration [15].

3. The ethical and privacy considerations in AI are in accordance with the legal and regulatory frameworks that oversee data protection and privacy. Adherence to legal statutes and mandates, such as the GDPR, is imperative in order to prevent legal ramifications. Disregarding these apprehensions may lead to legal transgressions, impairment of reputation, and monetary sanctions [16].

4. The mitigation of bias and discrimination is a crucial consideration in the development and deployment of AI systems, as these systems acquire knowledge from data and subsequently render decisions that can have significant implications for individuals. The incorporation of ethical considerations in the design and training of these systems is imperative to ensure their fairness, lack of bias, and nondiscriminatory nature. The act of addressing privacy concerns serves to mitigate the risk of unauthorized utilization or disclosure of confidential information, thereby minimizing the likelihood of discriminatory practices [17].

5. The promotion of social equity and mitigation of negative impacts of AI systems are contingent upon ethical and privacy considerations. Stakeholders can endeavor to achieve impartial access to social cybersecurity solutions based on AI, thereby promoting inclusiveness and bridging the digital gap, by addressing apprehensions regarding accountability, transparency, and fairness [18].

6. The promotion of sustainable and responsible innovation in the realm of AI is imperative in light of ethical and privacy concerns. Such concerns necessitate the guidance of AI system development, deployment, and usage toward responsible innovation. Through the incorporation of these factors in the initial phases, interested parties can preemptively recognize and alleviate possible hazards, guaranteeing the ethical implementation of AI in the realm of social cybersecurity [19].

The ethical and privacy considerations in AI-driven social cybersecurity are not only a moral obligation but also a pragmatic requirement. Through a comprehensive analysis of the effects of AI systems on various aspects such as individual rights, trust, legal compliance, fairness, and social impact, stakeholders can effectively cultivate a digital environment that is more secure and safe. The objective of this chapter is to furnish the essential perspectives and direction for proficiently addressing these apprehensions, thereby facilitating the conscientious and principled implementation of AI in the domain of social cybersecurity.

11.2   Ethical considerations

The deployment of AI technologies has the potential to significantly impact social cybersecurity practices [20]. However, their implementation raises a range of ethical considerations that require careful attention. The discourse pertaining to ethical considerations within the realm of AI in social cybersecurity is centered on a number of crucial domains that warrant careful consideration.

- The utilization of AI systems in social cybersecurity necessitates access to copious amounts of personal and sensitive data, thereby raising concerns regarding privacy and data protection. The acquisition, retention, and manipulation of this information give rise to apprehensions regarding the safeguarding of personal privacy and data security. Ensuring adherence to rigorous privacy standards, including, but not limited to, data anonymization, encryption, and secure storage practices, is of paramount importance for AI algorithms and systems. In order to establish trust with users, organizations are required to secure informed consent and maintain transparency regarding the utilization of data.
- The opacity of AI algorithms, particularly deep learning models, renders them inscrutable, thereby impeding comprehension of their decision-making mechanism. This poses a significant challenge to transparency and explainability. Insufficient transparency may result in a loss of confidence and give rise to ethical issues. In order to tackle this issue, endeavors ought to be undertaken to construct interpretable AI models that furnish justifications for their determinations. The implementation of explainable AI (XAI) can facilitate the comprehension of the decision-making process for both individuals and organizations. This can result in a higher level of accountability and the enablement of equitable treatment.
- The issue of bias and fairness in AI systems arises from the fact that these systems are trained on historical data that may contain inherent biases, leading to the perpetuation of discriminatory outcomes. Biases may emerge due to disproportionate training datasets or inherent biases embedded within the algorithms. The identification and mitigation of biases are essential to guarantee equity and impartiality in the treatment of all individuals. The process entails the proactive surveillance and assessment of AI systems to identify and correct instances of bias, as well as guaranteeing inclusive participation in the creation and assessment of AI models.

- The growing autonomy of AI systems has raised inquiries pertaining to accountability and liability. The attribution of accountability in cases where AI systems render decisions or inflict damage can present a complex predicament. It is imperative to establish unambiguous lines of accountability and legal frameworks pertaining to incidents related to AI, in order to ensure that both individuals and organizations are held responsible for the actions of AI systems. The aforementioned concerns pertain to the matters of accountability, openness, and the distribution of duties between human agents and AI systems.

- The establishment and maintenance of user trust in AI-based social cybersecurity solutions are heavily influenced by ethical considerations. It is imperative for individuals to possess a sense of assurance regarding the impartiality, protection, and dependability of AI systems. The integration of ethical principles, such as obtaining user consent, ensuring transparency, and establishing accountability mechanisms, can foster trust and promote user adoption. Clear communication of the advantages and drawbacks of AI systems is imperative, with the aim of ensuring that users comprehend the manner in which their data is utilized and safeguarded.

- The role of human oversight and decision-making in the context of AI systems should not be completely supplanted by automated processes. The preservation of human oversight is of utmost importance in order to guarantee the maintenance of ethical considerations. The active participation of humans can serve as a preventive measure against the indiscriminate deployment of AI systems that may result in unforeseen outcomes. It is imperative that human experts assume the responsibility of establishing demarcations, overseeing the performance of AI systems, and intervening as needed to alleviate potential hazards and ethical issues.

- The development and implementation of AI technologies ought to take into account their wider social implications, particularly with regard to social impact and inclusion. The evaluation of the impact of AI on social cybersecurity across diverse segments of society and the mitigation of potential disparities is of paramount importance. The ethical considerations of utmost importance include ensuring inclusivity, minimizing social biases, and accounting for the needs of marginalized communities. The mitigation of negative social impact of AI systems can be achieved through the active pursuit of diverse perspectives and the involvement of stakeholders in both the design and deployment phases.

It is imperative to acknowledge and address the ethical implications that arise in the context of AI utilization in social cybersecurity, in order to promote responsible and ethical deployment of AI technologies. Through the acknowledgement and proactive resolution of these issues, stakeholders can cultivate confidence, safeguard confidentiality, advance equity, and guarantee that AI systems make constructive contributions to social cybersecurity protocols while maintaining ethical norms.

Unscrupulous practices in the field of AI present notable hazards and may exert extensive effects on diverse facets of society. Comprehending and investigating these hazards is imperative in order to alleviate negative consequences and advance ethical AI creation and implementation. The discourse surrounding the possible hazards and ramifications of unethical AI practices encompasses various crucial domains that warrant thorough investigation [21].

- The perpetuation of discrimination and bias is a potential consequence of unethical AI practices, which can result in unequal treatment and the reinforcement of preexisting societal inequalities. AI systems that are trained on biased data or developed with biased algorithms have the potential to generate discriminatory outcomes, which can have an impact on various domains, including, but not limited to, hiring, lending, and law enforcement. The presence of biases has the potential to exert a disproportionate effect on communities that are marginalized, thereby perpetuating systemic injustices. It is imperative to mitigate these potential hazards through the utilization of equitable and impartial data gathering, algorithmic construction, and assessment methodologies.
- Unethical practices in the field of AI have the potential to encroach upon the privacy rights of individuals through the facilitation of unauthorized access, misuse, or mishandling of personal data. AI system mechanisms or superfluous or redundant data exhibit inadequate consent mechanisms or possess feeble security measures that can result in privacy violations and data breaches. The aforementioned transgressions can result in significant repercussions, such as the misappropriation of personal identity, monitoring, and unapproved categorization. Enhanced regulatory measures and comprehensive privacy protocols are imperative to safeguard personal privacy and alleviate associated hazards.
- Unethical practices in the field of AI can potentially lead to security vulnerabilities, thereby exposing crucial systems to cyber threats. AI systems are vulnerable to exploitation by malicious actors who can carry out various types of sophisticated attacks such as adversarial attacks, data poisoning, or model manipulation. The aforementioned attacks have the potential to jeopardize the integrity, availability, and confidentiality of both data and systems, resulting in financial ramifications, operational interruptions, and breaches of privacy. The implementation of proactive security measures, thorough testing, and ongoing monitoring is imperative in order to effectively reduce potential risks and guarantee the durability of AI systems.
- The implementation of unethical AI practices can result in notable disruptions to both the economic and employment sectors. Insufficient contemplation of workforce transitions and retraining during the automation of jobs may result in job displacement and worsen socioeconomic disparities. Unjust business practices, such as the exercise of monopoly power or the utilization of AI for market manipulation, have the potential to impede competition and impede the progress of the economy. It is imperative to mitigate these potential hazards by means of conscientious integration of AI, initiatives for retraining, and regulatory measures that foster equitable competition and safeguard the rights of laborers.

- The unethical practices of AI can result in the erosion of human agency and decision-making, ultimately leading to a loss of control over critical systems and processes. The utilization of AI systems without adequate human supervision and accountability measures may lead to inadvertent outcomes and ethical predicaments. The absence of human control in domains such as autonomous vehicles, healthcare, or criminal justice can result in significant consequences for safety, ethics, and justice. It is imperative to uphold human oversight and integrate ethical frameworks that prioritize human values and judgment in order to effectively mitigate these potential hazards.

- Unethical practices in the field of AI can potentially facilitate the dissemination of disinformation, deepfakes, and manipulative content. AI algorithms have the potential to augment the spread of fabricated news, influence public perception, and generate tailored disinformation initiatives. The aforementioned practices have the potential to erode democratic processes, diminish public trust, and weaken social cohesion. Enhancing digital literacy, advocating for algorithmic transparency, and establishing effective content moderation mechanisms are crucial in addressing the hazards linked to AI-powered manipulation and disinformation.

- The utilization of unethical practices in the field of AI can lead to intricate ethical predicaments and difficulties in attributing responsibility. The deployment of autonomous AI systems or those that make decisions without well-defined accountability frameworks can pose challenges in assigning responsibility in the event of errors, biases, or harm. The establishment of ethical guidelines, regulatory frameworks, and auditing and monitoring mechanisms for AI systems can effectively tackle the aforementioned challenges and promote accountability for the conduct and judgments of AI.

It is imperative to investigate and comprehend the potential hazards and consequences of unethical practices in the field of AI in order to cultivate confidence, guarantee impartiality, and advance responsible development and implementation of AI. Through a thorough exploration of these factors, it is possible to take preemptive measures to manage and alleviate the adverse effects linked to AI in the realm of social cybersecurity [22].

Foremost, it is imperative to increase awareness regarding the ethical considerations associated with AI in the realm of social cybersecurity. The recognition of potential harm that unethical AI practices can cause to individuals and society as a whole is facilitated by the involvement of stakeholders such as policymakers, researchers, and industry professionals. The consciousness of these hazards enables us to adopt preemptive measures to mitigate them [23].

Furthermore, through the examination of ethical implications linked to AI in the realm of social cybersecurity, it is possible to construct a structure for the conscientious advancement and application of AI. The framework ought to prioritize the incorporation of transparency, accountability, and fairness in AI systems. The utilization of ethical guidelines and standards can provide direction for the development, execution, and assessment of AI algorithms and models, guaranteeing their alignment with fundamental values such as nondiscriminatory practices, safeguarding of privacy, and upholding of human rights [24].

Moreover, the examination of potential hazards and consequences arising from unethical AI practices facilitates the identification of deficiencies in current regulations and policies. The assessment of the adequacy of current legal frameworks in addressing the distinct challenges presented by AI in the realm of social cybersecurity is made possible through this approach. By means of such deliberations, policymakers can formulate and implement suitable legal frameworks and standards that safeguard the rights of individuals and foster ethical practices in the field of AI.

Interdisciplinary collaboration is imperative in addressing ethical considerations. The integration of multidisciplinary experts, encompassing computer science, ethics, law, and social sciences, can facilitate a holistic comprehension of the intricate matters pertaining to AI in the context of social cybersecurity. The act of collaborating can facilitate a multifaceted strategy for tackling ethical issues, encompassing technical, legal, social, and ethical viewpoints [25].

Furthermore, a comprehensive examination of the ethical implications linked to AI in social cybersecurity prompts entities and programmers to incorporate ethical frameworks and guidelines into their developmental procedures. The significance of integrating ethical principles into the initial phases of AI system design, such as data collection, algorithm development, and model training, is underscored. Through the incorporation of ethical considerations, it is possible to pursue the development of AI systems that exhibit not only efficacy, but also accountability, equity, and deference to the rights of individuals [26].

Finally, the examination of ethical implications linked to AI in the realm of social cybersecurity elicits crucial introspection and discourse among the general populace. The deployment of AI technologies in the realm of cybersecurity prompts societal discourse regarding the associated values, risks, and trade-offs. The significance of public awareness and engagement cannot be overstated in the context of shaping policies, regulations, and norms that are in-line with societal values and that guarantee the utilization of AI in manners that safeguard and benefit individuals and communities [27].

Within the realm of social cybersecurity in the field of AI, a multitude of ethical frameworks and guidelines can be employed to guarantee conscientious and ethical conduct. The frameworks in question provide a fundamental basis for the creation of AI systems that place emphasis on equitable treatment, lucidity, liability, and consideration for the liberties of individuals. Let us examine a few instances of these frameworks:

- The ethical principle of ensuring fairness and nondiscrimination is a crucial aspect of AI systems. The implementation of ethical frameworks, such as the fairness, accountability, and transparency framework, is advocated to facilitate the creation of AI algorithms that do not propagate biases or exhibit discriminatory behavior toward individuals on the basis of protected attributes such as race, gender, or religion. These frameworks promote the utilization of fairness metrics and techniques to alleviate algorithmic bias and foster equitable treatment [28].

- Safeguarding the privacy of individuals is a crucial ethical concern. The GDPR in the European Union offers a set of principles that govern the ethical acquisition, retention, and utilization of personal data. The authors prioritize the acquisition of informed consent, the establishment of data security protocols, and the implementation of anonymization or pseudonymization techniques to safeguard the privacy rights of individuals [29].

- The capacity to provide explanations and comprehend the decision-making process of AI is of paramount importance in establishing accountability and fostering confidence. The XAI guidelines and other ethical frameworks espouse the creation of AI systems that offer comprehensible justifications for their decisions and behaviors. The utilization of interpretable models and algorithms is promoted by these frameworks, which facilitate the provision of insights into the decision-making process of AI. This, in turn, empowers individuals to comprehend and question the outcomes of AI [30].

- The development of AI is often guided by ethical frameworks that prioritize a human-centric design approach. The incorporation of end-users and stakeholders in the design process is advocated to guarantee that AI systems are in accordance with their values and requirements. The promotion of participatory design methodologies and user-centered approaches is advocated in order to integrate a range of perspectives and forestall the implementation of AI systems that could potentially have adverse effects on individuals or communities [31].

- The implementation of mechanisms for ethical governance and accountability is of paramount importance. Ethical frameworks emphasize the significance of organizational policies, guidelines, and review processes in guaranteeing the responsible development and utilization of AI. They advocate for the implementation of mechanisms that facilitate the auditing, monitoring, and assessment of AI systems, with the aim of identifying and addressing ethical concerns. Furthermore, it is recommended that organizations establish unambiguous roles and responsibilities to ensure ethical practices in the development and deployment of AI systems [32].

- The ethical frameworks underscore the importance of responsible and ethical utilization of data. The proponents of data minimization espouse the principle of limiting the amount of data that AI systems gather and store to only what is essential for their designated function. Frameworks emphasize the significance of data quality, data security, and refraining from utilizing data acquired through unethical channels [33].

11.3 Privacy concerns

The convergence of AI and social cybersecurity gives rise to noteworthy privacy apprehensions attributable to the acquisition, retention, and analysis of individualized information. In this particular domain, AI systems frequently depend on copious amounts of data, encompassing social media posts, online activities, and personal data, to scrutinize user conduct, identify potential hazards, and safeguard against cyber intrusions. Nevertheless, the utilization of data-intensive methods may have the potential to encroach upon the privacy rights of individuals. This domain gives rise to several significant privacy concerns.

- The phenomenon of invasive data collection refers to the acquisition of substantial amounts of personal information by AI systems without the explicit knowledge or consent of the individuals concerned. The aforementioned can encompass personal identifying information, browsing activity, geographic positioning data, and interactions on social media platforms. The unselective gathering of such information gives rise to apprehensions regarding the privacy rights of individuals and the possibility of unauthorized exploitation or abuse of their personal data.
- In the realm of social cybersecurity, AI algorithms frequently employ profiling and behavioral tracking techniques to discern anomalous patterns or recognize potential hazards. Although these methods have the potential to improve security protocols, they may also give rise to apprehensions regarding privacy. The practice of creating detailed profiles of individuals through the analysis of their online activities and behavior has the potential to encroach upon their privacy and autonomy.
- The sharing of collected data with third-party entities for analysis, collaboration, or other purposes is a common practice in AI systems. The aforementioned scenario poses potential privacy hazards, as individuals may lack agency over the distribution and utilization of their personal data beyond the immediate setting. The possibility of data breaches or unauthorized access by third-party entities gives rise to apprehensions regarding data security and personal privacy.

The utilization of AI in social cybersecurity is accompanied by various data collection, storage, and processing techniques that have been identified as potential sources of privacy concerns:

- The issue of overcollection of personal data by AI systems may arise, wherein an excessive amount of data may be gathered beyond the scope of the intended purpose, thereby posing a potential threat to the privacy of individuals. The act of collecting personal identifiers, location data, or sensitive information without explicit consent can give rise to significant privacy concerns.
- The storage of substantial amounts of personal data in databases or cloud environments necessitates the implementation of robust security measures to mitigate the risks associated with insecure data storage. Insufficient implementation of data security measures may lead to occurrences of data breaches, unauthorized entry, or loss of personal data. The compromise of individuals' privacy can occur due to weak encryption, inadequate access controls, or improper data handling.

- The implementation of anonymization or pseudonymization techniques is imperative for safeguarding the privacy and identities of individuals in AI systems utilized for social cybersecurity purposes. Insufficient anonymization or pseudonymization of data may lead to the reidentification of individuals, thereby linking their personal information to their identities and potentially jeopardizing their privacy.
- The utilization of AI systems in social cybersecurity frequently entails automated decision-making procedures that possess the potential to affect the liberties and entitlements of individuals. The absence of transparency and comprehensibility in such systems may give rise to apprehensions regarding the capacity of individuals to comprehend or contest verdicts that impact them, thereby potentially violating their privacy entitlements.

The collection, storage, and processing of personal data in the realm of AI in social cybersecurity are subject to various privacy laws and regulations. The objective of these laws is to safeguard the privacy rights of individuals and promote the responsible management of their data. Several noteworthy instances can be cited, such as

- The GDPR is a regulatory framework that imposes stringent standards for the handling of personal data, and it is enforceable within the European Union. The aforementioned principles, namely, data minimization, purpose limitation, and individual rights, are given significant emphasis. It is imperative for organizations to acquire informed consent, implement suitable data security measures, and ensure transparency in their data-processing practices [34].
- The California Consumer Privacy Act (CCPA) confers specific rights and authority to California inhabitants with respect to their personal information. Businesses are obligated to reveal their data collection procedures, provide opt-out alternatives, and abstain from trading personal data without explicit authorization. The CCPA enforces sanctions for failure to adhere to its provisions and confers authority upon individuals to pursue legal recourse in the event of privacy breaches [35].
- The Personal Data Protection Bill (PDPB) is a comprehensive legislation in India designed to regulate the collection, storage, and processing of personal data. Its primary objective is to ensure data protection. The aforementioned principles, namely, purpose limitation, data localization, and individual consent, are introduced. The PDPB institutes a regulatory body, known as the Data Protection Authority, with the mandate to supervise adherence to data protection regulations and administer sanctions for infringements of privacy and data security [36].
- The Health Insurance Portability and Accountability Act (HIPAA) is a regulatory framework in the United States that is designed to safeguard the confidentiality and integrity of personal health information. Its primary objective is to ensure the privacy and security of individuals' health data. The regulations mandate stringent obligations on healthcare providers, insurers, and their affiliates to guarantee the privacy of confidential medical information [37].

- The Personal Information Protection and Electronic Documents Act (PIPEDA) is a Canadian federal law that governs the collection, use, and disclosure of personal information by private sector organizations in the course of commercial activities. The private sector organizations in Canada are governed by PIPEDA, which regulates the collection, utilization, and dissemination of personal information. The concept places significant emphasis on the principles of consent, accountability, and individual data access. The PIPEDA mandates that organizations comply with privacy principles while managing personal information [38].

Adherence to privacy laws and regulations is of utmost importance for entities functioning within the realm of social cybersecurity in AI. It is imperative to incorporate privacy-by-design principles, perform privacy impact assessments, acquire informed consent, and guarantee secure data-handling practices. Through compliance with these regulations, entities can ensure the preservation of individuals' privacy entitlements and sustain confidence in the deployment of AI technologies for the purpose of social cybersecurity.

11.4   Responsible AI practices

The concept of responsible AI practices pertains to the conscientious and responsible deployment of AI technologies, with a focus on ethical considerations and accountability. Within the realm of social cybersecurity, the implementation of responsible AI practices is imperative in safeguarding the confidentiality of personal information, maintaining ethical principles, and minimizing the likelihood of prejudicial or detrimental effects stemming from AI algorithms. The implementation of ethical AI practices involves a range of principles and guidelines that strive to advance equity, clarity, and liability throughout the creation, implementation, and utilization of AI systems [39].

The implementation of impartial and lucid AI algorithms is of utmost importance in the domain of social cybersecurity, as it serves to prevent prejudicial practices, inequitable treatment, and adverse societal consequences. The presence of bias in AI algorithms can stem from a multitude of factors, such as partiality in the training data, decisions made in the design of the algorithm, or the unconscious biases of those responsible for its development. Algorithms that exhibit bias have the potential to sustain and intensify preexisting societal biases, resulting in inequitable consequences and prejudicial treatment toward specific individuals or groups [11].

In order to mitigate these concerns, it is imperative to construct AI algorithms that are intentionally crafted to be impartial and lucid. The objective of unbiased algorithms is to promote impartiality and equitability by reducing or eradicating partialities in the process of decision-making. Algorithms that exhibit transparency offer lucid explications and rationales for their determinations, thereby facilitating comprehension of the fundamental reasoning and identification of any possible partialities or inaccuracies by the users. The present chapter aims to investigate the significance of explainability and accountability in mitigating ethical and privacy concerns.

The incorporation of explainability and accountability is crucial in mitigating ethical and privacy issues that arise from the utilization of AI in the realm of social cybersecurity. The concept of explainability pertains to the capacity to comprehend and construe the manner in which AI algorithms reach their determinations or prognostications. Transparency is a crucial element in the development and deployment of algorithms as it fosters trust, facilitates critical inquiry, and allows for corrective measures in the event of inaccuracies, prejudices, or violations of privacy.

The concept of accountability pertains to the obligation and legal culpability of the persons or entities engaged in the creation, implementation, or utilization of AI systems. The implementation of ethical and legal compliance in the use of AI technologies necessitates the establishment of unambiguous lines of responsibility, oversight mechanisms, and accountability frameworks. The implementation of accountability measures can encompass a range of strategies, such as conducting audits, establishing monitoring systems, forming ethical review boards, and formulating guidelines to ensure responsible development and deployment of AI. The integration of explainability and accountability features within AI systems can enable stakeholders to effectively tackle issues pertaining to privacy breaches, discriminatory practices, and opacity. The aforementioned practices serve to foster ethical decision-making, incentivize responsible conduct among both AI developers and users, and streamline the identification and remediation of potential ethical and privacy hazards.

In the realm of social cybersecurity, ethical and privacy concerns can be effectively addressed through the implementation of responsible AI practices, unbiased and transparent algorithms, and the incorporation of explainability and accountability mechanisms. The implementation of these measures serves to guarantee the conscientious and principled utilization of AI technologies, safeguard the privacy entitlements of individuals, and uphold the confidence of the general public in the application of AI systems for social cybersecurity objectives.

11.5   Mitigation strategies

The effective management of ethical and privacy concerns related to AI in the realm of social cybersecurity necessitates the utilization of diverse strategies and techniques. An effective strategy involves implementing a proactive and iterative ethical assessment framework throughout the entire process of creating and implementing AI systems. The framework entails the identification of plausible ethical hazards, active involvement of stakeholders in the decision-making process, and the implementation of ethical impact evaluations to guarantee that the technology adheres to societal values and standards [40].

Furthermore, it is imperative for organizations to establish unambiguous ethical protocols and codes of behavior that regulate the implementation of AI in the realm of social cybersecurity. The guidelines ought to encompass concerns pertaining to data privacy, transparency, fairness, and accountability. It is possible to implement regular ethics training and awareness programs aimed at educating employees and stakeholders on the responsible utilization of AI technologies.

The implementation of data protection measures is of utmost importance in ensuring privacy protection and risk reduction in the context of AI in social cybersecurity. The utilization of encryption is a prevalent method for safeguarding confidential information. The process entails the transformation of information into an encoded format that is exclusively accessible to authorized individuals possessing the decryption key. Through the process of data encryption, unauthorized individuals are prevented from accessing and utilizing intercepted or compromised data, as it is rendered indecipherable and unusable.

The implementation of access controls is a crucial element in safeguarding data. Access control mechanisms are implemented to guarantee that solely authorized individuals possess the requisite permissions to access, modify, or utilize sensitive data. The aforementioned tasks encompass the deployment of procedures for verifying user identity, regulating access based on assigned roles, and establishing surveillance measures for the purpose of monitoring data usage and retrieval.

Moreover, it is recommended to implement data minimization strategies in order to solely gather and preserve the essential data for the purpose of AI. Organizations can mitigate the risk of unauthorized access or misuse of personal information by minimizing data collection.

Anonymization methods are used to eliminate or alter personally identifiable information from data, thus safeguarding privacy. The aforementioned techniques endeavor to disassociate data from particular individuals, thereby rendering it arduous to ascertain or establish a connection between the data and an individual's identity. Data masking is a widely used method for anonymization, which involves substituting sensitive data with either generalized or fictitious values. One possible approach to protect privacy in research is to use pseudonyms or aggregate data to conceal individual-level information. K-anonymity is a method that guarantees the anonymity of individual records in a dataset by making them indistinguishable from a minimum of $k-1$ other records. This approach effectively safeguards privacy [41].

Differential privacy is a sophisticated methodology that introduces perturbation to the dataset with the aim of thwarting the possibility of re-identification. The technique ensures that the inclusion or exclusion of an individual's data does not exert a substantial impact on the overall results of data analysis, thereby safeguarding confidentiality while enabling significant analysis.

The implementation of anonymization techniques is of paramount importance in the realm of social cybersecurity, as it facilitates the utilization of data for purposes such as research, analysis, and training of AI models, while simultaneously mitigating the potential for privacy violations. It is crucial to acknowledge that while anonymization is a widely used technique to protect privacy, it is not infallible. The possibility of reidentification attacks or the integration of anonymized data with external datasets poses a potential threat to privacy. Hence, it is imperative to conduct continuous research and assessment of anonymization methodologies to ascertain their efficacy in safeguarding confidentiality concerning AI in the domain of social cybersecurity.

11.6   Collaboration and governance

The importance of stakeholder collaboration cannot be overstated in tackling the ethical and privacy issues that arise from the implementation of AI in social cybersecurity. The intricate nature of these challenges necessitates the involvement of experts from diverse domains to formulate all-encompassing and efficacious resolutions. Collaboration is an approach that encompasses various perspectives, including technical, legal, ethical, and societal considerations, in a comprehensive manner.

The involvement of AI developers is crucial in guaranteeing that ethical considerations are incorporated into the design and implementation of AI systems. The individuals in question bear the responsibility of incorporating techniques that enhance privacy, mechanisms that promote transparency, and algorithms that ensure fairness into the AI models. The involvement of cybersecurity professionals is imperative in the detection and reduction of potential security threats, thereby guaranteeing the resilience of AI systems against vulnerabilities and attacks [42].

The regulatory framework surrounding AI in social cybersecurity is significantly influenced by policymakers who hold a pivotal position in shaping it. Engaging in collaboration with policymakers facilitates the alignment of the development and deployment of AI technologies with legal and ethical frameworks. Policymakers have the potential to make significant contributions to the regulation of data collection, storage, and usage, as well as the establishment of accountability and transparency frameworks in AI systems [43].

Privacy advocates are crucial in promoting and safeguarding individuals' privacy rights while also ensuring that privacy-related issues are appropriately resolved. Engaging in collaboration with privacy advocates can serve to increase awareness regarding potential privacy risks, facilitate the adoption of privacy-enhancing technologies, and incentivize organizations to implement privacy-centric practices in the development of AI [44].

Multi-stakeholder governance frameworks offer a forum for stakeholders engaged in AI in social cybersecurity to collaborate and coordinate. These frameworks facilitate the collaboration of stakeholders from diverse sectors such as academia, industry, civil society, and government, in order to jointly tackle ethical and privacy issues.

These frameworks serve to enable the creation of protocols, benchmarks, and optimal methodologies that foster ethical AI conduct. The platform offers a space for discourse, dissemination of information, and the transfer of specialized knowledge in order to tackle nascent ethical and privacy concerns. Multi-stakeholder governance frameworks ensure that decisions and policies are reflective of the interests and concerns of all stakeholders involved by incorporating diverse perspectives.

The utilization of such frameworks additionally facilitates the establishment of trust and bolstering of public confidence in the realm of AI technologies. The demonstration of a steadfast dedication to transparency, accountability, and fairness is crucial in promoting the responsible and ethical utilization of AI in the realm of social cybersecurity. In addition, governance frameworks that involve multiple stakeholders promote sustained communication and cooperation, facilitating perpetual enhancement and adjustment in response to evolving technological and societal contexts.

Several noteworthy collaborations and initiatives have demonstrated the favorable results of multi-stakeholder collaboration in tackling ethical and privacy issues in AI-powered social cybersecurity. An instance of collaborative effort in the field of AI is the Partnership on AI, which involves prominent technology corporations, academic establishments, and nongovernmental organizations. The primary objective of this initiative is to tackle the obstacles associated with the development and implementation of AI, which encompasses ethical deliberations. The collaboration is centered on the advocacy of equity, lucidity, and responsibility in AI systems, while also tackling apprehensions associated with partiality, confidentiality, and safeguarding [45].

An additional instance is the Global Network Initiative (GNI), a multifaceted entity that unites technology corporations, civil society groups, investors, and scholars. The GNI endeavors to safeguard and promote the fundamental principles of freedom of speech and privacy in the contemporary era of digital technology. The organization formulates and executes ethical standards and directives that govern the conduct of technology enterprises with regard to human rights, encompassing topics pertaining to AI and cybersecurity [46].

In addition, the formation of research centers and consortiums with a specific focus on AI ethics and privacy has been facilitated through partnerships among academic institutions, government agencies, and industry stakeholders. The aforementioned cooperative endeavors facilitate cross-disciplinary investigation, exchange of information, and formulation of policies.

11.7 Future directions and recommendations

The progression of AI technologies is anticipated to give rise to novel ethical and privacy predicaments within the realm of social cybersecurity. It is imperative to investigate these patterns in order to anticipate and proactively tackle potential issues [47].

An emerging phenomenon in the realm of social media is the growing utilization of social media analytics and monitoring tools that are powered by AI. Although these tools provide significant insights into cybersecurity objectives, they give rise to apprehensions concerning user privacy and surveillance. Achieving a harmonious equilibrium between efficacious cybersecurity protocols and safeguarding personal privacy will pose a substantial ethical predicament.

An emerging phenomenon in the realm of cybersecurity is the amalgamation of AI with Internet of Things (IoT) devices, particularly in the context of social cybersecurity applications. The phenomenon of convergence gives rise to novel intricacies concerning the acquisition, retention, and dissemination of data. It is imperative to prioritize the safeguarding of personal information gathered by IoT devices, while simultaneously upholding transparency regarding the utilization of said data.

The utilization of autonomous systems powered by AI for decision-making in the realm of social cybersecurity poses ethical quandaries. Inquiries pertaining to accountability, transparency, and the likelihood of algorithmic bias are raised. It is imperative to comprehend the effects of these systems on the rights and welfare of individuals and to establish accountability mechanisms.

In order to tackle the ethical and privacy dilemmas that arise in the domain of AI-powered social cybersecurity, a number of suggestions and optimal methodologies can be implemented:

- The principle of privacy by design advocates for the integration of privacy-related factors into the initial stages of the design and development of AI systems. To safeguard the privacy of individuals, it is recommended to deploy privacy-enhancing technologies such as access controls, data anonymization, and encryption.
- It is recommended to establish ethical guidelines and codes of conduct that are industry-specific to AI in the realm of social cybersecurity. Such measures would ensure that ethical considerations are taken into account and upheld across the industry. The guidelines ought to encompass the principles of transparency, fairness, accountability, and user privacy protection.
- It is recommended to perform thorough risk assessments and impact analyses in order to identify potential ethical and privacy risks that may be associated with AI systems. One can reduce these potential hazards by implementing suitable measures, such as conducting audits for algorithmic fairness and establishing protocols for safeguarding data.
- It is imperative to guarantee that individuals have authority over their personal data and are furnished with lucid and comprehensible consent mechanisms. It is imperative to clearly and openly convey to users the objectives and consequences of gathering and manipulating data.
- The implementation of regular monitoring and auditing processes is recommended to detect and address any ethical or privacy issues that may arise. This encompasses the continuous assessment of AI algorithms with regards to equitable outcomes, partiality, and inadvertent ramifications.

In order to tackle the ethical and privacy dilemmas that arise in the domain of AI-powered social cybersecurity, a number of suggestions and optimal methodologies can be implemented:

- The principle of privacy by design advocates for the integration of privacy-related factors into the initial stages of the design and development of AI systems. To safeguard the privacy of individuals, it is recommended to deploy privacy-enhancing technologies such as access controls, data anonymization, and encryption.

- It is recommended to establish ethical guidelines and codes of conduct that are industry-specific to AI in the realm of social cybersecurity. Such measures would ensure that ethical considerations are taken into account and upheld across the industry. The guidelines ought to encompass the principles of transparency, fairness, accountability, and user privacy protection.
- It is recommended to perform thorough risk assessments and impact analyses in order to identify potential ethical and privacy risks that may be associated with AI systems. One can reduce these potential hazards by implementing suitable measures, such as conducting audits for algorithmic fairness and establishing protocols for safeguarding data.
- It is imperative to guarantee that individuals have authority over their personal data and are furnished with lucid and comprehensible consent mechanisms. It is imperative to clearly and openly convey to users the objectives and consequences of gathering and manipulating data.
- The implementation of regular monitoring and auditing processes is recommended to detect and address any ethical or privacy issues that may arise. This encompasses the continuous assessment of AI algorithms with regards to equitable outcomes, partiality, and inadvertent ramifications.

11.8   Conclusion

The present chapter explored the convergence of AI and social cybersecurity, emphasizing the importance of tackling ethical and privacy issues within this realm. The discourse was initiated by presenting a comprehensive outline of AI and its significance in the domain of social cybersecurity, underscoring its prospective advantages and hazards. The significance of implementing responsible AI practices and the imperative for impartial and lucid algorithms were underscored.

This chapter delved into the ethical implications that arise in the context of social cybersecurity when employing AI, encompassing concerns related to privacy, impartiality, answerability, and the likelihood of algorithmic prejudices. The study analyzed the possible hazards and consequences associated with unethical practices in the field of AI, including, but not limited to, breaches of privacy, discriminatory results, and manipulation of social behavior. The presentation showcased real-life case studies that served as exemplars to demonstrate the ramifications of unethical practices in the field of AI.

The issue of privacy was thoroughly deliberated, with emphasis on the difficulties associated with the acquisition, retention, and manipulation of data. The chapter delved into pertinent privacy laws and regulations, including the GDPR and CCPA, and underscored the significance of adherence to safeguard the privacy rights of individuals. The study analyzed various data protection strategies, such as encryption, access controls, and anonymization techniques, and demonstrated their significance in safeguarding confidentiality.

The chapter underscored the significance of fostering collaboration among various stakeholders, such as AI developers, cybersecurity specialists, policymakers, and privacy advocates. The discourse revolved around the significance of multi-stakeholder governance frameworks in tackling ethical and privacy predicaments. The session also highlighted instances of fruitful partnerships and undertakings in this domain.

The study delved into the upcoming developments and potential obstacles in social cybersecurity that rely on AI, emphasizing the importance of ongoing surveillance and adjustment of ethical and privacy protocols. Effective mitigation of ethical and privacy risks was facilitated through the provision of recommendations and best practices, including privacy by design, ethical guidelines, and risk assessments.

The chapter highlights the crucial significance of addressing ethical and privacy concerns in the domain of AI-based social cybersecurity. AI technologies possess the capacity to yield substantial advantages; however, they also present intricate ethical predicaments and privacy hazards. Neglecting to attend to these issues may result in unfavorable outcomes such as violations of privacy, prejudiced behaviors, and a decline in the confidence of the general public.

The chapter elucidated the probable societal ramifications of unscrupulous AI practices, including the exacerbation of prejudices, manipulation of public sentiment, and infringement of privacy entitlements. The statement underscored the importance of implementing ethical AI methodologies that prioritize equitable outcomes, open communication, and responsible conduct. Through the consideration of ethical and privacy implications, stakeholders can facilitate the conscientious implementation of AI in the realm of social cybersecurity, thereby minimizing the likelihood of adverse effects.

References

[1]   Burton, J., and Soare, S. R. (May, 2019). Understanding the strategic implications of the weaponization of artificial intelligence. In *2019 11th International Conference on Cyber Conflict (CyCon)* (Vol. 900, pp. 1–17). IEEE.

[2]   Kalloniatis, C., Kavakli, E., and Gritzalis, S. (2008). Addressing privacy requirements in system design: The PriS method. *Requirements Engineering*, 13, 241–255.

[3]   Samtani, S., Kantarcioglu, M., and Chen, H. (2020). Trailblazing the artificial intelligence for cybersecurity discipline: A multi-disciplinary research roadmap. *ACM Transactions on Management Information Systems (TMIS)*, 11(4), 1–19.

[4]   Du, S., and Xie, C. (2021). Paradoxes of artificial intelligence in consumer markets: Ethical challenges and opportunities. *Journal of Business Research*, 129, 961–974.

[5]   Jobin, A., Ienca, M., and Vayena, E. (2019). The global landscape of AI ethics guidelines. *Nature Machine Intelligence*, 1(9), 389–399.

[6]   Binns, R. (2017). Data protection impact assessments: A meta-regulatory approach. *International Data Privacy Law*, 7(1), 22–35.

[7] Fjeld, J., Achten, N., Hilligoss, H., Nagy, A., and Srikumar, M. (2020). Principled artificial intelligence: Mapping consensus in ethical and rights-based approaches to principles for AI. *Berkman Klein Center Research Publication No. 2020-1*. Berkman Klein Center.

[8] Roberts, J. L. (2014). Protecting privacy to prevent discrimination. *William & Mary Law Review*, 56, 2097.

[9] Padden, M. and Öjehag-Pettersson, A. (2021). Protected how? Problem representations of risk in the General Data Protection Regulation (GDPR). *Critical Policy Studies*, 15(4), 486–503.

[10] Floridi, L. and Cowls, J. (2022). A unified framework of five principles for AI in society. In: *Machine learning and the city: Applications in architecture and urban design* (pp. 535–545). Wiley Online Library.

[11] Siala, H. and Wang, Y. (2022). SHIFTing artificial intelligence to be responsible in healthcare: A systematic review. *Social Science & Medicine*, 296, 114782.

[12] Paraman, P. and Anamalah, S. (2023). Ethical artificial intelligence framework for a good AI society: Principles, opportunities and perils. *AI & Society*, 38(2), 595–611.

[13] Kaloudi, N. and Li, J. (2020). The AI-based cyber threat landscape: A survey. *ACM Computing Surveys (CSUR)*, 53(1), 1–34.

[14] Foxman, E. R. and Kilcoyne, P. (1993). Information technology, marketing practice, and consumer privacy: Ethical issues. *Journal of Public Policy & Marketing*, 12(1), 106–119.

[15] Brinkerhoff, J. M. (2002). *Partnership for international development: Rhetoric or results?*. United States: Lynne Rienner Publishers.

[16] Rothman, D. J. (2017). *The discovery of the asylum: Social order and disorder in the new republic*. London and New York, (Taylor and Francis): Routledge.

[17] Wang, S., Jiang, X., Singh, S., *et al.* (2017). Genome privacy: Challenges, technical approaches to mitigate risk, and ethical considerations in the United States. *Annals of the New York Academy of Sciences*, 1387(1), 73–83.

[18] Bhatt, H., Bahuguna, R., Singh, R., *et al.* (2022). Artificial intelligence and robotics led technological tremors: A seismic shift towards digitizing the legal ecosystem. *Applied Sciences*, 12(22), 11687.

[19] Wyatt, A. and Galliott, J. (2021). An empirical examination of the impact of cross-cultural perspectives on value sensitive design for autonomous systems. *Information*, 12(12), 527.

[20] Taddeo, M., McCutcheon, T., and Floridi, L. (2019). Trusting artificial intelligence in cybersecurity is a double-edged sword. *Nature Machine Intelligence*, 1(12), 557–560.

[21] Mohamed, S., Png, M. T., and Isaac, W. (2020). Decolonial AI: Decolonial theory as sociotechnical foresight in artificial intelligence. *Philosophy & Technology*, 33, 659–684.

[22] Haluza, D. and Jungwirth, D. (2023). Artificial intelligence and ten societal megatrends: An exploratory study using GPT-3. *Systems*, 11(3), 120.

[23] Jayanti, R. K. and Burns, A. C. (1998). The antecedents of preventive health care behavior: An empirical study. *Journal of the Academy of Marketing Science*, 26(1), 6–15.

[24] Akter, S., Dwivedi, Y. K., Sajib, S., Biswas, K., Bandara, R. J., and Michael, K. (2022). Algorithmic bias in machine learning-based marketing models. *Journal of Business Research*, 144, 201–216.

[25] Sautermeister, J., Mathieu, R., and Bogner, V. (2015). Xenotransplantation—Theological–ethical considerations in an interdisciplinary symposium. *Xenotransplantation*, 22(3), 174–182.

[26] Orr, W. and Davis, J. L. (2020). Attributions of ethical responsibility by artificial intelligence practitioners. *Information, Communication & Society*, 23(5), 719–735.

[27] Rubinstein, I. (2013). Big data: The end of privacy or a new beginning?. *International Data Privacy Law*, 3(2), 74–87. NYU School of Law, Public Law Research Paper No. 12–56.

[28] Landers, R. N. and Behrend, T. S. (2022). Auditing the AI auditors: A framework for evaluating fairness and bias in high stakes AI predictive models. *American Psychologist*, 78(1), 36–49.

[29] Chassang, G. (2017). The impact of the EU general data protection regulation on scientific research. *Ecancermedicalscience*, 11, 709.

[30] Lim, S. (2021). Judicial decision-making and explainable artificial intelligence: A reckoning from first principles. *Singapore Academy of Law Journal*, 33, 280.

[31] Xu, W., Furie, D., Mahabhaleshwar, M., Suresh, B., and Chouhan, H. (2019). Applications of an interaction, process, integration and intelligence (IPII) design approach for ergonomics solutions. *Ergonomics*, 62(7), 954–980.

[32] Rakova, B., Yang, J., Cramer, H., and Chowdhury, R. (2021). Where responsible AI meets reality: Practitioner perspectives on enablers for shifting organizational practices. *Proceedings of the ACM on Human–Computer Interaction, 5(CSCW1)* (pp. 1–23).

[33] Hemker, S., Herrando, C., and Constantinides, E. (2021). The transformation of data marketing: How an ethical lens on consumer data collection shapes the future of marketing. *Sustainability*, 13(20), 11208.

[34] Hoofnagle, C. J., Van Der Sloot, B., and Borgesius, F. Z. (2019). The European Union general data protection regulation: What it is and what it means. *Information & Communications Technology Law*, 28(1), 65–98.

[35] Palmieri III, N. F. (2020). Who should regulate data: An analysis of the California Consumer Privacy Act and its effects on nationwide data protection laws. *Hastings Science & Technology Law Journal*, 11, 37.

[36] Bentotahewa, V., Hewage, C., and Williams, J. (2022). The normative power of the GDPR: A case study of data protection laws of South Asian countries. *SN Computer Science*, 3(3), 183.

[37] Edemekong, P. F., Annamaraju, P., and Haydel, M. J. (2018). Health Insurance Portability and Accountability Act. In: *StatPearls. StatPearls Publishing, Treasure Island (FL)*; 2022. PMID: 29763195.

[38] Jaar, D. and Zeller, P. E. (2008). Canadian privacy law: The personal information Protection and Electronic Documents Act (PIPEDA). *International In-House Counsel Journal*, 2, 1135.

[39] Morley, J., Machado, C. C., Burr, C., *et al.* (2020). The ethics of AI in health care: A mapping review. *Social Science & Medicine*, 260, 113172.

[40] Wirkuttis, N. and Klein, H. (2017). Artificial intelligence in cybersecurity. *Cyber, Intelligence, and Security*, 1(1), 103–119.

[41] Abouelmehdi, K., Beni-Hessane, A., and Khaloufi, H. (2018). Big healthcare data: Preserving security and privacy. *Journal of Big Data*, 5(1), 1–18.

[42] Floridi, L., Cowls, J., King, T. C., and Taddeo, M. (2020). How to design AI for social good: Seven essential factors. *Science and Engineering Ethics*, 26, 1771–1796.

[43] Jackson, B. W. (2018). Artificial intelligence and the fog of innovation: A deep-dive on governance and the liability of autonomous systems. *Santa Clara High Technology Law Journal*, 35, 35.

[44] Bennett, C. J. (2010). *The privacy advocates: Resisting the spread of surveillance*. Cambridge, MA: MIT Press.

[45] Ebers, M. (2019). Regulating AI and robotics: Ethical and legal challenges. *Algorithms and law*. Cambridge: Cambridge University Press.

[46] Maclay, C. M. (2014). *An improbable coalition: How businesses, nongovernmental organizations, investors and academics formed the Global Network Initiative to promote privacy and free expression online*. Boston, MA: Northeastern University.

[47] Dewani, N. D., Khan, Z. A., Agarwal, A., Sharma, M., and Khan, S. A. (Eds.). (2022). *Handbook of research on cyber law, data protection, and privacy*. Hershey, PA: IGI Global.

Chapter 12

Conclusion

Mohamed Hammad[1,2] and Ahmed A. Abd El-Latif[1,3]

In this book, we have delved into the intersection of artificial intelligence (AI), biometrics, and cybersecurity, exploring the advancements, challenges, and applications in these fields. Throughout the *12* chapters, we have provided a comprehensive exploration of various topics, offering insights into the integration of AI techniques with biometric authentication systems and their impact on cybersecurity.

Biometric authentication, utilizing unique biological traits, provides robust and reliable identification methods across various domains such as access control, surveillance, banking and finance, border control, healthcare, and time and attendance management. However, the widespread adoption of biometric security systems raises concerns regarding privacy, data security, and ethical considerations. Challenges, such as accuracy and reliability, vulnerability to attacks, data security, standardization, and interoperability, need to be addressed to maximize the benefits of these systems while minimizing risks.

To overcome these challenges, researchers are leveraging AI approaches to improve biometric systems. AI algorithms enable biometric systems to handle variations in environmental conditions, enhance feature extraction methods, facilitate continuous learning and adaptation, enable multimodal biometrics, detect and mitigate attacks, and counteract spoofing attempts. By analyzing large volumes of biometric data, AI algorithms can refine models, enhance accuracy, and reduce error rates over time. Moreover, the integration of AI algorithms with biometric systems allows for proactive defense mechanisms and the detection of fraudulent activities, ultimately strengthening security measures.

The book *Artificial Intelligence for Biometrics and Cybersecurity* explores these topics in-depth, covering a wide range of aspects related to the use of AI in biometric security systems and cybersecurity. The chapters discuss the advancements in AI techniques, evaluation of biometric security systems, integration of biometric technologies with cybersecurity protocols, and applications such as electrocardiogram

[1]EIAS Data Science Lab, College of Computer and Information Sciences, Prince Sultan University, Saudi Arabia
[2]Department of Information Technology, Faculty of Computers and Information, Menoufia University, Egypt
[3]Department of Mathematics and Computer Science, Faculty of Science, Menoufia University, Egypt

(ECG) identification and securing IoT hardware. The book also highlights the importance of standardized evaluation protocols, benchmark datasets, and ethical considerations in the development and deployment of biometric systems.

In this book, we started with the introduction of the book, which discusses several general definitions such as AI, biometrics, and cybersecurity. In addition, the chapter shows how these technologies can combine and finally give the structure of this book.

The second chapter focused on the improvements in biometric systems with the help of AI advancements. We discussed the challenges related to data quality, privacy, and security that need to be addressed. AI approaches, such as data pre-processing, pattern recognition, deep learning, and behavioral biometrics, were highlighted as means to overcome these challenges and enhance the accuracy and reliability of biometric systems. We emphasized the importance of responsible and transparent development and deployment of biometric systems, ensuring individual privacy, data security, and compliance with ethical and legal guidelines.

The third chapter emphasized the significance of evaluating the performance and security of biometric systems. We provided an overview of biometric security, performance evaluation metrics, and evaluation methods and tools. Standardized evaluation protocols and benchmark datasets were identified as crucial for future research. We emphasized the adoption of standardized protocols, relevant performance metrics, and regular monitoring and evaluation of biometric systems to ensure optimal performance and security. Open-source tools and platforms were recommended to facilitate the adoption of best practices and ensure the security and effectiveness of biometric systems.

In the fourth chapter, we explored the use of machine learning and deep learning algorithms, specifically generative adversarial networks (GANs) and federated learning (FL), in cybersecurity. We discussed how GANs can generate synthetic data for training machine learning models and simulate cyber-attacks, while FL enables collaborative training without sharing sensitive data. These approaches were highlighted for their potential to detect and respond to cyber threats while preserving data privacy. Future research directions, such as diverse network traffic generation, decentralized training using FL, and adaptive and resilient cybersecurity defenses, were proposed. We also identified potential areas of research for GANs and FL in image security and privacy-preserving image analysis techniques.

The fifth chapter specifically focused on the development and achievements of face recognition technology using FL. We discussed the success of deep neural networks in face recognition and raised concerns about privacy protection. The progress made in face recognition technology under the FL framework was analyzed, and potential future developments and problems were discussed.

In the sixth chapter, we explored the use of ECG as a biometric tool for human identification and authentication in highly secured systems. We highlighted the unique qualities of ECG, such as universality, uniqueness, permanence, collectability, and circumvention resistance. The chapter provided insights into the potential applications of ECG-based biometric authentication methods and the utilization of machine learning approaches for accurate identification.

Throughout the book, we also discussed other topics, including secure authentication, access control, intrusion detection systems, securing IoT hardware through biometric-based methodologies, and graphical password authentication. Real-world case studies demonstrated the practical implementation and effectiveness of AI in biometrics and cybersecurity.

Finally, this book has provided a comprehensive overview of the integration of AI, biometrics, and cybersecurity. We have explored the advancements in biometric systems, the challenges they face, and the solutions offered by AI techniques. The potential applications of AI in various domains, including secure authentication, access control, surveillance, banking, healthcare, and time and attendance management, have been discussed. We have also emphasized the importance of addressing concerns related to privacy, data security, and ethical use of biometric information. The book has highlighted the significance of evaluating the performance and security of biometric systems, recommending the adoption of standardized evaluation protocols and benchmark datasets. We have explored the use of machine learning and deep learning algorithms, GANs, and FL.

Index